It's hard to know where the hippie movement begins. It's even harder to know where it ends. There were hippies long before they were ever called hippies, and there were hippies long after the hippie movement was dead. What's certain is that it was a wild, visionary, revolutionary time. Especially as you could claim Social Security while you were at it.

C. J. Stone first saw Timothy Leary on TV in his living-room in South Yardley, Birmingham, when he was sixteen years old. He was impressed. Timothy Leary had probably never heard of Birmingham, let alone South Yardley, let alone set out to make his views known to a sixteen-year-old delivery boy; and yet here he was, in the author's living-room, telling him to 'turn on, tune in and drop out'. That's when C. J. Stone became converted. He'd already turned the telly on and tuned it in. Now all he needed to do was find the drop-out button.

The Last of the Hippies is about a generation of souls looking for the drop-out button. Part autobiography, part history, part travelogue, it recounts the author's adventures in that marginal realm: the mythical hippie's heavenly playground. Where LSD is the drug of choice, where evolution is the pastime, where revolution is the rhetoric, and paganism is the religion. It's a carnival of madness. Join it at your peril.

The Last of the Hippies

The Last of the Hippies

C. J. Stone

illustrations by Eldad Druks

faber and faber

First published in 1999
by Faber and Faber Limited
3 Queen Square London WC1N 3AU

Photoset by Faber and Faber
Printed in England by Clays Ltd, St Ives plc

A CIP record for this book
is available from the British Library

ISBN 0–571–19313–7

10 9 8 7 6 5 4 3 2 1

For John Pendragon 1946–1998. The last of the hippies

'Dear Oz,
Reading your mag makes me feel very small . . .
JF.'

From a letter to *Oz* magazine, quoted in *Hippie Hippie Shake* by Richard Neville

'Youthful Folly has success.
It is not I who seek the young fool;
The young fool seeks me.
At the first oracle I inform him.
If he asks two or three times, it is importunity.
If he importunes, I give him no information.
Perseverance furthers.'

The I Ching, Hexagram 4, 'Youthful Folly'

'Someone's had too much to THINK . . .'

Captain Beefheart, 'Sue Egypt'

Contents

Acknowledgements

I would like to say thank you to all of those people without whose help this book could never have been written.

To Julian Loose at Fabers for commissioning it, and for putting up with my doubts. To Steven Andrews, of course, for being himself (whatever that is). To Jon and Terry from Espionage Films who, although they don't appear in the book, were there at its inception. To Piers and Gill, for the wine and conversation. To Sue Rowley, for her well-being. To Graham Fowler, for remaining a friend. To Dave Westacott, for remaining a communist. To Nancy and Moffs of Groovy Movies, for the solar equipment (it never worked). To Des Moore, for his candour. To Susanna, for being a hippie. To Louie, for being a closet hippie. To Simon Rogers at the *Big Issue*, for feeding me work. To Terryl and Joe Bacon, for the use of their orchard, and for their kindness and generosity. To Karen and Tony, for their back garden and their patience. To Judith Roe, a good friend, and a source of inspiration. To Chris Craig, for distracting me with Karl Marx. To Lissie Freewoman, for distracting me with other things. To Michael Eavis and Andrew Kerr, for their time and their stories. To Glenn, for the jokes. To the Library of Avalon and the Assembly Rooms at Glastonbury, for the use of their space. To Paul and Nik, for the use of the room. To Simon and Bunny, for the lift and the squabbles. To Kevin and Roger of AD3000, for revealing what was hidden. And to everyone I met in the course of writing this book, whether you appear in it or not. It was better than a poke in the eye with a burnt stick.

The Last of the Hippies

1 Dear Pete

'He who knows no limitation
Will have cause to lament.'

The I Ching, Hexagram 60, 'Limitation'

We called you Piss-Off Pete. 'Piss-Off' as in: 'Go away, get lost, we don't want you round here.' Also you pissed people off.

As it happens it was Rod the Mod who first called you that. I met Rod for the first time this year and his name wasn't Rod the Mod at all, it was Tony. I was with Steve. It was Steve who told me that Tony was called Rod the Mod. But in those days (in the days when Rod the Mod was called Rod the Mod and you were called Piss-Off Pete) Steve was called Droid. Only my name hasn't changed. I was Chris Stone then, and I'm Chris Stone now. Except when I'm writing books, that is, when I get called C.J.

This was back in the early seventies: '73 or '74.

You were a rock-guitarist, very talented. You could play solos fast and hard and hit all the right notes. The trouble was, you couldn't stop yourself from playing solos. You'd launch into a

3

solo right where the chorus should be, or in the verse, or in the middle-eight. You'd launch into a solo when other people were playing solos, or when the singer was trying to sing. Sometimes you'd launch into a solo before everyone else had even started to play, when they were just setting up. Other musicians refused to play with you. No matter what you'd rehearsed only the day before, you'd suddenly launch into a ten-minute squealing, shrieking, wired-up ego-wank guitar solo when they least expected it, and then you'd be looking at them triumphantly as if to say, 'Look at me, I'm a fucking genius.' It had something to do with your ego, which was strangely out of kilter. Put you on stage and you were the embodiment of David Bowie's Ziggy Stardust: 'Making love with his ego, Ziggy sucked up into his mi-y-ind.'

You were obsessed with Bowie. You sounded more like Bowie than Bowie himself. Bowie was your God, your mentor. You even wrote to Bowie once, proposing marriage. Everything Bowie did, you wanted to do. So you started wearing make-up and dressing in women's clothing. This was the Glam Rock era, when what had started as the hippie revolution ended up wearing knee-length silver stack-heel boots over crushed-velvet loon pants with forty-inch flares. This was its slogan: 'Forward to the barricades! But first I must check my eyeliner.'

I liked you, Pete, though you were a little sad. You were craving attention. Maybe you were craving love. I don't think you ever found it. All anyone ever said to you was 'Piss off, Pete.'

When I first met you, you were fairly normal. It was Steve who introduced you to me. There were a few of us. We were on our way to a club down the docks.

Steve said, 'This is Pete. He's a good guitarist.'

I forget what you were wearing. I forget most things. I have the picture of a shiny blue velvet top with flared sleeves. And bangles too, lots of bangles, tinkling on your wrists as you moved your arms about. A set of love-beads maybe, or a choker. You were looking at me and smiling, a boyish, bashful, secretive smile. I never looked beyond the surface in those days. I still don't. So I had no idea what secrets you wanted to conceal. You seemed like a nice guy to me. I forget what you said. Something pretentious and airy, no doubt, something loopy but funny. I

4

seem to remember UFOs coming into the conversation, and LSD. I think you were already on your alien trip by this time. But we had a conversation nevertheless, while you continued to smile at me in your twinkling, friendly way, laughing at yourself. You laughed at yourself a lot in the early days.

You were strikingly good-looking, with blond hair and baby-blue eyes. All the girls adored you. You were pretty and unthreatening, an easy person to be around. There was a string of the most devastatingly good-looking girls in Cardiff. But then something wasn't quite right. Maybe you were bisexual. Maybe you were just straight gay. Maybe you'd bought all of that seventies Glam Rock rhetoric about sexual ambivalence and the androgynous spirit. But then again, maybe it was the LSD. Good old LSD, it changed everyone's life. In your case it turned you into a bad joke, a kind of tripped-out jester-fool in women's clothing. You were the butt of your own joke in the early days and it was possible to hold a conversation with you. In later years you stopped smiling and you stopped making any sense at all.

I'll have to ask Steve to help me continue the story. Steve was closer to you than anyone.

You know Steve, of course, don't you? How could you forget him? You'd remember him as Droid.

Steve is unique. There's nothing quite like him on this Earth. He's not really a hippie. He's an alien being from another planet. But he seems to be keeping the hippie faith, whatever that is. He's about six-foot tall, balding, with a sort of Egyptian head-dress of dreadlocks strung with beads dangling about his ears, and a goatee beard. That's how he looks now. Back in the seventies he wasn't balding, and his hair cascaded around his face like a curtain. I'd call him a saint, only he has this innate capacity to laugh at himself and the world. I don't know, maybe saints do laugh uproariously at jokes about their own misfortune while off their heads on cider or mushrooms. I haven't met all that many saints, so I can't say. He lives on a council estate on the outskirts of Cardiff with his son, Isaac, and has an as-yet unrealized ambition to be an International Rock Star; or, failing that, at least to have a slot on *Top of the Pops*. Maybe this book will help him realize his ambition. Then again, maybe not.

His full name is Steven Andrews. It was from his surname that his nickname derived. The kids at school called him Android. Later it was shortened to Droid.

He was one of your best friends, Pete. He was the one person who never told you to piss off.

'I must have met Pete probably about '73,' says Steve, now. 'I think I met him in the Claude, and then I'd see him in the Old Arcade, the Moon Club, and all those sorts of places. He was pretty together. I used to hang about with Geoff and Bruce Campbell. He could play the guitar, it was before he went really weird. He used to have various girlfriends in those days.

'Later he started going loopy. This must have been about '75. I was living in Cathedral Road then with a couple of other guys in a flat. And at that time Pete came round. We were in the living room, having a bit of a drink, a smoke, as you do, and Pete said, could he go and meditate in the kitchen? And we thought, *Yeah, let him go and meditate in the kitchen.* 'Cos he wasn't doing much in the room apart from staring around, making signs on his head. So we said, "Yeah, go in the kitchen." A bit later we heard this strange yelling from the kitchen, going, "Saaaaa-lllllll-eeeeeey!" Or that's what it sounded like. And we all went out in the kitchen, and Pete was there stark naked standing in front of the window with his arms outstretched towards the ceiling, yelling this strange cry, which sounded, to us, like "Sally". I think I probably shouted out, "Pete, what the fuck are you doing, get out the way of the window." 'Cos it was looking out over the street, with shops and people shopping down in the street. I think it was a Saturday and it looked out upon Pontcanna Street, which is one of the main streets in the area, and I was thinking, *Well, someone's gonna call the police or something ridiculous.* And he said that he was invoking the goddess Selene. But to us it was just like he was shouting "Sally" with his arms outstretched stark naked in front of the window. Which was, like, totally crazy; but there you are, that was Pete.'

Yes, that was you, Pete. That was you when you'd started to go really weird. It was like your mind had conked out or something, as if the brain mechanism had slipped a gear. The ego-wank guitar solos gave way to an ego-wank transcendentalism. Gobbledegook flying out of your mouth in the same way that screaming guitar solos had shrieked from your fret-board in an earlier era.

You began to develop strange ways of talking, peculiarities of intonation and reference that made your speech sometimes incomprehensible. For instance, you would refer to people as 'Creation' and then give them a number. You were 'Creation Number One', of course. Your girlfriend would always be 'Creation Number Two'. And then you would have long periods of silence in which you could only sign by pointing downwards at the top of your head and making this *tssssk-tssssk* noise, like the sound of static electricity crackling through your brain. It was as if you were trying to tell us something, as if your brain was really short-circuiting. 'Neural damage,' you'd say, in this high-pitched, camp, robotic voice, sounding like a computerized drag queen with a ferret up your bum. Well, it was funny. In the end it was tragic. But the most tragic thing of all is that no one could take the tragedy seriously. Your final tragedy, Pete, is that even your tragedy was funny.

I've often wondered where the shift came, from the merely eccentric to the psychopathically certifiable. A friend of a friend went out with you for a while. In those days you were only what you would call unconventional. And that was kind of the spirit of the time. Unconventionality was the norm; breaking the rules was the rule. People would be sitting round with you, usually stoned, when you would start breathing hard and gazing into the distance. 'Nirvana,' you might say, in a flat, nasal voice. And then you would start weaving tales of lotus flowers and other Far-Eastern religious paraphernalia with a kind of mad, twisted logic. You were fascinating, in the way that the way-out is often fascinating to the young. It was the kind of thing we all did. Almost everyone fancied himself a guru in those days.

At other times you might say, 'Meditate upon the causes of corruption,' or tell people that the ego should be abolished. That's another irony of the time (and one we shall come back to): that the demolition of ego was seen as the goal of all of our endeavours, and yet that there was more egotism about then than in almost any other decade. There can be nothing more egotistical than the declaration against ego. What else is making the declaration but the ego itself? Always beware of people who call themselves egoless beings. They're the biggest egotists of the lot.

You lived in a flat full of Indian cloth with tasselled drapes and incense, with dangly things hanging from the wall. Low table. A mattress on the floor. Pictures of the Buddha and Hindu gods. Rugs and cushions, like a dark, warm womb. And at first you were not without a certain sense of humour, as I said earlier. You'd say something kind of weird and wobbly and people would laugh, and you would laugh with them. Maybe you got addicted to the laughter. Maybe that was a front and you wanted to be taken seriously. After a while people started calling you Piss-Off Pete, and you even kind of liked it. 'Piss off' was said in an affectionate way: not so much 'Go away' as 'Oh, come off it, Pete, that's just crazy.' And yet everyone encouraged you to it. It was what they wanted. The bizarre, the strange, the deranged even. Syd Barrett's post-Pink Floyd meanderings had a cult status (they probably still do). Madness was all the rage.

I'm sure it was round at your place that I first heard *The Man Who Sold the World* by David Bowie. If it wasn't, it ought to have been. It's an album about madness and the fear of madness. But whereas Bowie's character was a tragic hero, yours was a tacky parody.

Obviously you were struggling with your sexuality at this time. There were no aid-structures as there are now for the potentially gay. You were a beautiful man, surrounded by women, and admired by other men. But in some secret part, maybe, you longed for something more than admiration: maybe you longed for the love of other men too. Who knows? Maybe in these days of open sexuality you would not have had to have gone through what you went through then. It was about this time that you shifted from the merely effeminate styles of early Glam Rock into total transvestism. Again, this was tragically funny. For all your blonde good looks, you were very much a man. The sort of man who needed to shave twice a day. No matter how much make-up you wore, you could never disguise the dark stain of stubble across your jaw, and for all the femininity of your clothing, your hairy, muscular arms still poked out from whatever off-the-shoulder little number you were wearing at the time. It was incongruous and comic in the way that the PG Tips chimps are incongruous and comic. Incongruous and comic and just a little sad.

One day you were sitting in your darkened flat with your girlfriend, Jane, and another girl, when you were suddenly gripped by the idea that the two women were the embodiments of evil spirits. There was a spear near by, just one of those things (along with the incense holders and brass gods and African masks) that you used to decorate your flat. You launched the spear across the room in a fury of sexual suspicion. The two girls were only saved by a washing line that was dangling across the room. The spear bounced off it and deflected harmlessly away. At the time that sort of thing just seemed normal. It was just another crazy moment in a season of crazy moments, lost in a daze of drug-induced confusion.

Later you had another girlfriend, Terry. You would order her around and treat her really badly. One day Steve was round your flat. You said, in your by now usual camp-robotic style, 'Woman, prepare carboniferous dehydrated material.' She knew what you meant. She was used to your way of saying things by now. And she went into the kitchen to make the toast. When she brought the toast back in and handed it to you, you refused to eat it. Instead you stood on the bed waving your arms about and going 'Tsssk tsssk, neural damage,' and all the rest, and doing one of your mad, camp performances. Terry didn't know what to make of it. She was confused by it all. Still, she must have loved you because she stayed with you quite a while.

Finally you became openly gay. There was a string of boyfriends to replace the girlfriends you'd had before. But things were swiftly degenerating too. You were making less and less sense of it all. The humour disappeared, and you stopped taking care of your appearance. You still wore women's clothing, but now you had dirty fingernails to go with the stubble and the muscular arms.

Steve went out with you for a while, as you know. The following is Steve's account of your brief time together:

'My relationship with Pete? Well that didn't last very long. Basically I was having no success with women, again, and Pete was sort of the next best thing to a woman that I could find. He looked sort of like a woman. One night in the Moon Club some guy came up to me and said, "Cor, who's that tasty blonde chick?" And I said, "That chick is a bloke actually." And he said, "Well I don't care, she's gorgeous." I was completely out of it on various substances most of the time anyway, so that was how it came about. But I can remember actually being out with him and holding hands and necking in a public place, and that this felt quite good. You know, when you're actually out with someone, you have a sort of sense of self-pride that, "Here I am walking down the street with a partner." And you can sort of show off to the world that you've managed to get it together to become an item with somebody else. And I can remember having that sort of feeling, being out with Pete. And also the idea that because this was a gay relationship being shoved in the face of the world, this was a good thing to do, sort of to liberate people, and this sort of idea. But basically I couldn't handle Pete, 'cos Pete didn't used to speak for ages, or he just used to mutter utter strangeness, and tap his head and make noises and all this stuff. So conversation-wise it was a waste of time. Also I felt that it wasn't right for me. I sort of learnt from it that I wasn't really gay, that I was basically heterosexual, failing as a heterosexual and going after the next best thing. And I also felt guilty in a way after that. Pete did want this relationship with me on a physical level, but I didn't want that with him. And I felt that my relationship with Pete was something like that, that if I could have had a real girl I would have dropped Pete like a shot. And I felt quite bad about that at the time. I used to have Pete running after me for some time after that.

'It came about that I was with Pete because I used to use his flat as another place I used to crash. I used to have a need for somewhere to stay on many occasions, 'cos I'd taken a load of downers, and Pete's was a place where I could almost guarantee I could go there and I wouldn't be turned away. Also, I used to understand some of his mystic psychobabble, some of that made a lot of sense to me, and I could relate to that, so I used to like listening to what he did have to say when he had something to say. And also 'cos my head was totally messed up around that time period, I could relate to his condition, so we did actually have some points of similarity. And so it came about that I was with him because I used to stay around his flat quite often.'

So – no maybes any more – you were gay, Pete. You were gay, but you didn't hang around with gay people. Why was that? They were probably telling you to piss off, too.

You see, you'd lost your sense of humour somewhere down the line. You just weren't funny any more. You'd started to take yourself too seriously. All the irony was gone. And this is another observation of mine, that it was the ones who could laugh at themselves who survived this time, and the ones who couldn't who went under.

'There was a time when I was in the Old Arcade with him once,' Steve continues, laughing, 'and he was just sitting cross-legged in lotus position on the floor, chanting "*Om*" over and over again. And he got chucked out that time. The bar manager came out and said, 'If you're not buying a drink or anything, if you're just gonna make this stupid noise, then you can just get out of here.' And he got thrown out.

'Later, it would have been about '77 or '78, Pete came round to see me. He had some trouble, they'd stopped his money, and he wanted me to go to the Social with him. So we went down the Social Security offices which is down the docks, and we were just waiting about there for bloody ages, as you do in these places. They say, "OK, take a seat and we'll get somebody to see you." Pete was dressed in his usual sort of gear, some sort of strange head-scarf that he had on and earrings and bangles and lipstick, some sort of glitzy top and leggings, platform boots, handbag, that sort of gear; and nail varnish on his nails, probably chipped.'

Eventually the man at the reception desk called you over, and Steve went with you.

'So you are Peter Alexander Pearce,' the Social Security Officer said.

You did your usual. 'Ooooooooooohhhh, ch ch ch ch,' you said, sounding like a mad robotic mannequin in the throes of a mechanistic orgasm, wriggling your bum about on the functional seating and pointing with your finger to the top of your head, signing in your inimitable way. 'Neural damage,' you added, as if that answered his question.

The bemused Social Security Officer had to pause. 'Well, I'll repeat the question again: you are Peter Alexander Pearce of Llandough Street, Cardiff?'

'Ooooooooooohhhh, Stel-lar Intel-ligence,' you said, emphasizing the syllables like some camp mantra, with a meaningful look in your eye. I can't imagine what the poor man was thinking at this point. He just looked back and forth at the two of you as if wondering which planet you'd recently arrived from.

Steve stepped into the conversation. He said, 'I'm sorry but my friend hasn't been very well, he hasn't had any money and he hasn't been eating properly, so perhaps it would be better if you had a word with me.'

The guy was relieved. At last, a normal human being, albeit one wearing tartan loon pants, a tartan jacket, tartan T-shirt and tartan shoes, with a mass of black curly hair almost covering his face and a beard the size of a battleship. At least the man made sense. 'Well yeah,' he said, 'we need some sort of confirmation that he's been paying rent at the address that we've got him down for. And if you can get a rent book or something, then bring that in or send it in and that will confirm his current status.'

'Yeah, OK,' said Steve, 'we could do that.'

And then you left, and went back to your flat.

When you got back Steve asked you for your rent book. 'Tssssk, tssssk, ch ch ch,' you said, staring and signing and waving your arms about, casting meaningful glances around the room and letting out the occasional tripped-out orgasmic giggle.

Steve had had enough. 'Look Pete,' he said, sternly, 'we need this rent book, 'cos I've told the social security people I'm gonna get this information to them.' And then, after a long wait, and more signs and performances, you finally brought out a really tacky rent book, battered and stained and looking like it had been used for drying the washing-up over a number of years. Steve opened it up and there was nothing in it. Well the first page was filled, but the rest of it was blank, which showed that for the last two years you hadn't actually paid any rent to anybody.

Steve said, 'Look, this is no fucking good. We want proof that you've been paying rent. This is crazy, I can't show them this, it basically shows that they've been paying you money and you haven't been paying it to anyone. I don't understand this. I've got to show them something, so can you explain yourself here. Why hasn't the landlord filled it in? What's happened to the money? I hope you haven't wasted it all.'

Finally you signalled to Steve to give you the rent book, which he did. And you scrawled across it, in block capitals, PSY-CHOPATHS STOLE MY RENT SAVINGS.

Steve said, 'I definitely can't show them this, Pete, you've basically ruined the rent book now. Who are the psychopaths? Where are the bloody rent savings?'

Well you could be lucid at times, especially when you were in a corner. You went on to tell Steve that the psychopaths were some people who were living upstairs, squatters, and they'd moved out now, and apparently they'd bust into your room, and you'd put the rent savings in a box and they'd stolen the box with all the money in – all told like that, in a breathless rush of uncharacteristic normality – these were the psychopaths who'd stolen the rent savings. Steve thought that the whole thing was totally ridiculous, even that you'd put all the money in this box, which was asking for trouble; but anyway, that's what you had done. And you wanted to know what would happen to you then.

Steve said, 'I dunno, I can't show them this, I just don't know what to say really.' He was trying to think what he could do. He said, 'Well you could either end up being chucked out of here, or you could end up in Whitchurch, the mental hospital, or maybe in trouble with the police, I just don't know. Maybe you'll end up on the street.'

You said, 'Ooooooooooohhhhh Droid, can I move in with you and Susan?'

'I don't think so, not really,' said Steve, nonplussed. He didn't know what to do. He didn't know what to say. You were a puzzle to him like you were a puzzle to everyone else by this time. He just couldn't handle it. He made his excuses and left. And shortly after that somebody told him that you'd been taken into Whitchurch, which is where you were for a long period. There was just nothing that Steve could do about it.

'Pete said to me once that when he was in town people would cross the street to get out of his way and he used to see these people and it used to affect him. He said, "People never come up to me and say, 'Oh hi, Pete, why don't you call round sometime, or, let's go for a coffee or something.'" They used to go, "Oh fucking hell, it's Piss-Off Pete," and make a beeline to get out of his way. And he used to be aware that people were calling him Piss-Off Pete and doing all they could to keep out of his way.'

The story continues. Steve's common-law wife, Susan, had given birth to their son in 1979. And then Susan had cracked up too, and was waving her hands about and locking herself in the bathroom and talking all sorts of babble. Steve just seems to have this innate capacity to draw madness to him. It's like some sort of magnetism, unhappy serendipity.

He asked you what you thought the reason for all this was, why Susan was locking herself in the bathroom and waving her arms about. Maybe he thought, since your conditions were so similar, that you might have some answer to this. And this was your diagnosis: 'A Thetan is in a body or approaching a body,' and then you did some more of that *tsssht, tsssht, ooooooohhhhh* stuff. 'And that was it, that was the Pete diagnosis of what Susan's condition was: "A Thetan is in a body or approaching a body."'

'Thetan' is a Church of Scientology word, by the way. It refers to the soul as an alien being from another planet.

You'd use Scientology terminology quite a lot, Steve remembers. You did a song which basically consisted of you calling out numbers at random, for the numbers of UFOs. It went something like this: 'UFO 4, operating Thetan 7, advance Org A.L.O.A.' And then maybe something like, 'UFO 51, operating Thetan 75,' and on like that.

'Later I went round to see him. Susan said to me that she was concerned about Pete. This was before he was hospitalized. Around the time he was sort of resurrected in a way, and he was coming round to see us. Susan was concerned about him, and she said, why didn't I go round to see how he was, and if I wanted I could invite him round. So I went round to see him. I just walked in 'cos the door was just left open, and at that particular point his front windows were smashed through and there was nobody else living in Llandough Street then, the squatters who he called the madmen psychopaths from upstairs, they'd gone, and he was there in the bottom flat, and he was just lying on his mattress.'

You were like a wounded animal, Steve told me, lying there on your mattress, in that filthy, cold flat. It was no longer a womb. More like a ruined sepulchre, waiting for the coffin to arrive. Steve asked you what you were doing and, after one of your customary long silences, you said you were waiting to die. Steve told you what Susan had said, and that if you wanted to come round and see them, then you could. At which point he could see the life and the energy rushing back into you. It was like some-one had switched the lights back on. Your face lit up. You were enthused by the whole idea of it, that somebody actually wanted to know. 'Uh oh oh, oooooooohhhh Droid, oh,' you squirmed in appreciation. And on and on like this. 'Droid, ooooooooo,' rolling round on your mattress, wriggling with pleasure. It was at this point that Steve noticed that across your wall you'd scrawled, 'David Bowie SOS.' That was your last plea for help when you were waiting to die.

'Then he came round to see me and Sue, and within about two days she was totally pissed off with him, and she couldn't handle him. He was coming round on a regular basis everyday, and he was throwing stones at the window, he was waiting outside at the flat, tapping on the door, and going, "Oooohhhh, it's me, Peter, don't keep me outside like a cheap whore," and stuff like this.'

This could be at three o'clock in the morning. Or you'd be out-side and they'd hear stones tapping on the window, and they'd look down and see you in the garden with this total Pete expres-sion on your face, plastered in make-up with a headscarf on. You'd be looking up pathetically, like a dog, the way an animal looks at you, for sympathy, for attention, and begging for hospi-tality, for love, and Steve would think, *Oh, there's Pete*, and feel that he had to do something. And this went on day in and day out until Susan had had enough. She couldn't handle it any more, she said. And the truth is Steve couldn't handle it either. After that you were taken into Whitchurch.

'The last time I saw Pete,' Steve tells me, drawing the story to its lonely end, 'was in Richmond Road where I was living with Susan. Susan was still freaking out at the time. Pete was in Whitchurch, but he was allowed out on day release with the stu-dents from upstairs who used to go and collect him. Pete's mother had come round the house for some reason.'

Fiona, one of the student girls from upstairs, was taking it upon herself to be responsible for you, Steve says. At the begin-ning she was moralistic about the entire thing, about psychiatric treatment and the drugs they seemed to be handing out like Smarties, which she thought was wrong. She thought that there had to be some other way. But when confronted with the reality of yours and Susan's madness she changed her mind. 'Well

15

maybe, you know, the things I thought were wrong, maybe they aren't wrong. Maybe they should give them all these drugs, whatever drugs they need to control it, 'cos I just don't know how to handle it,' she said to Steve.

Steve continues:

'Pete was upstairs lying on this couch thing, staring at the ceiling, and his mother was in the room and was over by his head and was waving her hands about and saying, "Peter my son, we're all praying for you, there are angels all around your head." And Pete's just looking into space and squealing, "Ha ha ha ha ooooohhhh." And I'm thinking, *Fucking hell, it's not surprising that he's fucked up if his mother is telling him that there's angels all around his head*. He's from this religious background, as you know. And it gave some idea to all of us what was wrong with him. I think that was actually the last time I saw him. He had to go back to Whitchurch after all that, and then I heard that he was transferred to this mental hospital up North. I didn't see him again.'

No one in Cardiff saw you again after that. No doubt, that's what your mother was doing there that day, coming to pick you up to take you back to your home town. And after that, you were gone. It was like you'd stepped through a door into some other world, like you'd joined the Carnival of Madness and couldn't get off the ride. There's no saying where you are now.

And that's it, Pete. What more can I say? You were a good man dragged down by madness. Many people were dragged down by madness in those days. Syd Barrett of the Pink Floyd, Peter Green of Fleetwood Mac, Brian Wilson of the Beach Boys. These were the celebrated cases. Ordinary people thrust into genius by a drug which knew no limits, but who had no mechanism for dealing with the responsibilities of genius. And many, many more like you, whom no one remembers but their friends.

And who is there to blame? It wasn't your fault, was it? It wasn't Steve's fault. It wasn't my fault, though maybe I could have done more at the time, if I'd have known what you were suffering. But I was a selfish young man, too caught up in my own concerns to notice what was going on in anybody else's life; too busy pursuing my own salvation to notice that there were others more in need than me.

That was what it was like at the time. Vanity and indulgence. The search for salvation had become a personal pursuit. Each looking to his own. The hippie dream, expansive and outward-looking though it had been in its early years, had turned in on itself. It was all 'me, me, me, self, self, self'. It wasn't anybody's fault. It was the era in which we lived. And if we were mad in our own ways (and you were mad in a certifiable way) then it was because the era was mad.

What follows is the story of that era, and of its aftermath. I've addressed it to you, Pete. But actually it is for anyone who cares to listen.

2 Hippies, Heads and Freaks

'A spring wells up at the foot of the mountain:
The image of youth.'

The I Ching, Hexagram 4, 'Youthful Folly'

Pete wasn't a hippie. He called himself 'a fragile Ladytron from Sirius'. He was a loony. I wasn't a hippie either. Rod the Mod certainly wasn't a hippie. But, then again, he wasn't a Mod. The only person who might fit the description is Steve, and even Steve didn't call himself a hippie at the time. He was a freak. We were all freaks.

The word 'hippie' is a media invention. It's a diminutive of the word hip. It was meant as a term of derision. It was always a term of derision. It's still a term of derision to this day.

According to Richard Neville (of *Oz* fame) the word was invented by the *San Francisco Chronicle* as a warning to its readers. Unfortunately its readers refused to heed the warning. Either that, or hippies never read the *San Francisco Chronicle*.

Hippies never read newspapers. That's a fact.

I spoke to my editor at Fabers before I started writing this book. I was worried about the title. 'There's no such thing as a hippie,' I told him. 'Can't we call it *The Last of the Freaks* or something?'

'Of course there's no such thing as a hippie,' he said. 'But everyone knows one when he walks into the room. And everyone wants to punch him in the face.'

Another term that was often used was 'heads'. This one always disturbed me. It invokes the image of something alien and strange: a disembodied head floating about, like some creature from a nightmarish fairy tale; or, even worse, of the body it leaves behind, crashing about blindly (having no head, and therefore no eyes), into walls and under cars and over cliffs, arms outstretched in an effort to feel its way around.

Who on earth would want to call himself a head? It's such a meaningless term. You might as well call yourself an elbow, or a large intestine. Me, I often get called a prick. Sometimes I get called an arsehole. They're both bodily parts reduced to terms of abuse. Which is what I take 'head' to be.

Someone told me that the term 'head' predates the hippies. Heads were beatniks who got into dope. They'd get into their own heads. Sometimes they'd get off their heads too. Presumably they did a lot of thinking. The term survives to this day in the head shop, those emporia of strange tat that still exist on the occasional high street, selling hash-pipes and chillums and psychedelic posters and other such arcane, drug-related paraphernalia. No one ever buys anything in a head shop. They walk in, puzzled, and then they walk out again, none the wiser.

I met someone once who must have thought of himself as a head. This was in a council estate in Sheldon, in Birmingham. He said, 'Are there many heads round here?' I had to do a double-take. I couldn't imagine what might have given him the impression, this being an area of neat privet hedges, net curtains and horse-and-cart pottery figurines: nothing remotely like Greenwich Village or Haight-Ashbury. I guess he was asking me that because he was looking at me at the time, and I had long, straight hair and flared loons. But – as they say – one swallow doesn't make a summer, one long-haired person doesn't make a Haight-Ashbury and, by the same token, one social movement doesn't make an era.

These days I'm constantly astounded by the sheer vanity of those commentators who – having been through the experience themselves – want to characterize the entire decade we refer to as the sixties in terms of one small, brief, Western, predominantly middle-class social movement. I mean, my Dad lived through the sixties too, and I don't remember him ever dropping out, not even for a second. He never took LSD. He never went to the UFO club in Notting Hill. He never protested against the Vietnam war, nor practised free love (or if he did, it was without my Mom knowing about it). He was still a relatively young man, but he was a factory worker. And, like most workers the world over, he was far more concerned with the day-to-day needs of his growing family, with keeping a roof over our head, and providing for us, than with the particular indulgences and peculiar forms of rhetoric going on in parts of London at the time. We tend to forget this, that the lives of the vast majority of people were simply untouched by the so-called spirit of the sixties; that most people went through most of the decade hardly knowing what a hippie was, still less interested in what hippies had to say.

And it's the same commentators, too, who always want to emphasize the fundamental importance of the use of LSD in fuelling this grand social movement. Again, I'm astounded at their vanity. Their lives were changed by LSD, so they presume that everyone else's life was changed too. LSD certainly helped inspire a number of people in Europe and America. But what about the rest of the world? This was the era when the peasant army of the Vietcong were challenging the hegemony of American power in South-East Asia, and winning; it was the era of the student revolt in Paris in '68, and the so-called Prague Spring in Czechoslovakia in the same year; and almost through the entire decade, it was the era of the Cultural Revolution in China. And most of this in the name of youth and idealism, in challenging the forces of age and conservatism, in seeking out a new vision and a new hope.

How many Red Guards were taking LSD, I wonder? How many Vietcong or Prague revolutionaries? I venture to suggest: precisely none. How many of the French workers who joined the students briefly in that heady summer of 1968? Again, at the most, not very many at all.

If you were to believe those books – and they abound – then the sixties was a decade of flower power, LSD and dancing to the Pink Floyd at the UFO club. Nothing can be further from the truth. For some people – a few thousand maybe – for a few years, this may indeed have characterized the sixties. But for the vast majority of people throughout the world, the sixties was just the same old dull round, the urge for survival, the daily routine of work–eat–sleep, the quiet struggle against the forces of oppression, the grinding reality of poverty. The same as any other decade.

The sixties? All right if you happened to have money. All right if you happened to know the right people. All right if you happened to live in London. But if you were poor, working class, and lived anywhere else, then forget it. The sixties never happened.

Parts of this book were written in a pair of old Letts diaries, dated 1967 and 1968, the years of the great hippie explosion. They belonged to a council buildings work inspector from Barton-on-Humber in Lincolnshire, where I'd lived for a while, many years later. The diary entries consist of things like:

'Friday 19th May 1967. One block No. 4 houses concreted OK, but too much concrete was used.'

And again:

'Tuesday 13th June 1967. Weather Fine. Sewer cleaning men arrived late owing to breakdown. Found blockage on straight length on Butts Road. Our men will have to dig free the hose pipe.'

Not one mention of an LSD party or a free-love orgy, you'll notice. There's no free-love orgies in either of the diaries. Mind you, I expect he liked to imagine free-love orgies in his spare time. Who doesn't?

By the time I entered the movement it was all but dead. In fact, in terms of the sixties, it was literally dead. It was 1971.

I was eighteen years old. I'd grown my hair, just a little bit (it kind of dangled limply over my ears, much to my mother's annoyance) and was wearing ripped, faded cord jeans. My mother never understood why I wanted to wear ripped, faded cord jeans when she was perfectly happy to buy me a brand new pair. Ah, mothers! They never do understand, do they?

I was on my way to Cardiff University to study English Literature. Maybe I imagined that going to Cardiff University to study English Literature was the height of rebellion. But it wasn't exactly the LSE. In fact even the LSE wasn't exactly the LSE by 1971. The student rebellion was all but over.

The day I left I went for a drink with my friend Rose. Actually, she was much more than a friend. I fancied her like crazy. She was small and compact with a halo of flaming red hair and large breasts. I'd always had a thing about her breasts, ever since I'd seen her a couple of years before leaning casually back against a desk, pressing her breasts out into the welcoming air and being playfully flirtatious with some other kid. I'd always hoped that she might one day be equally playfully flirtatious with me.

Just before we'd left school – after the A levels were over – I'd gone to a party with her. It was my first ever party. We'd ended up sleeping together: us two and about half a dozen others. But she'd stripped down to her bra and knickers and let me nuzzle up to her back. I think I was nuzzling up to her in more ways than one. I guess she was starting to get playfully flirtatious with me by now. We began seeing each other occasionally – whenever her boyfriend wasn't around, that is.

On the day in question, Rose had come over to my house to see me off. I was packed and ready to go. My Dad was going to drive me. And then – when the moment came – I just didn't want to leave. I didn't want to leave Rose. I didn't want to leave home. I didn't want to leave Birmingham. I didn't want to become a student. I didn't want to go to Cardiff. I burst into tears.

This is something I have always been able to do. I've never been one of those men who complain that they can't cry. I often cry. I still cry. I cry at *Casablanca* every time, especially when Humph clutches his whiskey and his eyes go all watery in the close-up and he slams down his drink and says, 'Play it.' And Sam does: he plays 'As Time Goes By'. I think 'As Time Goes By' is one of the best songs ever written. I always cry when I hear it. This isn't because I'm a New Man or anything. I don't even know what a New Man is. I'm a wimp, that's all.

I cried so much Rose had to travel down to Cardiff with me. I cried all the way, much to my Dad's eternal embarrassment.

We were almost boyfriend and girlfriend then. She talked about me to all my friends. She couldn't wait till I came back.

And then when I did get back, she dumped me. I never did understand why she dumped me. I wasn't even going out with her. Probably I was too much of a wimp.

Rod Stewart was in the charts about this time, with a double A-side. 'Maggie May' and 'Reason to Believe': *Someone like you makes it hard to live without somebody else.* It was my song for Rose.

Anyway, thus began my illustrious career as hippie king of Cardiff City. In floods of tears, being a wimp.

Well, I wanted to be a hippie. I'd always wanted to be a hippie. I had visions of myself returning to school after – say – a year, dressed all in denim, with long curly hair and a big bushy beard, with a pair of cowboy boots and a leather cowboy hat, with sunglasses shading my eyes, looking cool, leaning casually back on my chair and saying 'man' a lot. It was absurd of course. For a start, no matter how long I grew my hair, it was never curly. And even my beard, when I did manage to grow it, was as flat and straight as an ironed vest. As for the cowboy boots and the shades, I always had this streak of uncontrollable uncool in me that made the wearing of such items simply absurd. I could never wear anything that didn't seem ironical in some way. But still I dreamed. Being a hippie was better than being a schoolboy. It was better than being a wimp. It was certainly better than being a Brummie at the time. Being a Brummie seemed the worst thing anyone could be. I quickly dumped my accent, taking on a sort of Mid-Atlantic-Cockney-hippie drawl instead.

These days I'd rather be a Brummie than a hippie. At least Brummies don't have to wear such ludicrous clothes as the mark of their identity. They often do wear ludicrous clothes; it's just that they're not the mark of their identity.

I soon settled into the life and began to make friends. One of the first people I spoke to was Dave. He was hanging around outside the lecture theatre wearing tight black leather trousers and a short nylon furry jacket. He was dressed like Jim Morrison. It was the sort of outfit no one would be seen dead in these days. No one but a raver, that is.

He was tiny, about five foot two, with thick black hair just curling over his collar and ears. I guess I thought he was a hippie. Who else but a hippie would want to go around dressed like Jim Morrison?

I can't remember what I said to him. Something inane, no doubt, masquerading as cleverness. 'Are you a new boy too?' Something like that.

And then he replied and I nearly fell over. Out of that tiny, frail-looking, diminutive frame boomed this mighty, grumbling, gravelly voice, like the rumble of thunder from the bowels of the earth.

I asked about his leather trousers. I was impressed. 'I bought them in this shop in Camden,' he growled. 'I couldn't do up the zip, so the shop assistant helped me. She helped me to pull up the zip.' I liked that. I imagined that it was all part of the service in hippie shops: shop assistants that helped you pull up your zip. But – being terminally shy – it meant I could never go into a hippie shop again.

Actually Dave didn't turn out to be a hippie at all. He was a communist, which was even worse. He dressed like Jim Morrison, but he talked like Karl Marx. Karl Marx in leather trousers.

I think it was probably in that lecture that I first saw Simon. The lecture was by Terry Hawkes. I realize now that it was an early piece of radical structuralism. I remember the lecturer telling us that *Coronation Street* was as good as Shakespeare. And he used the phrase 'What's for tea, Mum?' to illustrate how intonation can change the meaning of a sentence. He repeated the sentence several times, emphasizing different words. The final example made it sound as if it was Mum herself we were expecting to eat for tea. Everybody laughed. Everybody but Simon, that is.

'Are there any questions?' the lecturer asked.

'Yeah,' said Simon, slouched down in his chair, his long black hair falling across his face. 'How few books do we have to read to get through this course?' There was a certain snarling drawl in his voice. His whole body language – leaning back in his seat, with his foot resting on the seat in front – spoke of insolent disdain. His dark, hooded eyes flashed defiance.

The lecturer was taken aback. He was preaching a new, radical approach to English Literature. Unfortunately his new, radical approach didn't involve rejecting English Literature altogether.

The two of them were soon squabbling across the room: the urbane, sophisticated lecturer from his platform, trying to argue the case for a committed new approach to this tired old subject;

and the insolent young man, much older-looking than his years, from his slouched position, rejecting the whole hierarchical system, questioning the very basis, the very platform of secure academia, on which the lecturer stood.

Later I spoke to Simon in the junior common room. I offered him lunch. I had potatoes and eggs and wanted to make egg and chips. The only trouble was, I had no idea how to cook chips. I had to get Simon to show me how. There was I, dressed in my ripped, faded cords, looking like I'd been living in a squat for years, and I didn't even know how to make myself a plate of chips.

That evening we went back to Simon's place in Penarth, just outside Cardiff. We went by train. He had a top-floor flat. I remember the rickety stairs leading up. I remember an old woman on the first floor listening to Radio 4 very loud on an old radiogram. I'd never heard Radio 4 before. I remember the tiny kitchen on the landing, tucked beneath the sloping roof, with the bedroom to the side, and the living room in front. I remember the sloping roof of the living room, and the dormer window. I remember an electric fire and a stereo.

Simon introduced me to his wife. Her name was Jeannie. That's how grown-up he was compared to me, that he had a wife. I didn't even have a girlfriend. She had long, reddish hair and a frail, birdlike appearance. She had a thin nose and spoke nasally. I remember her fine, long fingers and brittle wrists. I can still hear her voice echoing down the years: not the words, just the tone, like a garbled whisper in an acoustic chamber.

We spent the evening together, the three of us. Jeannie kept looking back and forth at Simon and me and exclaiming, 'You could be brothers!' We both had long, black hair and dark eyes and were the same height, but I was slightly podgy (having only just left home) and Simon looked like an escapee from a concentration camp. He had broad shoulders and a bony chest. We went for a walk, and I borrowed Simon's jacket. Jeannie said, 'You look just like Simon in that jacket.' It was far too big for me. It dangled over my hands. We walked through the park and down to the seafront. We drank coffee in the café there.

Later Simon read a story. It was called, 'The Time, The Place, The People'. It was the story of a master singer and his pupil. I think now that it probably presaged my future relationship with

Simon. It said that only when the time was right, and the place was right, and the people were right, only then would the master singer sing, and awe his pupil with the beauty of the song. Then he let me read one of his own stories. It was about his first ever girlfriend. It ended up with him asking himself why he was writing this story. It's for an unknown friend, he answered, someone he hadn't yet met. I felt I was that friend.

I was always in awe of Simon. At the time I would have considered him a hippie. He had the hair and wore the right clothes. Once he wore a red bandanna as a headband and a rabbit-skin waistcoat. I tried wearing a headband too, but my ears stuck out. He was two years older than me and had lived in Notting Hill Gate. He was full of questioning new ideas. His defiance was palpable. He was a blaspheming, arrogant, sternly uncompromising young man with an acid wit and uncanny observational powers. He would pick up on things. Sometimes it seemed he knew what you were thinking.

But he wasn't really a hippie, any more than a man in a leather jacket is necessarily a biker. He was too much of a rebel to be a hippie. He was a bright kid from a poor background, still railing violently against the class system that had made his childhood so miserable. You couldn't go anywhere with Simon: the merest hint of a posh voice in the room would have him snarling with anger. He called posh people 'scum'. It was no wonder he couldn't stand the college.

These days Simon is far mellower. He even has a few posh friends.

And now we get to the difficult bit. Whenever I stayed with Simon and Jeannie, I would sleep with them. I kept my pants on at first, which they found amusing. I would lie there, sweating with frustration, feeling Jeannie's warm body pressed against my back. They were always fast asleep long before me. Then one night I took the pants off. Jeannie was very excited. She had her arms around the two of us. She was pinned to the bed, writhing with pleasure, while we stroked her lean, smooth body. Simon got up suddenly to make a cup of coffee, and the next thing I knew Jeannie's legs were around me and I was coming over her. It was as quick as that. I nearly cried with humiliation. I'd always imagined that I was such a stud.

26

They say that the first time that you make love affects you for the rest of your life. I would say that this is true. I've been caught, half-unconsciously, in threesomes ever since. Perhaps it explains why I've never been able to hold on to a relationship. I'm always waiting for the other person to come and join in.

Christmas that year I started going out with Rose again. I bought her a copy of 'Sticky Fingers' by the Rolling Stones for her Christmas present. She hadn't bought me a present, so she consented to having sex with me instead. That was my Christmas present: sex on my Mom and Dad's living-room floor. She seemed indifferent to it, like it was a duty to her rather than a pleasure. I gave up halfway through.

We went shopping one day. Rose wanted to dress me up. She bought me a pair of blue flared loons with pockets down the side, like overalls but far more expensive. Then we went to an Indian Restaurant for a meal. We ordered our meal from the menu and then sat and waited. The waiters were hanging round eyeing us up suspiciously, talking amongst themselves. Eventually someone came out. 'We can't cook that,' he said.

'OK, what can you do?' I asked.

'Chicken curry.'

So we had chicken curry instead. It was a quarter of chicken on the bone with some thin sauce dribbled over it, plopped onto a bed of rice. Then we ordered a cup of tea. The tea came with the tea bag still floating in it. Rose and I were laughing. It was obvious we weren't supposed to be there, as if the restaurant was a front for some other, more dubious operation. We were imagining drugs, or the white slave trade.

I hadn't tried LSD up till now, though I really wanted to. LSD was the hippie drug. I was an LSD-virgin, and therefore not yet a hippie.

A friend of mine, Graham, had got some black microdots. I'd only met him recently but there was an immediate bond between us. He lived in Chelmsley Wood, near my Mom and Dad's house, so we'd often walk home from the pub together. One night we stood by a little stream under a bridge and smoked cigarettes while we talked. We smoked cigarettes lit with matches from cupped hands. We talked about anything and everything –

all the things we enjoyed, all our beliefs and enthusiasms – in that lush, rushed, wild, enthusiastic way that young people often do talk. We still have conversations like that to this day.

Rose and I met him in the pub one day, and he was tripping. He was funny and perceptive. I could see that Rose liked him. I bought a few microdots from him. He was supposed to come over to my house in a couple of days to take one with Rose and me. I guess even then I must have known that something was going to happen between them. He could make her laugh. So I took a microdot with Rose the night before instead. She became like a little girl, dependent on my company, while I was like some dribbling Lothario lusting after her. I tried to snog her, pushing my tongue deep into her mouth, but she pushed me away. We walked into a pub and it was like Dante's Inferno. It was swirling with a fiendish red light and everyone had horns. We had to run away. On the way back we went to visit a friend. He came to the door in slow motion, and then speeded up, like a film put through a broken projector. I said, 'I can smell the green haze.' The friend sniffed, and realized there was a gas leak somewhere. He called out the gas board. Rose and I slept together that night, on my parents' living-room floor, with her huddled up to me for protection, and in the morning she left.

Then Graham came round ready to take the trip with us. It was about nine o'clock in the morning by now. So I had to take one with him too, to save his disappointment. We took a copy of Joyce's *Dubliners* with us, and went over to the park. We were like a couple of kids, playing on the swings, running around under the trees. We read from *Dubliners* and it didn't make any sense. I found it funny. Then I said, 'I've taken two trips, and had sex twice. You've taken ten trips, but you've never had sex.' We were sitting on the swings, dangling our legs. He appeared to be crying. I said, 'Are you crying?' and then he definitely was.

Later he told me that the reason he was crying was that he knew that he was in love with Rose, and that hurt. The second he'd seen her he'd fallen in love with her, he said; and in that moment, sitting on the swings, in a park in Birmingham, tripping with me, he knew that his childhood was over. He was crying for his lost childhood.

But after this the atmosphere changed. Something had crept in between us, like a sort of snarl. I kept looking at my watch. Time stood still. A minute was like eternity. All of a sudden I knew what it was to be mad. I was mad now, and it would last for ever. Then Graham started talking. He was making things up, playing the experienced tripper, the psychedelic teacher. He was bamboozling my mind, running rings round everything I said. We started walking while Graham just talked, on and on. I looked at him and I suddenly didn't know who I was. I'd forgotten my name. How could I answer when I didn't even know my own name? I couldn't even hear what he was saying. I kept thinking, What if we meet someone I know? How could they know me, I thought, when I didn't even know myself? How would I answer if they asked me a question about myself?

Who am I?

Later he took a trip with Rose as he'd wanted to. He was the trips king, unafraid, always funny. They started going out together. One night we were all at a party. They were going out together then. I was on the stairs, and she came up to me, laughing. I pushed her away from me violently. She laughed again. I was jealous.

I went back to Cardiff after the holidays dressed in all this new hippie gear Rose had bought for me. The first person I went to visit was Simon. I stood at his door and held out my arms. Simon was startled at the transformation. 'What's happened to you?' he said. I'd still got some of those microdots, and Simon, Jeannie and I took one each. It took a while for it to come on. Then I was looking at a stain on the wall, and it started moving. After that we were on the switch-back ride at the Carnival of Madness, once again. Jeannie was saying she wondered what it would be like to have two pricks inside her at the same time. Simon looked like Mephistopheles, with a thin goatee. We were in the bedroom, Jeannie and I sitting at the head of the bed, with Simon lying down at the foot. He started snarling at me, picking my character to pieces. I was pressed against the wall wondering what was going on, scared to death, unable to answer. I thought he must be telling me the truth. Later he told me that he thought I was an arrogant Indian prince looking down my nose at him.

Simon believed in free love. He wanted to abolish jealousy. He had another girlfriend besides Jeannie. One day the three of them shared a bed, and the two women were at each other's throats, cursing and snarling at each other. Simon was surprised. He was hurt. He'd shared Jeannie with me, so why couldn't she share him with someone else? He couldn't understand it, he said. He cried.

Later in the year Jeannie was away. Simon and I shared his bed. We masturbated each other. The day after, Simon said, 'That will hurt you more than it hurts me.'

Another time we were all in bed together and I could feel Simon's hand writhing around my penis. He was asleep. I told him what he had done the following day. He grew very sharp. 'Then you must have a very small prick,' he said. 'I thought it was your little finger.'

Simon and I shared birthdays. His was the day after mine. We were planning to have a party together. I said something inconsequential and he snapped. 'I apologize excessively,' I said, in an exaggerated manner, bowing like an eighteenth-century Lord.

'Yes, you do,' he said, putting me down. We'd been such good friends, and now we were squabbling all the time. He was always picking holes in my character.

The truth was that I was in love with Simon. I was having sex with his wife, but I was in love with him. And the other truth was that he was jealous of me. We did a lot of talking in those days. We preached our radical philosophies with a breezy indifference to the facts of our lives. We declared ourselves in favour of freedom. But Simon was jealous of me because I was having sex with his wife, and I was in love with him.

Jeannie put the dilemma very succinctly. She said, 'We're always talking about our conditioning. We're always saying we should break it down. But I don't think we can. We're stuck with it. It's what we are. And how can we change what we are?'

We were into fads. One time it was jacks. We played jacks for days on end, bouncing a tiny rubber ball and picking up the little moulded metallic stars in ones, twos, threes and fours. I became very good at it. Later it was the I Ching, the ancient Chinese oracle. You throw coins to read the future. I asked it a question: 'Should I stop seeing Simon and Jeannie?'

This was the answer it gave:

'Six in the third place means:
When three people journey together,
Their number decreases by one.
When one man journeys alone,
He finds a companion.'

Did I follow this wise advice?
 No.

Rose came to Cardiff to visit me. She was being awkward and grumpy the whole weekend.

Jeannie was walking up ahead one evening, looking very sexy in a pair of high-heeled boots. I was behind, with Rose. 'Jeannie walks like a film star,' I said.

'No she doesn't. Everyone walks like that in high-heeled boots.'

There were a few of us around Simon and Jeannie's flat one day. I'd got one last microdot, and we cut it into six. Imagine it! A microdot is about the size of a pin-head. It was a precision operation. We went for a walk down the front. We were walking on the grass. In the distance we could see the promenaders walking along the footpath. Rose laughed. She said they looked like they were on a conveyor belt. We got back to the flat and someone put on Radio 4. The voice of the newsreader sounded so pompous we all laughed. Then we couldn't stop laughing. It became like purgatory, to be laughing at precisely nothing.

I think Rose had already started going out with Graham by this time, or she was thinking about it at least. This weekend was my last attempt to get her back. It failed. Rose and Graham were together for a number of years.

Rose wasn't a hippie either. No one in this book so far has been a hippie. She was a working-class Brummie from a council estate, with aspirations to be an artist. The fact that she wore flares and took LSD is neither here nor there. Everyone took LSD and wore flares, or everyone I knew, all the people of my age. It was fashion, rather than philosophy. The hippies, really, were a vocal minority making a great noise in the capital and the media at the time, a group of people we aspired to emulate. They were the people who had led the fashion. But they were not the same as us.

What's the difference between a working-class Brummie from

a council estate and a hippie? A hippie can be an artist if he or she wants to be. People from council estates aren't allowed. Or this is Rose's opinion, anyhow.

Rose had a nervous breakdown in 1979. She was diagnosed manic-depressive. She's been on medication ever since and virtually housebound for the last two years. She never did fulfil her ambition to be an artist.

I saw her recently. I told her about this book. 'What do you think about hippies now then, Rose?' I asked.

'Grrr,' she said.

3 Free Love

'To make a fool develop
It furthers one to apply discipline.
The fetters should be removed.
To go on in this way brings humiliation.'

The I Ching, Hexagram 4, 'Youthful Folly'

I first met Steve in the Buccaneer. Actually there's some dispute about this. I always say that we met in the Pig and Whistle. Steve then says that, no, we met in the Buccaneer. I defer to his better knowledge of these matters. I accept that, yes, it probably was the Buccaneer. But this is all a play. After the first time that Steve had corrected me, I remembered very clearly that it was actually the Buccaneer. I only keep the dispute going in order to defer to Steve in the end. Let's face it: someone has to defer to Steve occasionally – Steve usually being the deferential one – and deference has always been one of my special talents too.

He was going out with a girl called Mandy at the time. She was very pretty, petite, with shoulder-length blonde hair. Steve was very much in love with her.

He was wearing this green and white striped public school

33

blazer. Public school blazers were quite the thing with hippies, a fashion statement that probably goes a long way towards revealing the social origins of most of them. I don't know where Steve got his from, though. I don't think that in Steve's case it was actually his old school blazer, though he had been to a posh school. I was wearing a prison bomber jacket, even though I'd never been to prison. And this kind of illustrates what we were all about: Steve in the blazer of a school he'd never attended, and me in a prison bomber jacket, though I'd never been to prison. It was an act, it was a game, it was a put-on. It didn't mean anything at all.

I'd bought the jacket at a jumble sale during an ill-fated trip to the south coast a couple of years before. As such it had a certain sentimental value. Steve and I swapped jackets. After that, I'd see him in my jacket and he'd see me in his. It kind of sealed the bond between us. I don't know how it came about, us swapping jackets. It was one of those spontaneous acts that young people are prone to. I remember feeling a sort of smug pleasure in the act. I think I thought I was being radical.

I was quite the radical young man by then. I spouted free love freely to anyone who would listen. Of all the monuments to hippie ideology, free love was possibly the most defining. We spoke of love and peace. What we meant was sex. There was an awful lot of sex, but not all that much love. Or rather, there was an awful lot of sex if you were young and attractive and stylish and straight, and you had an intelligent sounding array of bullshit at your disposal.

I was still the pupil, remember, singing the master singer Simon's favourite song. Also, after the failure with Rose, and the emotional confusion of Simon and Jeannie, simple sex seemed the obvious solution.

I was living with Steve and Dave the communist in Mackintosh Place. This was a few months later. Simon and Jeannie had gone to live in London, Simon having dropped out of college.

Dave was a satyr: there's no other word to describe him. His enthusiasm for anything sexual was boundless. He couldn't stop himself. It was as if there was direct connection between his eyeballs and his testicles, with no resistance in between. He would simply launch himself at women, a quality that I believe some women found attractive. There's nothing like enthusiasm to spark off enthusiasm in another human being.

One day I was in my bedroom, with whatever girlfriend it was I was going out with at the time. The room was tiny, barely large enough to fit the double bed in. The gap between the door and the foot of the bed was less than three feet. The girl and I were naked on the bed. Suddenly Dave walked in. He saw us there. He was fully dressed, but by the time he'd covered the distance between the door and the bed, his clothes were off. He was like an arrow: straight in there.

Dave and I had this league table going. We wanted to fuck as many woman as possible. It was a race. Well, I would be embarrassed about this now, if it wasn't for the fact that there were women involved too. Everyone I knew was promiscuous – or everyone I wanted to know, rather.

But there's a difference between being promiscuous because you happen to like fucking, and being promiscuous because you see it as your civic duty to act in this way. The free love concept was promiscuity disguised as a philosophy. It tied the whole thing up in rhetorical wrapping paper, like some cheap, useless toy in a flashy package. It's the packet that sells, not what's inside. I was always very lyrical. Also I had the advantage of being fairly good-looking, in a wimpy sort of way. So I used to say things like: 'Sex is an act of love, which is an act of friendship.' And then I might add, 'What's the hang-up?' The implication being, if you didn't go along with the philosophy, it must be your problem.

I can't remember the things I said now. I wish I could. I'm sure I had a whole array of arguments at my disposal. I was good at talking, good at sounding like I believed what I was saying, good at mixing logic with sincerity in a way that gave credence to both. Whatever it was I said, I know that it launched me into the hearts, not to say the loins, of a number of attractive young women I knew.

One of them was a girl called Gaynor. I'd seen her in the Pig and Whistle once, and been struck by her quiet, dark beauty. She had long black hair and wore large, circular, Gypsy earrings. It turned out that she was going out with someone from Newport. That didn't stop me, though. I managed to persuade her to fuck with me. Even as we were doing it – and as we were sitting naked on the bed afterwards – she was saying, 'I don't know what's come over me. I don't usually do this. I'm faithful. I've only ever slept with two people in my life, and my boyfriend is the other one.'

Gaynor was a woman I could really have loved, and she was definitely in love with me. I slept with her two or three times and then moved on.

You'll be pleased to know that vanity on this monumental scale never lasts. Not in my life it doesn't. Even before we reach the end of this chapter, that sly, vain young man will have met his first obstacle. And by Chapter 8 he will be facing his Nemesis, all his luck stripped away. So maybe there is such a thing as Justice after all. Who knows?

Steve and Mandy would listen to this free-love stuff, too. Steve kind of liked it, although he was never promiscuous, being a romantic at heart. He was always a sucker for anything alternative-sounding. But – like I say – it was the package that sold, not the contents. It didn't sound like a chat-up line. It sounded like a true-love concept.

And Mandy liked me, and Mandy's friend Gill liked Steve; but for Steve, Mandy was the only one, the love of his life. And I quite liked Gill, but I also liked Mandy. And Dave liked just about anything that moved and even, occasionally, things that didn't move either. And the whole thing was a convoluted, extraordinary, ridiculous mess.

And then one evening, after some typical lyrical diatribe, Mandy, Steve and I ended up in a threesome. I felt that it was my duty to mankind to instigate this. It was a philosophical statement. Afterwards Mandy said to Steve, 'What sort of guy are you? What sort of boyfriend are you? Any other boyfriend would have thumped him one.' But Steve couldn't see that. What I'd said had made a certain amount of sense to him. Not that Mandy had resisted during the lovemaking. In fact she had been excited. And then it dawned on Steve that Mandy liked me. He was working at the time, some telephone office job. He was being responsible and together because he loved Mandy so much. She gave him a sense of pride and self-worth, a feeling like he had some meaning and direction in life. He used to ring her up all the time at her Mum's house, and she would come round to the flat to see him. But he was becoming consumed with jealousy. There was a deep suspicion gnawing away at him. And one day he had this sensation while he was at work.

I've got this phrase going through my head. 'Like unquiet ghosts in the bones of my house.' It's a line I made up to explain a feeling. Something is stirring, something deep and alien, foreign to the rational mind; something that is communicated in dreams and premonitions alone, wafted on the air, like a strange breeze blown from some other country. Whenever someone feeds me with rational bullshit about free love, I remember that phrase and the feeling it conveys. There are deeper things than words. There are things that go beyond the rational or explainable. I've no doubt that was the feeling that Steve was having that day.

Something was up. He knew that Mandy was round at Mackintosh Place with me. And then, when he got home, there she was. Not that we were doing anything, but the suspicion remained. He knew that she'd come round specifically to see me. And as soon as he walked through the door he caught her eye, and there was this furtive little flash of guilt there. 'Like unquiet ghosts in the bones of my house.' A chill ran through him, a sudden pang of fear.

The atmosphere closed in around us, dense, heavy, oppressive. I said: 'What's the matter?' But no one answered. We were going out together that night, all three of us. We walked into town and no one was talking. I kept saying, 'What's the matter with you two?'

Mandy finished with Steve that night, there in the Park Lane Bar, with its plain linoed floor and strip-lights, its cheap Guinness, its bare wooden tables. She said, 'I don't want to see you any more.' And he blacked out.

After that he started taking downers. He lost his job, and Mandy started going out with Dave. Steve told me that it always hurt him to see those two together. I can't say I noticed.

Steve and I took a trip. Steve is the kind of person who everyone said shouldn't take trips. He was already in a world of his own. He would get so high that you feared he would never come back. But he decided to take this trip anyway. He didn't care any more. We were walking by the weir, and the water seemed to freeze. He thought, *Oh good, the trip's coming on.* But that was it. Nothing else happened for him. He was so miserable about Mandy that even the normally devastating LSD didn't affect him. It affected me though. I saw two trees over the river and their leaves had turned to letters of the alphabet. One of them spelled out the word 'FANG', while the other one spelled out 'HELP ME'. I was babbling on about this. 'Look at those trees. One is saying . . .' Steve couldn't see it at all. All he could see were two ordinary willows, very nice in their own way, but not in the slightest bit psychedelic. Anyway, he was bored. He wanted to go to the pub. So we did. We had a few drinks, and I discovered the extraordinary adaptability of the word 'Wow'. It could be said in so many different ways. You could say it like a question: 'Wow?' Or like a bold assertion: 'Wow!' You could say it like a proposition: 'Wow.' Or like box of chocolates with boiling water poured over them: 'Wo-o-o-o-o-o-o-o-o-o wwwwwwwwwwwwwwwwwwwww.' In fact you could say it in so many ways that my poor old computer doesn't have enough grammatical symbols to cover them all: 'Wow: Wow; Wow> Wow^ Wow* Wow< Wow} Wow~ Wow# Wow/ Wow| Wow+ Wow=' and on and on and on. I said 'Wow' so many times that the bouncer in the pub chucked me out. 'Wow,' I said, as I landed on the pavement outside. Steve followed me out. We went to a club and I carried on saying 'Wow' until even the normally faithful Steve had had enough. *Fuck this*, he thought, and went home to bed.

There's no such thing as freedom without limits. There's no such thing as simple sex. It's the limit that defines the freedom. It's the complications that make sex interesting. The opposite of freedom is not oppression. The opposite of freedom is too much freedom. Real freedom requires discipline. The problem with hippie philosophy was that it arose mainly as a reaction to what went before. But it was never discerning. It rejected the old, laced-up, patent leather, corporate world of the company man and replaced it with . . .

With what? With tennis shoes. With baseball boots. Anyone who's worn baseball boots for more than half a day will know the drawbacks. Stinking sweaty feet, the outrageous pong of terminal athlete's foot.

My Uncle George had several pairs of shoes he'd kept for twenty-five years or more. He polished them all every Sunday morning. They had leather soles. Every time the soles went he'd have them fixed. They were shiny and soft and beautifully crumpled and kept his feet dry in all weathers.

There always was a difference between the mind-numbing respectability of the American corporate man and the cautious respectability of the British working class. The hippie philosophy had come out of America. It had arisen from all that was alienating and destructive in American life. It had been taken on initially by well-off people in Britain (many of whom had private incomes). Rebellion was in the air. Everything was to be thrown over. Conditioning. Capitalism. All the token constraints of so-called straight society. 'Kick out the jams, motherfuckers!' as one song so succinctly put it. Put the whole stinking mess of it in the rubbish bin. And so began the throwaway society.

Working-class respectability included such out-of-date notions as mutuality, decency, respect. Certain people still believed in notions of honesty and trustworthiness. They were concerned for the welfare of others. They wanted to work. They thought work created dignity. They had a vision of the future that included everyone. Or my Uncle George did, at least.

In rejecting all that was old we were also in danger of rejecting many things that were good. We were throwing the baby out with the bath water, and leaving the world open to the libertarian philosophies of the far right. It's no accident that a number of prominent hippies went on to become yuppies. It's no accident that the anarchistic individualism of the seventies gave way to the free-market individualism of the eighties. What's the difference between doing-your-own-thing off your head on acid at a festival, and doing-your-own-thing off your head on cocaine in the City of London? Nothing but the location. Libertarianism is a disease not a philosophy.

I'd left college by this time. Still Simon's follower, I'd 'dropped out' in good old hippie style. Not that I had any idea what to replace it with. I had no allowance. I had no private income. I couldn't travel the world. So I got a job.

I was a machine operator in a steelworks for a time. That was interesting. The machine was called a grit-blaster. It literally blasted grit at the freshly forged bars of steel as they came off the rolling mills, leaving the surface of the bars mottled and matt-grey. A huge crane would drop the glowing bars of steel onto the top of my machine. Then I would shuffle them down through a succession of mechanical platforms, working them up and down to get them straight, until they fell, one at a time, onto the rollers taking them into the grit-blaster itself, and on, past my jurisdiction. Or that was the idea anyway. Occasionally more than one bar would fall onto the rollers causing the machine to clog up. Then everything would have to stop while labourers down below man-handled the bars into their proper order. Once, one of the bars came off the machine altogether and into the passageway. It kind of rose up and leapt off the machine onto the floor with a vicious clanging insistence. No one quite knew what to do. No one had ever prepared for this eventuality. There were sliding cranes bringing steel from the rolling mill to the grit-blaster. And there were sliding cranes taking steel from the grit-blaster to wherever it went next. But there were no cranes that could reach the passageway, and no human could lift the huge bars back onto the machine. For some unknown reason, it seems, the man who designed the machine had failed to include an anti-C. J. Stone device in his plans. The machine was on halt for a whole day.

From the grit-blaster I moved into the accounts department. I seem to remember someone suggesting that I might prefer it in there. Obviously I was too much of an intellectual to work on a machine. Maybe they thought I'd find safety in numbers.

I made myself smart. I had a black, floppy-collared shirt and a black kipper tie. I had the black loons that Rose had bought me, and a black jacket. I was an existentialist trainee accountant. All that remained was the shoes. I bought myself a pair of white pumps.

Well I thought I looked smart: all in black with white pumps. The office manager thought otherwise. After about a fortnight he called me into his office to ask if I'd make some alterations to my dress. He didn't object to the floppy collared shirt and the kipper tie, though he had grounds to. He didn't object to the hair dangling round my chest, nor the beard. He didn't even object to the frightful flares on my black, cavalry twill loon-pants. No. It was the pumps. You weren't allowed to wear pumps in the office. So I left. It was a matter of principle. I was a hippie. I liked to smell my feet at the end of the day.

Actually I was very happy during the time I worked in that office. I'd just learned to meditate. Every evening I would do my meditations, and every morning I would wake up with the sun streaming through my window, and eat egg and tomatoes on toast. It was a boundless, optimistic time. I even liked going to the office. All I had to do was to add up lists of numbers on an adding machine. All the numbers were minus numbers, this being a Nationalized Industry, so my sartorial stance was a statement of another kind. The steelworks were in the red, but at least the accountant was in the black.

And then, when I'd done the work, I would spend time looking out of the window at Caerphilly mountain in the distance, or reading books tucked into the drawer of my desk. I was at the back of the office, so no one noticed. And when I looked up and across at the mountain, hazy in the sunlight, it seemed I was seeing my future there, bright and full of hope.

After that I moved back to Birmingham and got a job in a social security office. I was a runner. This was in the days before the files were kept on computer. I had to find the files and bring them to the office staff. You literally had to run from department to department along the polished corridors. So the white pumps came in handy in the end. We were encouraged to wear them. They stopped you from falling over.

Eventually I moved in with Auntie Elsie and Uncle George in Burton-on-Trent, where I worked as a dustman.

Actually Elsie and George weren't really my Aunt and Uncle. Elsie was my Grandmother's sister, so they were my Great Aunt and Great Uncle. Also they were my godparents. They were a childless couple. I guess that's why they took their godparenting duties so seriously. Seriously enough, in fact, to invite me to their home. Elsie was a plump, merry, kindhearted woman with an infectious laugh and a real love of animals. I've no doubt that, were she still alive in the nineties, she would be one of those people protesting at the export of live animals. George was a wiry, old, bent-backed Staffordshire man with a clipped, dry sense of humour. He'd been a printer, but these days had become a gardener. He was also a socialist and a republican. We used to laugh at the royal family together. They lived a life of order and simplicity, where the very routine was their source of pleasure. They did the same things every day and in the same order. For instance, George would always go to the same pub every day at six o'clock, and drink the same amount of the same beer, and smoke the same number of cigarettes. Ten cigarettes a day, starting at six o'clock. And then he'd go home and watch the nine o'clock news with Elsie while they made toast on the fire's embers. After that they would go to bed.

George said, 'Man, know thyself.' He meant, know your limits.

I learnt from them that the questioning spirit was not a new thing. Rebellion wasn't invented by the hippies at all. George would tell me tales of working-class struggle, of strikes for better pay and conditions. He said, 'I don't know why people do overtime. We fought for the forty-hour week.' And despite the fact that he was always laughing at Elsie and calling her fat, you could tell how devoted they were to each other. For George and Elsie, free love would have been a ludicrous concept. To them, love meant loyalty and respect.

It was while I was staying with them that I met Beverley. I was back at my Mom and Dad's for a weekend while they were away. Simon had come to visit. It was my sister who introduced me to her. She was one of my sister's friends. And she wasn't a hippie either; she was a *Cosmo* girl, into make-up and how to achieve the perfect orgasm.

We were all planning to go for a drink: Beverley, my sister, myself and Simon. But somehow Beverley and I ended up going out alone. I think that my sister engineered it that way.

We had a few drinks and chatted. I wasn't chatting her up. I was being philosophical, spoon-feeding her Simon's thoughts on love and freedom in bite-sized pieces. I was very intense in my own right, but the philosophy wasn't mine. Nevertheless, I must have seemed impressively different.

I put my arm around her jokingly. 'How y' doin' darlin'?' I said, again aping Simon. She nestled into the crook of my arm, and the next thing I knew we were kissing.

We walked home hand in hand. We got to my front door and it

was like a switch going on. No words. We went straight upstairs and made love.

It was magical. It was free. It was my first real taste of love. We were going out for a month or two after that.

Beverley was very beautiful. She was also very intelligent. She was in love with me, and I was in love with her. In any other age, maybe, she would have been the girl that I married. But this was the seventies and I was still jabbering on about free love. I guess she felt threatened. She wanted a normal life. She wanted to have a family. She started seeing her ex-boyfriend again.

Well that was all right, wasn't it? Free love meant sharing. She wasn't my 'possession'. She was her own person, free to do what she liked. I wasn't jealous. Jealousy was a selfish emotion. Why bind each other with promises? I could see other women and she could see other men. Of course she could see her ex-boyfriend. After all, he loved her too. We both loved her. And what is sex but an expression of love? What is love but freedom? I was free. She was free. Everybody should be free.

That's how I talked, on and on and on. Blah, blah, blah. They were not my words, they were Simon's.

When the note came saying she couldn't see me any more, I threw it in the bin. My sister laughed.

'What are you laughing at?' I spat peevishly.

'What did you expect?' said my sister, and laughed again.

I saw Beverley recently. She still lives in the same part of Birmingham as my Mom and Dad. I went round to her house to see her and we ate chicken tikka sandwiches and drank coffee. She has four children and is training to be a Church of England priest. She's had various mystical experiences in her life, she told me. One day she felt the love of God permeating the very air around her, suffusing the planet with vibrancy and light. Everything in the world was right, a perfect expression of the love of God, she told me. She felt high for a couple of weeks after that. So she's not a *Cosmo* girl any more. She's a Cosmic woman.

4 Oops

This story has several starting points. There's Palo Alto, California, sometime in the early sixties, and Ken Kesey's Acid Tests. The Grateful Dead, the acid revolution. There's Haight-Ashbury, San Francisco, 1967. The Summer of Love, the Grateful Dead again, Be-Ins, Happenings. There's Notting Hill Gate, 1968, the UFO club. Light shows, acid, the beautiful people. There's Death Valley, California, 1969, and the Sharon Tate murders. There's October 1971, and one young Brummie's journey to discover his fate. And there's sometime in 1997, over thirty years from the first date, when the young man's successor, a bemused old poker player, sits down to write a book about hippies.

No, I'm not really a poker player. Poker players have poker faces, and you can read me like a book. In fact, you're reading me like a book right now. I only said that so that I could go on to say that sometimes it seems as if life has dealt me a bum hand. But, then again – as any genuine poker player will tell you – it's how you play the cards that matters.

At this stage in my life – when I was starting to write this – I was living in Birmingham again. So research involved taking the same route down to Cardiff that I'd taken that very first time, and many other times since. I was on my way to see Steve.

You leave Birmingham on the M5. After that you take the M50 to Ross-on-Wye, and then the A40 and the A449 until you hit the M4 just outside Newport, which takes you the rest of the way. Well, I love the M50. I love slipping out of the hectic, hectoring, fuming, angry traffic on the M5 and onto this peaceful, westward-sweeping dual carriageway. There's hardly ever any traffic on it, which begs the question, really, of why they built the road in the first place. Obviously Cardiff people don't want to go to Brum, and you can't blame them for that. And as for Brummies: well I like to think that I'm the only one who's ever wanted to make this journey. It makes me feel important.

Steve lives in Ely, a large council estate to the West of Cardiff. You follow the signs to Cardiff West off the M4, and you're there. So you arrive in this ordinary street on this ordinary council estate, where ordinary people are getting on with their ordinary lives – washing their cars and weeding their gardens, cooking the dinner, taking their dogs for a walk – and then, in the midst of all this, you come across this extraordinary man with extraordinary ambitions and extraordinary beliefs, living in an extraordinary house. Well, on the outside it doesn't look all that different from the houses around it. Same pebbledash exterior, same council-issue window frames and door. Maybe the garden is a bit more overgrown and – were you a horticulturist – you might just recognize an unusual plant or two; and, as you approach the front door, you'd see a garden gnome peering at you through the window. But you wouldn't think much about this. A little bit of whimsy, that's all. It's when you enter the living room that you recognize it as what it is: a shrine to chaos. Steve's house is a jungle. It's a jungle of strange plants, mostly grown from seed. It's a jungle of wildlife, including stick-insects and cockroaches, toads and axolotls, which glare at you grimly or strangely from a variety of tanks and bottles and sweetie jars

45

scattered about the place. He even has a pet fungus: a huge, rubbery blob that lives in a beer bucket under the cactuses and feeds off sweet tea and herbs and produces a tart, sparkling beverage called Kombucha which Steve is brave enough and foolhardy enough to drink. And then there's the walls, another jungle: a profusion of images, photographs, drawings, paintings, slapped up indiscriminately, and charting, in a higgledy-piggledy way, the entire history of Steve's life and friendships, a testament to the extraordinary profusion of his mind. There's crop circles and UFOs, Arthurian characters and ancient magicians, various gods and goddesses from the East and from the West. There's black-and-white and coloured photographs from around the globe, all of the people he knows or is in contact with, from Germany, from Finland, from America, from Australia. There's a whole, vast world in there; or rather, two worlds: the world of the natural and the world of the supernatural, coexisting in delicious harmony, like the fairies and the spirits and the little people frolicking amongst the foliage in a Richard Dadd painting.

There's also a table covered in books and magazines in the middle of the room, several bookshelves weighed down with arcane literature, a cupboard full of tapes and books and loose sheets of paper chronicling his continuing quest to become an international superstar. And some ordinary things too: a small black-and-white TV, an old-fashioned video, a cheap midi-system, and one or two incongruous items of weight-training equipment. The weight-training equipment belongs to his son.

Well, I know the place, of course. I've visited it many, many times. I always like to visit Steve. I've always felt extraordinarily at home there. How can you tell if a friendship is real or not? I'll tell you. A friend is someone you feel comfortable with.

Steve is just himself. He's always been like this. You could call him a hippie, and certainly that's what he looks like. But it's not specific enough. It's lumping too many things under one label, like looking at a rose bush and calling it a plant. Steve is far too weird to be a hippie.

Actually he's an alien. He was dropped off by some passing starship some time in the late sixties, in order to scout the Earth for a possible future invasion. The only trouble was, they forgot to tell him what the Earthlings would look like, and then they forgot to pick him up again. He's been stuck here, confused, ever since. There are things here that were abolished from his galaxy a billion years ago: like money, supermarkets, washing machines and seatbelts. Consequently he's under the confused impression that all of these creatures harbour intelligent life. As for us human beings: well, we must be their slaves, naturally enough.

The best way I can illustrate this is to tell you a story. I was giving him a lift once. I opened the back door so he could load his luggage, but was surprised when he started getting in the back himself. 'You can sit in the front you know, Steve,' I said. 'I don't want to feel like a chauffeur.' He gave a kind of resigned huff and got in the front seat. 'Fasten your seatbelt,' I reminded him. It was at this moment that I caught his confusion. He simply didn't understand what a seatbelt was. He was holding it with a look of consternation on his face, poised in a moment of dread, as if I'd just caught him out at something. He was holding the thing gingerly, waving it up and down. He didn't know whether to kill it, talk with it, or bow down to it and address it as Sir.

'Come here,' I said, and leaned across and did it up for him, while he let out one of his characteristic, spluttering guffaws.

That's what I like about Steve. He's absurd, and he knows it.

Here's another story that illustrates this aspect of Steve's character. This happened sometime in the late eighties. Steve was working for Robin Williamson at the time, as his secretary. In case you don't remember: Robin Williamson had been a member of the Incredible String Band, a spectacularly popular folk/rock/poetry duo of the mid-sixties, who had just as spectacularly bombed into glum obscurity in the mid-seventies. Robin Williamson was a member of the Church of Scientology, as Steve was at the time. That's how they met.

So Steve was round at Robin Williamson's house one day, typing up letters, filing correspondence, answering the phone and all the rest, when there was a phone call.

'Hello, is Robin in?' asked a voice from the other end.

'No. Who is this speaking please? Would you like to leave a message?' said Steve in his best efficient secretary's voice.

'This is Van Morrison,' said the voice.

Steve is a devotee of Van Morrison. He adores the man. So you can imagine it, can't you? It's Van Morrison on the end of the phone. The Van Morrison, Van the Man, the international super-star, a world-famous singer/songwriter of almost mythical stature, and one of Steve's greatest heroes. Steve was just dumb-founded, dumbstruck, stunned by the enormity of the occasion. He started to babble incoherently down the phone.

'Oh, um, yeah, like,' he said. 'Um.'

Meanwhile Van Morrison was on the other end of the phone, waiting to get on with his phone call. He, too, was a member of the Church of Scientology. He just happened to be in town, and was ringing up to make arrangements to meet his old friend. Not that he got the chance to say any of this. Steve was still burbling on in a fit of excitement.

'I've always been a, well, like, a great fan of yours,' said Steve.

'Yeah?' said Van Morrison.

'Yeah, yeah, really. I really love your music,' said Steve. 'So what, er, what shall I, er, is there any . . .?'

'Just tell Robin that I'm in the area and that I'll call again later,' said Van Morrison.

'Oh yeah, yeah, right, I'll do that,' said Steve, doubly excited now because he was performing a service for Van Morrison too, 'yeah.'

'All the best,' said Van Morrison, and put down the phone.

Well Steve was really excited as he placed the phone back on its receiver. He thought, *Wow, that was Van Morrison on the phone, and he spoke to me. Van Morrison said 'All the best' to me. This is brilliant.* And he buzzed about the rest of the day performing all his tasks with a new energy and purpose, before passing the message on to Robin in the evening.

Well, that was all earlier in the year, and simply provides the backdrop for this tale. It was Steve's first contact with Van Morrison.

Later, Robin Williamson was holding an outdoor concert in the grounds of the folk museum in St Fagans, near Ely. Steve and his son were invited, and decided to go along. It was a spectacularly dismal midsummer's day, lashing with rain, and the concert was moved into a marquee tent. You could hear the rain beating on the canvas as it collected in pools on the roof.

So after the concert was over Steve noticed two men standing by the exit. One of them was Van the Man. Robin Williamson went over to talk to them. Steve was eavesdropping on the conversation. Van was introducing the other man to Robin Williamson, saying that he lived in Ely. This was Steve's cue. He thought, *Van Morrison is friends with someone who lives in Ely, and I live in Ely. I'd better introduce myself.* And he went over to talk.

'So you're Van Morrison then, are you?' he said, and then immediately regretted it. As if Van Morrison didn't know who Van Morrison was.

'Yeah?' said The Man, in that indifferent way of his, part-question, part-answer, part-yawn. Van Morrison is notoriously uncommunicative.

'Yeah, yeah. I spoke to you before.'

'Yeah?'

'Yeah, on the phone, you remember. I'm Robin's secretary.'

At which point Robin Williamson intervened. 'Yeah, Van: this is Steve Andrews. He helps me out occasionally. He's a good bloke.'

Yeah, yeah, thanks for that, Robin, thought Steve.

'Yeah?' said Van Morrison again. Nothing was going to break his ice.

'Yeah, I've always been a great fan of yours,' said Steve, still sailing blithely on, despite the difficulties.

'Yeah?'

'Yeah, and I've always loved your music.'

Things weren't going too well. He'd even forgotten the reason he'd started the conversation. He hadn't mentioned Ely at all.

At this point Isaac came up.

'Dad,' he said.

'Yeah?' said Steve.

'See this rope,' said Isaac, pointing to one of the guy ropes just outside the exit.

'Yeah?' said Steve.

'Can you put your face by it,' said Isaac.

'Yeah?' said Steve, beginning to sound like Van Morrison now, always saying yeah.

'Well go on then.'

So he did. He put his face by the guy rope, just inches away, while the rest of them looked on. He put his face by the guy rope and he waited. At which point Isaac shrieked with laughter, and twanged the rope, and a veritable deluge of water that had been collecting on the roof all afternoon cascaded down over Steve's face and down his neck and over his clothes. Steve stood up, mortified. After being frozen out by his hero, now here he was being humiliated too. He didn't know what to do. He dared not look at the others. Instead he took Isaac's hand and, muttering incoherently, led him out to the exit.

So what on earth was Steve doing? Why did he bow down before a guy rope in this way? Probably because he thought it was an Earthling commander, and he was showing it proper respect. Like I said: Steve is an alien, not a hippie. Hippies only give obeisance to guy ropes when they're off their heads on strange drugs.

I was in Cardiff to begin investigations for this book. Not that Cardiff was ever the centre of the hippie cult. People don't refer to Cardiff in the same breath they refer to Haight-Ashbury, Palo Alto or Notting Hill Gate. Ken Kesey never visited here. Alan Ginsburg never Ommed here. There never was an *Oz* 'Cardiff Edition' to shake the foundations of the State. John Lennon didn't live in exile here. There wasn't ever a free festival here. They didn't make drugs here. There wasn't a single LSD factory in the whole town. Jimi Hendrix wasn't born here, nor did he die here. No one famous died here. It's a dull but pleasant provincial capital. People don't even speak Welsh here, let alone study the Vedas in Sanskrit in order to discover the mathematical formulae that underlie Creation. They watch the telly. They go to the Bingo. Occasionally they go to the shops.

But Cardiff does have one distinction in the history of the hippie cult: that once it had taken root here it never died out. People still wear velvet cloaks and loon pants. They still wear bangles and patchouli oil. Girls wear long, fringed skirts and huge earrings. Men part their hair in the middle and say 'man' a lot. They think this is the fashionable thing to do. It's hard to tell them that none of it was fashionable in the first place. Steve even has a pair of tartan loon pants he bought sometime in late June 1971. He gets them out occasionally to wear at seventies revivalist nights and he invariably wins the first prize in the 'look a prat' competition. But then, Steve has an excuse. When he was dropped off from the Mothership all those years ago, everyone was dressed in similarly stupid clothes. He's been trying to blend in ever since. He thinks that's what Earthlings look like.

My original conception for this book was that I should be in pursuit of Piss-Off Pete. I wanted to interview everyone who remembered him and, perhaps, get their own stories in the process. I felt I needed a hook to hang the story on, and Piss-Off Pete seemed the ideal candidate, not only because he seemed like a victim of the era, but also because he was so memorable. The only trouble was, hardly anyone remembered him.

It was in this context that I contacted Piers and Gill through Steve, and made an arrangement for us to go round. I wasn't sure if I knew them or not. Steve told me that Piers was a fan of my writing. 'But Gill doesn't like you,' he said.

'Why doesn't she like me? I don't think she even knows me,' I said.

'Yes she does,' Steve said, 'she remembers you all right. She says you're dodgy, but she won't say what happened. Something to do with sex. That's all I know.'

We went round to see them anyway.

They live in a beautiful, quiet little cul-de-sac near a park, in a smart, suburban house. Piers answered the door. I wasn't sure if I'd ever met him. He seemed vaguely familiar, tall and lanky with a dark moustache, but he was obviously never a close friend of mine. We shook hands and he showed me through into the kitchen; and there was Gill, sitting at the kitchen table, giving me this look, guarded but friendly. She must have caught the look on my face too. Oops. I remembered her all right.

'Hello Gill,' I said.

'Hello Chris,' she said, and her smile was suffused with an amused kind of scepticism.

It must have been October 1973. I'd gone back to Cardiff, after the disaster with Beverley, to resume my college course. I'd gone round to see Dave, who was living with Richard and Jude at the time. Jude was a hippie Earth-Mother type, who later changed her name to Willow and became a witch. (Actually, she's not in the slightest bit like a hippie Earth-Mother type, but more of this later.) Richard was this mad scientist with soulful, hooded eyes. Gill was staying with them at the time, though I'd never met her before. I needed a place to crash for the night, and Jude said I could use Gill's bed. They weren't expecting her back that night. 'But if she does come back, you'll have to leave,' said Jude. So I went to bed, and sometime later Gill walked in.

Well I was naked. I had a hard-on. There was a woman in the room. I guess I must have been fairly persuasive, because we shagged. I don't remember much about it, but I expect it was very nice. I also expect that I made promises that I later failed to keep. So the free-love concept had now taken another turn. I no longer spouted it as a philosophical statement. I was practising it, but without telling anyone.

It's funny how things go out of your head. I hadn't thought of Gill or that night for years. Not since that night, in fact. We spent some time together, and that was it. I forgot about it. And now here she was, a face from my past, unforgettable.

This whole visit to Cardiff had been like that. Memories flooding in from all over: places I'd been, places I'd seen, people I'd known, things I'd done, things I'd left undone. But it wasn't like the memories were in my head. It took walking down a certain street to remember. It was as if I'd planted the memory on that street ready to return in twenty years time. It was as if I'd left a little bit of myself in that place, and then, when I returned, that bit of myself was still there, but grown abundant, a fruit-laden plant. It was the same with Gill. I'd left a little bit of myself inside her that night. It took seeing her again to remember it.

Well I was here to interview them about Piss-Off Pete, not to recall sexual indiscretions from my past. We were sitting around the kitchen table, the four of us, drinking a variety of alcoholic beverages. I switched on my Dictaphone. Piers was remembering Pete wearing a frilly pink tutu, but Gill disagreed. She said that, no, it wasn't Pete in the tutu, it was somebody else, the man who later became Roland Rat. They had a squabble. Gill told me that a friend of hers had gone out with Pete for a while. 'Then she started noticing that he was more interested in her male friends than he was in her,' she said. That was all either of them remembered about him.

Piers started telling me about a trip he'd taken in the Top Hat, a seedy café a lot of the freaks used to frequent, along with dossers, drug addicts, night workers and the rest, mainly because it was open all night. He has a very deliberate way of talking, as if he's expecting to be recorded. Which in this case was perfectly reasonable as he was being recorded. He only got halfway through his story before Steve and Gill, being bored, began a conversation of their own. So that's what I have on tape. Piers, in his declamatory style, telling me a story about some guy in the Top Hat stirring his tea, while Steve and Gill are rambling on about something else entirely. Actually Steve was talking about the Top Hat too, about when he was busted for Mandrax in there. But none of it was about Piss-Off Pete, and very little of it was about hippies.

Later I asked Gill to tell me about her first trip. We were all quite drunk by this time.

'So what happened was,' she said, 'what happened was that Ed and I – you remember Edwina don't you, very pretty, stunning – me and Ed, coming from Cardiff and all the rest, had done a lot of drink, lots of drugs and things, so we finished our A levels off and off we went to Butlin's. But the only thing we hadn't touched was acid. I was into mandies to the point of being found asleep in shop doorways . . .'

'And in the Students' Union,' said Steve.

'Oh yes! I'll tell you about the night I got locked in the Students' Union. That's a hilarious story, that is: everyone gave me everything . . .'

'No,' I said, trying to keep some order in this conversation, 'you were telling me about your first trip.'

'Yes, what happened was, that off we went to Butlin's and we were there as chalet maids. And Ed and I were already into flowing robes and the hippie bit and the flowers painted down the face and not wearing shoes and all the rest of it. And we were there in this row of chalets in Pwllheli in 1971 and I suppose we were looked upon as a little different. And, what happened was, we'd had the way with drink, we'd had the way with the holidaymakers' pills, that you'd clean their chalet and rip off their medication, and you'd sort of go out and fall asleep. But somebody came on the camp that was flogging acid. They were part of some team of entertainers that were passing through. The acid was on blotting paper. I realize now, with hindsight, that if you had acid on blotting paper, it must have been quite strong. So, one of the other fellow chalet maids was Willow – Jude at the time – who had taken to borrowing our clothes and things, and when we met her she was terribly straight, terribly shy, terribly focused, and she sort of joined our brigade. And we said, all right, we'll all drop this acid together. We thought, Ed and I, that we were so sophisticated, so into drugs, that we knew exactly what would be happening. And I just presumed I'd be feeling terribly drunk. Little did I realize that it would be totally different. And when I get nervous I grind my teeth. So I decided I was going to drop this acid and be drunk as a skunk within five minutes. I went and sat in this lounge area. You sat on couches and things, and it covered an arcade. And under the arcade the happy holidaymakers would walk through for their joyous Saturday night's entertainment. We all had this terribly cynical view of the happy holidaymakers. It was Saturday, so there was a new crowd in, meaning that you'd have Liverpool and Manchester United supporters all sleeping on the block. So the first night they would fight, the second night they would puke together, and the third night they were all jolly good buddies. So you had blood to clean up on Sunday Morning, puke to clean up on Monday morning, and . . .?'

'Piss?' I suggested.

'Yes, piss to clean up the other one.

'Anyway, so I'm sat there thinking, oh, I'm gonna be perfectly fine and . . . Good God! Look at the happy holidaymakers, aren't they just a bloody pathetic crew. And I'm looking at all the happy holidaymakers and I realized that they were all growing pouches, huge enormous pouches that were getting bigger and bigger and bigger. I thought, good God, they're a greedy bunch this week, they're all turning into the seven dwarves. And I realized, Christ Almighty, I'm not pissed, I'm in some other weird vein. I've got to get out of here. Got to go and find my friends. Got to get back to security. So I thought, right, get on the elevator. And then I thought, fuck a duck, I'm not on the elevator, I'm going to hell. So there's all these happy holidaymakers looking at me because suddenly I was thinking, yes, I'm going to go to hell. And their faces became bigger and bigger and their eyes suddenly focused in . . .

'Thank God, some bloke, who was a really old hippie, realized what was happening, found me, took me down the elevator, and across to the bar. So I got there and, in fact, the six of us were all having equally bad trips. Terrible trips. One woman thought she was a ghost, and the only way she could walk was to hold her shoulders down by her arms because ghosts were coming out of everywhere. We realized she was nuts. I'm not sure what Ed was into, but she was no security whatsoever. Someone else had little men running up and down her legs. It was total horror time.'

I said, 'And you still took acid after that?'

'Yes,' she said. 'As my first trip was the most horrendous trip under the sun, every other trip after that was really good.'

During the conversation one of their kids had come into the room. Gill said to Piers, 'It's called being a parent. Take it to bed.'

Piers said, referring back to an earlier part of the conversation, 'My wife doesn't like me to go into town.'

'Even though I didn't get in till three o'clock last night,' she said to me, in answer. It was as if they were negotiating their marriage through me. 'Would you take the offspring to bed?' she said, sharply, directing her words at Piers.

I liked that. 'Good night offspring,' I said. 'See you later.'

Piers and the boy had an argument over what time it was. 'I said nine o'clock.'

'Yeah, but it's seven o'clock.'

It was neither. It was 8.15.

Steve asked if the tape was still running. 'Yeah, it is,' I said, leaning close to take a look. 'It's just not going to make any sense. Conversations going all over the place. Everything's going in different directions, kids walking in. It's not going to have any logic to it at all.'

Which is precisely true, of course. There was no logic in our conversation whatsoever.

I also discovered that Steve and Gill went to the same school, and that Gill was born in Ely. 'That's interesting,' I said. 'You're an Ely girl, and you've ended up living in a nice place like this. But Steve is a Llandaff boy, who's ended up living in Ely.' It seemed to me that if anything characterized the era, it was this fact. Social mobility simply didn't exist before the sixties.

Gill said, 'I married a Canadian to get away from Cardiff, and he ended up falling in love with the place. Typical.'

55

And then she leaned close to me, while Steve and Piers were chatting, and said, very quietly so that only I could hear, 'I felt conned, I did. You made a fool out of me. You made all sorts of promises.'

'What?'

'You know what I'm talking about. That night. At Jude's house.'

'Oh. Yes.'

'You said all sorts of things. I felt like I'd been taken for a ride.'

'Sorry,' I said. 'That's what I was like in those days. I was a wanker.'

'Yes,' she said, 'you were.'

5 Rod the Mod Takes the Plunge

'To bear with fools in kindliness brings good fortune.'

The I Ching, Hexagram 4, 'Youthful Folly'

It was during this same trip to Cardiff that I met Rod the Mod for the first time. Like I said, his name isn't Rod, it's Tony. And he isn't a Mod. He got called that because he used to wear modish, fashionable clothes. Floppy-collared shirts with kipper ties. Multicoloured tank tops. High-waisted baggies. Platform shoes, that sort of thing. When Steve described him to me I imagined him as like a German porno movie star, with dangly, blond hair, sideburns and a Mexican moustache. But he's not like that at all. He's just a regular bloke really.

He's very sexist though. He referred to his two ex-wives as 'Bitch Number One' and 'Bitch Number Two'. He said: 'Women. They're always trying to get their hands on your wedge.' By which he meant his money, not his sexual organs.

He said, 'I don't think I'll get married again. I'll just find a

57

woman I don't like and give her the house.'

I asked him if he remembered Piss-Off Pete. 'Pete, yeah. Piss-Off Pete. He was a nice bloke. He used to wear women's clothes and stuff. A nice bloke.' And that's all he said, aside from informing me that it was he, Tony, who had first coined the nickname 'Piss-Off Pete'.

We met him in a pub called the Crwys, on Crwys Road. Steve – who's lived in Cardiff all his life – got lost taking us there. But I knew the way, even though I hadn't been in Cardiff for nigh-on twenty years. It was all coming back to me now.

The reason I'd wanted to meet Rod is that I'd written about him before, in my column in the *Guardian*. When the story had come out Rod had shown it to all his friends. 'That's me, that is,' he said.

'Come off it, Tony. You're pulling our leg. Your name's Tony, not Rod.'

And none of them believed him.

So I'm writing about him again now to correct a misunderstanding. To all of Tony's friends: yes it was Tony in that story. Tony who drinks at the Crwys. He and Rod the Mod are one and the same person.

But there's another reason I want to write about him again. I want to re-tell that story. It's all very well writing for a newspaper. But not everyone reads newspapers. And not everyone who does reads every single word. Add to this the fact that I only had 1,200 words to tell the story in, and that I had to miss out many points of importance, and that people who read newspapers tend to throw them away the day after, or use them for lighting the fire, and you can see why I prefer books. Books last for years. Someone may find this book in a second-hand bookshop in twenty years time, and still be able to enjoy it. So this is for you, my reader in twenty years time, who's just picked up this book from the shelf of your local Oxfam (assuming Oxfam shops and shelves still exist, that is) and who has accidentally opened it on this page. What follows is an extraordinary story. I only hope I do it justice in the telling. Coincidentally, it also reveals a lot about Steve's character, and the time that we were all living in.

Rod had never wanted to marry the woman in the first place. But somehow she'd wheedled and cajoled him into accepting her proposal. Maybe he was drunk at the time, or stoned. Maybe he just wasn't thinking right. Perhaps, in the throes of some aberrant romantic urge, he had even momentarily considered it a Good Idea. Whatever the case, now he was regretting it, and the awful moment of terminal wedlock was drawing ever closer.

Rod was Steve's landlord. He had money from somewhere or another. There were a bunch of guys living in the place. Steve himself. Ade the Suede. Mike. And Freaky Frenchie, as he was called at the time. That's Piers, who you met in the last chapter, before he started going out with Gill.

Rod had a plan. He decided he would hoist all of his gear into the attic of the flat that he rented to the lads, and stay there until the fateful day had passed. He asked them if this would be all right, and added that he would appreciate it if they could all say that they had no idea where he had gone if Andrea happened to turn up. They agreed. They were masculinists. They felt they had to stand by their troubled brother against the forces of female oppression.

So Rod made a start moving his hi-fi player, his alarm clock, his tapes, his toiletries, his girlie mags, his bedding, along with several changes of clothing and anything else he could think of, into the loft-space. The idea was that he would stay holed up there until after the wedding day had passed, like an outlaw waiting for the heat to die down after a bank job. That's how he felt: like an outlaw. As opposed to an in-law, which is what he didn't want to be.

The next day Steve was getting ready for an appointment. There was a knock at the door. Steve went to answer it. It was Andrea.

'Oh hi, Andrea,' said Steve, innocently enough. 'Lovely morning?'

'I want to see Rod,' she said.

Well Steve was about to fulfil his part of the contract. Rod? Rod? No, I don't know where he is. I haven't seen him for days, weeks, years. In fact, who's Rod? I'm sure I don't know anybody by that name. But he'd barely opened his mouth to speak when Andrea, glancing past him up the stairs to the landing, noticed Rod, halfway up the ladder leading to the loft, pushing a large bag of stuff before him. He was even now trying to speed up the process in the vain hope that he might yet escape her notice. Unfortunately that bulging bag of stuff was impeding his progress somewhat.

'Oh, there you are,' said Andrea. 'But what on earth are you doing? And what's that you're taking up into the roof?'

'Shit! That's done it,' said Rod, aware that he'd been caught red-handed. 'I suppose I'd better come clean, now that you've caught me in the act.

'What it is, Andrea,' he continued, 'what it is, I've told all the boys to say that they've not seen me, like, and I was goin' to hide up in the roof till the wedding day had come and gone, and then you'd've never been able to find me and I wouldn't have to marry you, see.'

Andrea just looked dumbfounded at this.

'But Rod, how could you? I love you.'

'Fuckin' hell,' said Rod, still up the ladder with the bag perched precariously over his head, 'I don't need all this right now.'

At which point Steve made his excuses and left.

And neither do I, he thought.

Well, all of this was ages ago. The wedding day had come and gone, and Rod and Andrea were now happily married with a baby. Or not so happily, as it happens. She'd chucked him out.

It was like this. Andrea had found a bunch of Rod's dirty magazines in the sock drawer, beneath a pile of washing. 'What's this?' she said.

'It's my girlie mags,' he said. 'What d'y' think it is?'

'But why?' she said. 'Why do you want these things? Aren't I good enough for you, then?'

'As it happens: no, you're not. I'm bored,' he said.

The inevitable happened. They traded insults of increasing viciousness until, at last, they were embroiled in a full-scale row, screaming abuse and throwing things at each other.

Well Rod kept tropical fish, upon which he lavished the most careful attention. And Andrea was jealous of these. So in the midst of the row she'd thrown an ornament which had, accidentally-on-purpose as it were, hit a tank of breeding Angel fish on one of the shelves. The tank had cracked and was sending little pulsing rivulets of fish-tank water down over the shelf and onto the floor. Rod had to rush to the fishes' aid, netting them out lovingly to place them in another fish-tank.

'Get a mop,' he said. 'Look, it's leaking out all over the floor.'

'Fuck off,' she said. 'You mop it up. It's your fault anyway. And after you've finished you can get out. I've had it with you and your bloody fish and dirty magazines. I don't know what you see in them. It's disgusting, a married man carrying on like that, looking at all that filth. And you spend more time with the fucking fish than you do with me and the baby. I want a divorce, and I want you out of the house right now!'

'Don't worry, I'm going,' said Rod. 'And another thing, I'll be back for my stuff, and you'd better not harm my fish or it'll be real war.'

By this time Andrea was storming out of the house, slamming the door behind her. 'And you can clean up you're own bloody mess,' Rod shouted after her, oblivious to the fact that she was no longer listening. 'You made it so you can clean it up. I'm going down to see my mates!'

Which is what he'd done. He'd gone round to stay with Steve, despite the fact that Steve was no longer his tenant.

Now at this time in his life, Steve was a Valium addict. This had come about because he'd been addicted to downers, and the psychiatric profession had decided, in its wisdom, to get him addicted to Valium instead. And one morning, not long after he'd moved onto Steve's sofa, Rod had asked for 'one of those little pills'.

'They're Valium,' said Steve, 'and you better be careful 'cos they're quite strong.'

'I don't care,' said Rod. 'I want to get stoned or pissed or both. Let's get pissed, Droid. I've had enough of all of this shit.'

So, pills already pulsating in their bloodstream, they got dressed up ready to go out and get pissed. Rod was in his usual gear: tank top, pastel shirt and baggies, with a smart jacket. Steve had on an oriental-style mandarin-collar caftan, in white, with gold and maroon printwork on it, and a psychedelic batik Indonesian T-shirt, plus flares and assorted strings and beads and bangles: the whole hippie works.

They had a day out on the town, compounding the booze with Valium, and the Valium with more booze. And all the while there's Rod going on in the same vein.

'I never wanted to get married in the first place, as you know. It was a fucking shotgun wedding, that's what it was: a shotgun wedding.'

'Yes it was,' said Steve.

'I don't know what she's going on about. What does she expect? I mean: I'm out working all bloody day, and if I can't have some enjoyment in my life, then what's the fucking point?'

'Yes, you're right there, Rod. What's the point?' said Steve.

'And what's the matter with my magazines? Other blokes have a much better deal, you know. They have their wives posing naked for Readers' Wives and all the rest. And they're going out to wife-swapping parties. I'd swap her any day, the bitch.'

'Yes, Rod, I know,' said Steve.

'And she won't let me have any booze in the house, not even a few cans. It's bloody ridiculous. What's a working man supposed to do? A man's got to have some relief in his life and some fun, don't you agree?'

'Yes, Rod, I do,' said Steve.

'So we're gonna get totally and properly pissed, right? And I don't know about you, but I'm on the look-out for a proper woman and a good time, not life with that miserable cow. What d'y' think?'

'Yes Rod, I agree, it's a good idea,' said Steve.

You've probably noticed by now that Steve was always agreeing with what Rod said. Steve always agrees with whatever anybody says. It's a trait of his. That's because, on his planet, there's no such thing as the word 'no'. It hasn't been invented yet. Which often gets Steve into all sorts of trouble, as this story will testify.

Well Rod is one of those old-fashioned, working-class, sexist blokes. He really does wolf-whistle at passing women, and make comments about them. 'Wouldn't mind giving her one.' 'Show us yer tits then.' 'Cor, look at the arse on that', etc., etc. So that's what they spent the day doing: getting drunk – Rod complaining and Steve agreeing – and looking at women and making comments. Rod, that is, not Steve: Steve is a complete romantic, and when he meets a girl all he ends up doing is holding hands with her and gazing into her eyes. Not that Rod ever got much further. For all that ribald rhetoric of his, he's a wimp really. All his remarks tend to do is put people off.

They ended up at Cardiff's famous docklands, outside some club after chucking out time, at about two thirty in the morning, totally legless. Steve was ready to go home. But by now a new idea had entered Rod's head. 'We could rip off a boat,' he was saying. 'Look, one of those boats over there. We could rip one off and go to St-Tropez. Think about it,' he added, a mad glint in his eye. 'Yeah, yeah, beautiful girls, bars, beaches, the works. And we'll send postcards to all the people we know: 'Bet you wish you were here with us, sharing all the wonders of St-Tropez.' Come on Droid, let's do it. Let's go to St-Tropez.'

Steve was sceptical. He thought, *I really can't see this happening.* But, then, it is a measure of his extraordinary gullibility that he didn't just laugh and walk away right then.

Meanwhile Rod was looking for a boat. He was walking along the dockside, peering into the gloomy depths, to try and find one. There were dinghies moored along the dock, and rowing boats. Steve said, 'You can't get to St-Tropez in one of those.'

'No, you don't understand,' said Rod. 'The whole thing is, we're gonna use one of these things to get out onto one of those bigger boats.' And he pointed out into the dock. There were speedboats and yachts moored out there.

Steve said, 'Can you navigate one of those things? I mean, do you know how to drive them?'

'Yeah, yeah, sure,' said Rod dismissively, 'we'll figure that out when we get there.'

The problem now was that all the boats were chained and padlocked, and Steve just wanted to go home. He said, 'Listen, Rod, we've been here for ages, we're wasting time. I'm going home.'

But he wasn't going home. Fate intervened. Just at that moment, as Steve, in a rare moment of decisiveness, was about to turn away, Rod spotted a boat without padlocks. 'Here, here,' he called, and climbed down into the boat. Steve jumped down after him.

'Rod,' he said, puzzled, 'there's no oars in this boat.'

'That's all right,' said Rod, 'we'll paddle with our hands.'

So they started paddling out into the gloomy docks. And they hadn't gone more than a couple of yards, when Steve noticed that his feet were getting wet. 'Rod,' he said, 'this boat . . . I think it's leaking.'

Rod agreed. 'Yeah you're right, there's a bit of water coming in. Don't worry about it.'

'No, Rod, you don't understand, this boat is leaking fast. The water is coming up. It's up to my knees. It's up . . . blub, blub . . .' And the boat sank.

Steve found himself under water. The boat banged his head. He was thrashing about, flailing his arms in the blackness, and swallowing mouthfuls of the foul ooze of the dock water, trying to get to the surface. They surfaced at the same time, rushing up with their arms in the air, gasping for breath. And then they did what you're not supposed to do. They grabbed hold of each other and sank again.

So they were splashing about in the filthy slime, wondering what to do next. Steve got cramp in his leg and had to hang on to the rope of a nearby buoy. There wasn't much he could do. Rod, meanwhile, swam to the nearest boat. He grabbed hold of it and was trying to pull himself onto the deck. And then he, too, was stricken by cramp, unable to move. So there they were, in a state of shock, numb, stuck, treading water, freezing cold, covered in black mud, breathing-in the noxious stench of this vile, polluted dock water, boozed-up, drugged-up and help-less. Steve started to black out. He thought, *This is it. This is the end.*

There was a man walking his dog by the dock. He glanced out and saw the two of them in the water not far away. He said, 'What're you two boys doin' then? Havin' a bit of a midnight dip, is it?'

'No we're not. We're fuckin' drowning. You know, like: help!' And they screamed.

It didn't sink in. The man thought they were having him on. 'What's the matter then?' he asked.

'Help! For fuck's sake, help!' Rod screamed at him. And then Steve added, 'We've got cramp. It's all gone wrong. We are: we're drowning. We can't swim. We can't do anything. Please: just get help.'

The man disappeared. He didn't say anything. First he was there, and then he was gone. No mention of what he was intend-ing to do. No 'Hang on in there, I'll go and get help.' A terrible silence descended into the deathly night air. Steve thought, *Shit, this is really the end now. Our only potential rescuer has just cleared off. We've had it.* And he blacked out.

He came to on a police launch with a concerned-looking police constable leaning over him. 'You all right?' he was saying.

After that they were taken to the edge of the dock and into a waiting ambulance. Steve blacked out again, and when he finally awoke, he was in a hospital bed, naked, his clothes in a plastic bag by the bedside. He leaned over and peered in. There they were, drenched with mud, and stinking like a chemical plant.

Rod the Mod was across the ward in another bed. He was embroiled in a heated argument with a nurse. 'I want a fag,' he was saying. 'I was nearly drowned and now I want a fag.'

'Well you can't have one,' she said.

Steve's head felt like a booming cavern, complete with stalagmites. His tongue felt like he'd been licking a camel's bottom, and his stomach felt like he'd downed the entire year's production of the British Nuclear waste industry in one headlong binge. He felt horrible.

Sometime later the ward sister came over to talk to them. It was 6 a.m. and the shift was changing. She said that they would have to wait in the hospital lobby until an ambulance was found to take them home. So they were dumped into wheelchairs and trundled down to the lobby area, trussed up in their hospital sheets like creatures recently awoken from the dead. Which is what they were, really. They had their bags of rotting clothes with them. Rod reached into his to find a cigarette. He brought out a crumpled packet, and then emptied the contents. It was full of some half-rotten, mouldering sludge. Well, they were both dying for a fag, and they spent the next hour or two asking round to see if anyone had got one. No one had.

They were in that waiting room for what seemed days. Time just dragged. They were bored, tired and uncomfortable, and indeed sick. Eventually Steve's nerves cracked. 'I've had it!' he said, and went into the toilet to put on his clothes. It was a nauseating, uncomfortable feeling, trying to pull the icy, sodden pants and trousers over his legs. He gave up, put the clothes back in the bag, and came slop, slop, slopping back to his wheelchair, leaving a trail of drips behind him.

When he got back, Rod was involved in another argument. A

sister had come over to remonstrate with him for showing off his chest. His sheet had slipped from his shoulders. 'It's disgraceful,' she was saying. 'It's disgusting. You should be thoroughly ashamed of yourself. There's teenage girls present, you know. At least your friend' – indicating Steve – 'has the decency to keep himself covered up properly.'

'Afraid they'll get turned on by my manly physique, is it?' said Rod.

'Right! That's it!' said the sister. 'Any more of your behaviour and I'm calling the police to have you taken away.'

'I wish they would,' muttered Rod, under his breath. 'Anything to get out of this place.' But he covered himself up anyway.

After that he phoned up Andrea. He made a full confession and begged her forgiveness. 'I didn't mean it, Andrea,' he said. 'I'll clean up the fish-tank water. I promise I'll spend less time with the fish and more time with you and the baby. I won't drink beer in the house. I'll throw away my dirty magazines. Just rescue me, will you? Get a taxi and come and pick me up. I'm going mad in here.'

She agreed.

Which left Steve contemplating God knows how many more hours waiting for an ambulance all by himself. He decided to give it one more try at getting dressed. He went back to the toilet and began the awful job of sliding those sodden, stinking clothes over his body. They were prickly and slimy and cold next to his skin. It was like dressing himself in rashers of salty bacon soaked in old chip-fat. But he did it. And, tired, hung-over, sodden and hungry, he walked out into the morning sunlight.

It was about 10 a.m. by now, an ordinary Saturday morning, as Steve made his way through the town centre towards his home. He still had on his oriental-style mandarin-collar caftan and his Indonesian batik T-shirt, but you could no longer see the colours. He made a squelching noise as he walked, and left a string of dark mud-prints behind him. He was dripping with this loathsome, black, chemical slime as a foul stench wafted from his clothes. His beard and face and hair were caked in mud. All the families were out shopping, mums and dads and kids enjoying the bright sunshine. Normal people, happy-go-lucky people, out doing their ordinary things. Suddenly Steve realized he was causing a sensation. Kids were screaming and hiding behind their parent's backs. 'Mam! Mam! Dad! What's that?' they were shouting. They were pointing at him. He looked like the creature from the black lagoon. People were backing off from him in horror. At which point he started giggling to himself, which only made matters worse. So now he was not only a loathsome monster dripping with horrible slime, and leaving a trail of stench behind him; he was cackling with mad, hysterical laughter too. A creature from another planet: his true identity revealed.

He got home and had a shower, and then dressed in fresh, clean clothes. Later Rod the Mod came round to see him. He'd squabbled with Andrea again. 'Fuckin' bitch. What's a man supposed to do? Got any more of those pills, Droid? Fancy a pint?'

Months later Steve was out in a club somewhere, when this bloke came up to him. 'I thought it was you. It is you, isn't it? Let me buy you a pint.' It was the police constable who'd fished him out of the water. He'd got a life-saving award for that. Shown great presence of mind, they'd said. 'My uniform got splattered with that dock's water, you know. It started to come apart at the seams. God knows what was in it. And there was you drinking the stuff. No ill effects, I hope?'

'None whatsoever,' said Steve. He neglected to add that, on his planet, that's what they serve in pubs. Dock water.

He still has the batik T-shirt he wore that night. It's full of holes.

6 Druid Time

*'I have always felt that Crowley's "Do What Thou Wilt" is good
. . . The question then becomes "What do we will to do?" Most of
the Crowleyites I've met . . . seem to have decided they will make
pompous asses of themselves . . .'*

Timothy Leary, quoted in *Cosmic Trigger Volume I*,
by Robert Anton Wilson

I wrote that last chapter sitting in a converted ambulance. It's a
1983 Ford Transit Disability Transport Vehicle converted into a
camper van. It's where I'm sitting right now, writing this.

There's a table and two seats that shift to become a double bed,
with boxes underneath for storage. And a row of seats along the
side, with boxes underneath for storage. And storage space
above the cab, where I keep my bedding. And a combined stain-
less steel cooker and sink, with space below for storage. It even
has a toilet: one of those chemical toilets in a wooden cubby-hole,
which I also use as a wardrobe. So it's a storage vehicle really. It's
where I store my dreams.

I got it from a man on the Chelmsley Wood council estate, not
far from where my Mom and Dad live. This was about a month
after the trip to Cardiff to interview Piers and Gill.

Chelmsley Wood – so I've heard – is the largest council estate in Britain. I don't know. I haven't made enough of a habit of measuring council estates to make a judgement on the matter. But it's huge. Larger than a few cities I can name. So big, in fact, that it even has its own shopping centre, with a market beneath, and several multi-storey car parks. Any place that can boast multi-storey car parks in such profusion deserves its place on the map.

I used to go there as a boy, when it was really a wood. I'd go there on camping trips with my friends. There was a rippling little stream with a ford, some fields and a wood. Most of it is gone now. There's still a bit of the wood left, though, nestled between the prefabs. It's where the drinkers go to consume their lager. The woods are full of empty cans and used condoms.

The man who sold me the van was Irish. He'd done it out himself. He had to sell it because his wife had recently had a brain haemorrhage and she was scared to travel down the motorways in it. It's a huge, rattly old thing that bangs and creaks and sways about making mysterious groaning and clanking noises as it rumbles along. No wonder she was scared of it. It scares me.

The reason I'd bought it was because I'd become homeless. I was living at home with my Mom and Dad, and was becoming mortally afraid that I was about to end up as that saddest of all sad creatures: the middle-aged bachelor living at home with his mother. I just didn't fancy ending up like Jack Kerouac, even if he did write good books. Good books are no compensation for being dead at forty-six.

It's a good job I've got a disability transport vehicle converted into a camper van. I've gone undercover. I've been researching for this book. I have to look the part. What's another way to describe a disability transport vehicle converted into a camper van? It's a hippie bus.

To complete the disguise I have a hand-drawn map of the Glastonbury region on my wall, done out to represent the area in the Dark Ages, when King Arthur was about. This was before the Somerset Levels were drained. The Isle of Avalon really is an Isle, and there's not a motorway in sight, not even an A road. And in the front, in the wind screen, there's a plywood sign from the first ever Glastonbury free festival, given to me by someone I shared a room with in Cardiff once. 'Worthy Farm' it says in crudely painted letters, the colour of dried blood, with a Star of David at the point. And on the floor there's a swirling turquoise and red and green and purple and blue rag mat made by my grandmother on my father's side. Very psychedelic. I wonder if my grandmother on my father's side ever took LSD? Probably not, though she certainly had a thing about laxatives. LSD is a laxative for the mind.

So this is more than just a camper van, then. It's my home.

Before I bought it my Mom and Dad went on holiday. They went to Tenerife, where my sister lives. They always go to Tenerife. They're creatures of habit. So I had two weeks to myself to begin work on this book. I made several false starts, none of which got me passed the first page or two. I gave up in the end.

One day there was a phone call. Earlier in the year I'd sent a letter to Rose, my first ever girlfriend, to say that I was now living in Birmingham and that we should get together for a drink. She'd not replied. And then, suddenly, while I was back at home in my parent's house, she rang me up. She'd decided she wanted to go out for that drink with me after all.

So it was back to square one, back to where I'd started all those years ago. Me in Birmingham, living at home with my Mom and Dad, going out for a drink with Rose.

Well, it wasn't quite back to square one. Rose was married by now, with a child. So we'd all gone out for a drink together: me and Rose, her husband, their five-year-old child, and their scatty dog whose name I forget. Actually we went out for several drinks, always at lunchtime. Rose had been living back in Birmingham ever since that breakdown in 1979. She said it had been a long, hard struggle to get herself back even into the semblance of health. She could cope with the depressive element of her illness. It was the manic phase that caused her panic. She said she did things that she would later regret. It was all rooted in her past, she said. Even that bubbly girl I had known as a schoolboy, and fancied so much, was a front. Underneath it something dismal and confused was already stirring. She was working painfully upon herself now to uncover the sources of her illness, with the aid of a psychotherapist. Her husband was being paid care allowance to look after her. This was the first time in over eighteen years that she'd actually had enough money to survive comfortably. She was very bitter about hippie culture and the hippie era.

One day we were sitting in a pub just outside Birmingham, drinking a pale, tasty Summer brew. She'd been talking about herself in her usual way, and a slight, disparaging thought crossed my mind. I thought, *This illness of yours is just a form of self-indulgence: it's an excuse.*

Suddenly Rose's eyes became round, and a flicker of panic crossed through them.

'I'm nervous of you, Chris,' she said. 'You're making me paranoid.'

I decided that she must have read my mind.

Well I can't prove this, but it has always struck me that mental illness is when the barriers of the mind come down. All sorts of things float in, good as well as evil. Very often the mentally ill person is telling us something which is true, it's just that our minds are so closed off that we cannot understand them. The only difference between a person who is mentally ill, and a genius, perhaps, is that the mentally ill person feels their thoughts as a form of punishment, whereas the genius celebrates them.

Rose had felt my criticism as a sting to her self-esteem. She was like a person who had been through some terrible accident which had somehow exposed her nerves. Even the slightest vibration was painful to her. I had no more doubts as to the authenticity of her illness.

It also struck me that it was no accident that she'd had her breakdown in 1979, just as Thatcher was coming to power. Greed and viciousness had become the ruling ideology. There would be no room left for compassion, no protection for the weak, no shelter for those who, by accident or carelessness, had not prepared themselves. An icy wind was blowing through the land. A storm was brewing up. Rose found herself suddenly on a ledge, dreadfully exposed, and she fell.

The reason that Rose is so bitter about the hippie experience is that she believes it was middle class. Drop out, they told us, so we did. Then, at the end of the seventies, there was little choice but to drop back in again. All the middle-class hippies had nice homes to go to. They had allowances and shares in their father's business. Maybe they'd opened a Carpet Emporium and Ethnic Clothes Shop with stuff they'd brought back from their trips to the Far East. Some of them became Druids. They were protected. But we weren't. Those of us from working-class backgrounds who'd bought the hippie dream found ourselves struggling on alone. There was no safety net for us. So when it came to dropping, there was only the cold, hard floor to break our fall. I got a job in a rope factory. Rose ended up in hospital.

And then – in the same week Rose had rung – I got a phone call from Graham, too. He also lives in Birmingham now. We met in the pub.

I'd seen more of Graham over the last twenty-five years than I had of Rose, but not a lot. In the last fifteen years or so we'd lost contact completely.

It was Graham I gave Steve's green and white striped public school blazer to, in another act of spontaneous radical jacket-swapping. Jacket-swapping was the thing to do. We swapped jackets almost as often as we swapped personality. Things were very fluid in those days.

When I'd first known him he was a slight, blond hippie with a sharp sense of humour. People used to make comparisons between us. They said he was angelic, whereas I was devilish. But he'd aged suddenly. I'd bumped into him at a Captain Beefheart concert a couple of years after we'd stopped hanging round together. He'd put on weight, was balding and had a beard and glasses. He looked about forty-something years old even though he was only twenty-six. He looked like a probation officer, which is what, in fact, he'd become. But he's not changed since then. Now that he really is forty-something years old, he still looks forty-something years old. Which is lucky really. At that rate of ageing, he could have looked a million by now.

I aged suddenly too, although a lot later. I managed to look fairly young until my late thirties. But then, one day, somewhere in my fortieth year (on a Tuesday, I think, sometime in September), I was middle-aged. It happened overnight. On the Tuesday I was twenty-nine, by the Wednesday I'd become forty. That's an advantage that Graham has over me. He's been forty years old for the last twenty years. I'm still trying to get used to it. So now Graham and I look the same age again. Two middle-aged men, sitting in a pub, reminiscing about old times. Sad, isn't it?

Graham, too, turned out to be angry about the seventies, and bitter about the hippie philosophy. He was full of scorn for all the wild and airily pretentious notions we'd shared at the time. It's odd, that. All the people I've met since who remember the hippie era or had anything to do with it, and who were around in the sixties, think of it with affection. They consider it an optimistic, hopeful time. But those of us who only experienced the hippie era in the seventies are invariably bitter. We think of it as an awful time. Everything that came out of it, from floppy-collared shirts to free-love philosophy, was dumb. We're all just profoundly embarrassed that we ever had anything to do with it.

It's a bit like the atom bomb really, but on a different scale. The people who made the hippie philosophy, like the people who made the atom bomb, were all very clever people. But it was still a stupid thing to have done, all the same. And once they'd been invented, they couldn't be uninvented. We've had to learn to live with them both.

There was something the hippies used to believe about the atom bomb. They used to believe that LSD was an inert substance until the first atomic explosion. It was that first atomic explosion that activated it as a spiritual tool, they said. God had given us LSD in order to effect a fundamental change in human evolution.

And with beliefs like that, who needs reality?

So, armed with the criticisms of my contemporaries from Birmingham, I set out in my new van to take a look at the current state of hippie culture. My aim was to take Brummie culture with me and – unashamedly this time, unlike the first time round back in the seventies – to confront the pretensions of hippiedom with it.

The first journey was down to Chippenham in Wiltshire. I slept on the side of the main road. Every time a car went by the van thudded. Every time a lorry went by the van thudded and juddered and went *whump!* It was the *whump!* I liked best. I thought I was going to take off.

The following day I drove up a track and parked up in a field for the afternoon. There were houses near by. I was soaking my feet in a washing-up bowl full of disinfectant water, when one of the people from one of the houses came out to talk to me.

'I've brought my guard dog with me,' she said, pointing to a cat that was rubbing itself against her leg and purring.

'I'm soaking my feet,' I told her.

I was sitting in the van, and she was outside behind me. I had to crane my neck to speak to her through the open window.

'Will you be staying here all night?' she asked.

'I'm not sure. Why? Is there a problem?'

'Are you on your way to Stonehenge?' she asked.

'No,' I lied. And then I changed my mind. 'Well, actually I am. I'm going there on the solstice with the Druids. I'm meeting up with them in Glastonbury. Do you want to come in?'

She came in and sat next to me. So I didn't have to crane my neck any more.

'I was a bit worried,' she said. 'You're not going to bring all of your friends here to stay are you?'

'I haven't got any friends,' I said.

'Only it's the solstice. This is Wiltshire. We were a bit worried in case thousands of you turned up.'

'There's only one of me,' I informed her, accurately.

'Thank God for that,' she said.

'Yes, thank God for that.'

As I said, I was on my way to Glastonbury to meet the Druids. Well, when I say 'Druids' I think I'd better explain. I don't mean Druids as in the ancient Celtic priest caste. They had their last stand at Anglesey and were exterminated by the Romans in the first century AD. I'm also not referring to that group of eighteenth-century intellectuals and crackpots who donned the white robe and declared Stonehenge as their temple, and whose spiritual descendants were still holding summer solstice rituals there as late as the eighties. No, the Druids I am referring to – or some of them, at least – are veterans of the Stonehenge Free Festival, which took place every year over the Solstice period from 1974 until it was brutally suppressed in 1985. They'd observed the Druid rituals taking place year by year and, perhaps, absorbed some of the mystique. Later they'd begun to wear the white robe themselves, both as a way of claiming access to the stones and also in order to continue the traditions of those earlier Druids. It was a political manœuvre as well as a spiritual statement. Many of them were hippies, in other words.

It was Steve who introduced me to them. He'd donned the

white robe himself a few years earlier. It suited him. He thought it was the latest thing in Earthling casual attire, the perfect wear for an average Saturday morning down at your local stone circle. I used to go over to see him in Avebury in Wiltshire whenever I could manage it, on the nearest Saturday to the so-called cross-quarterly festivals that are the basis of the Druidic and pagan calendar. The cross-quarterly festivals take place eight times a year. They consist of the two equinoxes, the two solstices, and the four ancient Celtic fire festivals of Imbolc, Beltane, Lughnasadh and Samhain: celebrated around 2 February, May-eve, August-eve and Hallowe'en respectively.

Druid festivals seem to consist of a lot of people in white robes standing round in a circle in the freezing cold making noises at each other. They do a lot of chanting. 'I-A-O,' they moan, like that, as the letters of the alphabet drawled out into a monosyllable. And then the High Priest will explain what it means. 'The letter I stands for the phallus of the sun god at sunrise,' he will say, 'the first ray of light over the horizon. The downstrokes of the letter A stand for the earth goddess opening her legs to receive the first beam of light as it enters the temple. And the O stands for the magnetic pull or attraction of the earth as it circles the sun, which keeps us all alive.'

'I-A-O' we all chant energetically, sounding like a family of demented vacuum cleaners with frogs up our nozzles, 'I-A-O,' over and over again. We I-A-O this and we I-A-O that. We I-A-O the grass and we I-A-O the sky. We I-A-O whatever plants are in season at that time, and which are usually piled up in the middle of the circle, looking bedraggled and cold. We I-A-O anything and everything, in fact: the trees, the birds, the stars and the sun, the lovely open legs of the goddess and the huge, erect penis of the god. Perhaps it's not the god's penis the High Priest is thinking about; it's his own.

No, sorry! That wasn't what the High Priest was thinking about at all. That was what I was thinking about. That's what I'm always thinking about. I have no idea what the High Priest was thinking about. No doubt he had higher things on his mind.

The I-A-O, of course, though of possibly ancient origin, was popularized back in the twenties and thirties by Aleister Crowley, himself a High Priest of sex magic. Aleister Crowley was very popular amongst the hippies. His slogan was 'Do What Thou Wilt', or, in its longer version, 'Do What Thou Wilt Shall Be The Whole Of The Law. Love Is The Law, Love Under Will.'

Students of hippie culture will immediately recognize echoes of the hippie's own favourite slogan, 'Do Your Own Thing', which was first coined by Ken Kesey in the sixties, without reference to Aleister Crowley.

Great minds think alike.

'Do Your Own Thing.' It may well turn out to be the most fatuous political slogan in history.

As if any one could just Do Their Own Thing. As if the postmen and the railway men and the steelworkers and the miners could. As if the lorry drivers and the builders and the plumbers and the electricians could. As if the fire-fighters and the ambulance drivers and the police officers could. As if the nurses and the doctors and the other health workers could. 'Sorry, Doctor, I know you're in the middle of a life-or-death operation at the moment, but well, I just want to Do My Own Thing. So, if you don't mind, I'll drop this tab of LSD and commune with the godhead instead.'

And as if the Oligarches of the Capitalist Ruling Class weren't already Doing Their Own Thing.

The High Priest has a habit of looking at you languorously from beneath drooping eyelids as if he's listening to you most deliberately, weighing up your words with deep consideration. It's a very self-conscious expression. It says, 'I am now thinking profound thoughts.' Which he might be, who knows? He's the High Priest after all.

This is one of the aspects of modern paganism I have had occasion to note: people who declare themselves as this, that or the other, with no reference, really, to anyone outside themselves. The High Priest is the High Priest because he says he is the High Priest. And some people actually believe him. It must have something to do with the way he dresses. He wears a white robe and a black cloak and an incongruously modern hat. I always think that the hat is the most authentically Druid thing about him.

There are several of these Druid orders. There's the Glastonbury Order of Druids (G.O.D.'s). The Secular Order of Druids

(S.O.D.'s). The Loyal Arthurian Warband (L.A.W.). It's like they're asking, 'So which is it: God's Law or Sod's Law?' Then there's the Cotswolds Order of Druids (C.O.D.) There are only eight of them. They're trying to get new members. So they're fishing for C.O.D.

Someone said, 'And there's S.A.D.'

'What's that mean?' I asked.

'Self-Appointed Druids.'

The High Priest was the first person in my quest this year to unselfconsciously admit that he had ever been a hippie. He went to the UFO club in Notting Hill in 1968, he told me, saw his first light-show, and was never the same again. He's still a hippie to this day. Or he seems like one to me.

I went round to his house at about ten thirty on the evening before the solstice. After that there were several hours waiting while various people turned up. I hardly knew any of them. We drank mead and ate lasagne while the High Priest showed us his home videos. Well, not home videos exactly. They were videos of the High Priest performing druidic ceremonies. 'I-A-O,' he was going, 'I-A-O.' I guess he was trying to get us into the right mood.

There was a squabble. Some film-maker was there. He kept trying to get the High Priest to put on this video he'd made, of some guy who had stood at the general election on the 'legalize cannabis' ticket. He was chattering away excitedly while the High Priest on the screen was I-A-O-ing the lovely open legs of the goddess. The High Priest in the room was having none of it. If it didn't have Druids in, it didn't count. Eventually I got bored and went to lie down in my van.

And then, about two o'clock in the morning, we set out for Stonehenge in a procession. I had three or four people in the back of my van. There was Ellie and Galahad, from the Loyal Arthurian Warband, and one or two others. Ellie is one of the nine Faery Queens of Britain. At this point in time she was also being referred to as Queen Gwynevere. Galahad is – well – Galahad. He's had his name changed by deed poll. People call him 'Gallie' and he has the worst sense of humour in the world. Instead of saying 'me too' he says 'me three' and thinks it's funny. It must have something to do with being so pure of heart that he can't tell a good joke from a bad one. Neither of them is a hippie. Ellie is a biker girl and Galahad is simply bonkers.

The High Priest's car was soon disappearing into the distance, and we were left on our own, rumbling through the deep night like a party of excited grannies on our way to see the Blackpool Illuminations. After a while we turned off the main route. Galahad was directing. We were trundling down little country lanes no wider than my van, as the sky began to turn golden behind the trees turning them into eerie silhouettes. Galahad was saying, 'There's a turning on your right,' or 'There's a turning to your left,' only there never was. We were lost.

Eventually we arrived in Amesbury, the nearest town to Stonehenge, by the strangest circular route, and were waved down by a policeman. It was almost light by now.

'I have to warn you,' he said, amiably, 'that if you proceed any further towards Stonehenge you will be arrested.'

'That's all right,' I lied, 'I just want to stop somewhere for a cup of coffee.' And he waved us on. He was being very friendly. It was probably the thought of all that overtime he'd just earned. We pulled away and I headed for Stonehenge.

At the roundabout just outside Amesbury there was a road block. The police were lined up across the road and the High Priest was parked on the slip road. I pulled up behind him. Eventually the police agreed to let the Druids perform their ceremony on the traffic island, which was apt enough, really, in a twentieth-century sort of way; the traffic island being round, just like Stonehenge.

I went off to make myself a cup of coffee in the car park of the nearby Little Chef, having seen plenty of Druid ceremonies in my time. But I performed a little ceremony of my own. I I-A-O-ed silently to myself in gratitude that I didn't actually have to spend time, freezing cold, in a Druid circle on a traffic island on the A303 saying I-A-O to anything and everything that moved. At least I had the decency to restrict my I-A-O-ing to one issue.

Actually I'm lying to you here. I didn't go off into the Little Chef car park in quite the disdainful way I suggested in the last paragraph. I went off into the Little Chef car park because I'm shy. We're all shy about different things. Some people are shy of writing books, even though they could. Some people are shy of addressing an audience or of reading out loud. Some people are shy about talking in front of a camera or a microphone. I'm not shy about any of these things. But I'm desperately shy when it comes to groaning on like a demented vacuum cleaner with a frog up my nozzle.

When I got back to the traffic island the ceremony had just finished. Perfect. The media were there. The media were there in strength. There were more of the media than there were of the Druids, which is always the way at Druid ceremonies. They were fighting over themselves to get an unimpeded view of a Druid or two who wasn't, at the same time, being shot by a dozen other cameras. The trick was to keep the other cameras out of shot. And, of course, they liked their Druids to really look like Druids (or how they imagined Druids to look). A simple white gown wasn't enough. The more regalia you had on, the more authentically Druid you were. So it was wands and staves and cloaks and headbands and arms full of flowers with ribbons attached; and necklaces and insignia and brooches and bells and wide leather belts with daggers attached, and piercings and tattoos and brass buckles and beads and green velvet hats with feathers attached; it was all the superficial things, in other words, that drew the media's attention, as is the way of the media. And meanwhile, these more picturesque Druids were standing self-conscious and stony-faced as dozens of cameras clicked or whirred at them, over and over and over again. You could see they were used to it. Why else would they dress like that, except to get the attention?

The High Priest was giving interviews, basking in the media gaze. This is actually what he's good at. He's a fine orator and an articulate spokesman, as well as a consummate self-publicist. He knows how to do interviews. He intones stentoriously in his public-school voice. He knows how to work the camera.

He was talking about the importance of Stonehenge as a ceremonial and ritual site and defending the Druid's right to be there. When one bank of cameramen and journalists left, they'd be replaced by another. He did TV interviews and radio interviews and newspaper interviews, one after the other, answering their questions with a politician's ease. Which is what he is really, a politician: a politician of the new magical left.

So, aside from me and the High Priest and all those banks of cameras, there was Des and Denny, and Susanna and her daughter Rainbow, and Galahad and Ellie, and one or two others whose names I forget, standing round on this midsummer's morning in the red glow of the sunlight beneath the shivering trees (indeed, despite the fact that this was a traffic island on a busy A road, it was almost like a sacred grove), just hanging about on the newly trodden paths through the rough grasses and chatting. 'I'm writing a book,' I told them, 'about hippies. Are any of you hippies?'

'I'm a hippie,' said Des, a craggy-faced man with a floppy Tibetan hat and a grumbling, nasal voice.

'I'm a hippie,' said Denny, a petite, handsome woman with a green velvet hat, clutching a bunch of flowers and looking suitably fey.

'I'm a hippie,' said someone else.

'I'm a hippie.'

'Me three. I'm a hippie too.'

There were hippies everywhere. I was surrounded by hippies.

We all agreed to meet up later.

Most of them were off to the Glastonbury festival site to perform another ritual in the stone circle on the sacred field. The Glastonbury festival was due to start at the end of the following week. Me, I'd had enough of rituals for the time being. My ritual cup of coffee in the Little Chef car park had exhausted me. I went over to Avebury instead, where I was hoping to meet Steve.

Avebury is a pretty little village at the western end of Wiltshire, which is completely enclosed within a massive stone circle. It's the largest stone circle in the British Isles. There's a pub, a vegetarian café, a shop, some public toilets, and a number of houses, all made from the same creamy-coloured stone. The houses look suspiciously as if they're made from the same sort of stone as the stones in the stone circle, some of which are missing. Which leads you to think that they've been busily bashing away at the standing stones for centuries in order to build the village.

It's where all the hippies come these days, in lieu of their old festival at Stonehenge. There are a number of prehistoric monuments near by, including Silbury Hill, a massive, conical, man-made hill of mysterious purpose, and West Kennet Long Barrow, a burial mound, all with their English Heritage car parks attached. This is where the hippies gather, in the car parks. I pulled into the car park at Avebury, also provided, thoughtfully, by English Heritage. I had Galahad and a couple of others with me. There were a number of hippie buses parked up. One or two of them were Ford Transit Disability Transport Vehicles like my own. I was dishevelled and bleary-eyed from the previous night's exertions. Everybody thought I was a hippie too.

I went off to find Steve. I knew Steve would be there, some-where or another. He's a fixture of the place, like Scottie on the Enterprise. The place wouldn't be the same without him.

I eventually found him in a tepee tucked away at the bottom of the great earthwork that surrounds the site. I ducked through the entrance. Steve was on the floor, surrounded by acolytes. He was his usual ebullient self. 'Chris!' he cried, and handed me a beer. So it was beer for breakfast. I spent the rest of the day getting drunk, which was my personal sacrifice to the goddess at this sacred time of the year.

We went back to my van. Steve was telling me about a cere-mony he'd attended at dawn.

'It was a really good ceremony,' he said. He'd observed it from the top of the earthwork overlooking the circle, and moved into it. The woman who was conducting the ceremony was called Amma Ra, a devotee of the Mayan thirteen-moon calendar. She'd done the usual, dividing the circle into the four quarters and invoking this, that and the other arcane or obscure presences, chanting, Omming, visualizing and all the rest. But there was one invocation Steve didn't join in with as he couldn't make out the name. 'It sounded like Key,' he said. 'I don't like invoking unknown entities. You never know what you might be letting yourself in for.' And then, at the end, they'd embraced the nearest person to them. 'That was the best bit, hugging the lady,' he said.

'Who, Steve?'

'The lady who was conducting the ceremony.'

'I thought you were outside of the circle when the ceremony started.'

'I was.'

'And then, at the end, you were standing next to the woman who was conducting the ceremony, and you gave her a hug?'

'Right.'

'So, let's get this right Steve. You were away from the circle when the ceremony started. And by the time it was finished you were standing right next to her. You fancied her, didn't you? You spent the entire ceremony edging your way round the circle so you could be next to her. It wasn't the ceremony you were interested in really, was it? It was her.'

'It's not true,' he said, laughing. 'My interest was entirely spiritual!'

Galahad was sitting in the van with us. He decided he wanted to score some acid, and someone from a nearby hippie bus came in to sort out a deal.

'What have you got?' asked Gallie.

'I've got acid, ecstasy, 2-CBs and DMT,' he said. He was getting out all these little packets and sorting through them. He had bags and bags of the stuff. 'This is DMT,' he said. 'It's stronger than acid. I like to take it once in a while. It's like being thrust into orbit where fundamental beings lay you out on an operating table and tinker with your psychic machinery. The acid's good. Pure Californian.'

'How much is it?' Gallie asked.

'Two pound fifty each. Three for a fiver. I got it from . . .' and he mentioned the name of a well-known pop group. 'I'm going off to California with them in the summer,' he added, boasting. 'They think I'm really cool.'

Gallie was impressed. 'I'll have two tabs,' he said. And then, by way of conversation, he said, 'I'm a road protester. What do you think of road protesters?'

'They take the wrong drugs,' the drug dealer said. 'They like alcohol and roll-ups. They should take better drugs.'

I looked at my bottle of beer and my roll-up, and then back at him and spluttered derisively. I thought, *At least the road protesters are doing something. So you got your acid from some pop group, and you're going off to America with them in the summer, and they think you're cool. So fucking what?* I was visibly sneering. He didn't seem to notice.

'He was an interesting bloke,' said Gallie, after he was gone.

'He was a prat,' I said.

The drug dealer was a young hippie. If you thought that hippiedom was an exclusive phenomenon of the sixties and seventies, you'd be wrong. It's one of those philosophies. It just won't go away.

I spent the rest of the day getting progressively drunker and drunker at the pub. Denny and Des turned up. They'd been elected King and Queen of the Summer, which meant they had to go off and do a lot of fucking. All in the name of the fecundity of the Earth, you understand, completely unselfish. We made arrangements to meet up later in the week. Eventually I was so exhausted from all the booze and the sacred exertions of the previous night that I had to go back to the van. I fell asleep. When I woke up it was morning. I looked out of the window and saw all these vehicles parked up on the dirt tracks. For half a second I was lost. I didn't know where I was.

Fucking hell, I thought, *I'm on a racetrack.*

It was quite a disappointment to discover that, after all, I was only at a hippie festival.

7 Huna Druzz *or*
   Another Failed Love Quest, an Apple,
   and a Cup of Coffee

I've said a number of times now that Steve is an alien being from
another planet. You probably think that's a metaphor, or a
snazzy way of explaining away difficult things. Actually it's
both. But it's also true.

It's probably too obvious to say that everyone lives as much in
their own heads as they do in the real world. It's so obvious that
I'm not certain that anyone has ever said it before. People tell
themselves stories, and then live by them. Everyone has a screen-
play or a novel (or possibly both) going on in their heads all the
time. Sometimes the novel is a detective novel. Sometimes it's a
love story. Or a cowboy book, or a war story, or a spy novel. Or
it's a kitchen-sink drama. In a kitchen-sink drama someone is
always doing the washing-up. Sometimes the story is a tragedy,
sometimes it's a farce. Usually it is both. In every case the person

is the hero of their own ongoing tale, and that tale is as real to them as the world. It motivates them in the world, tells them how to act, and therefore it, in turn, affects the world, affecting other people in their ongoing story-lines too. What's a fiction and what's a fact? How can you tell the difference?

In Steve's case the story is a kind of tripped out, mystical science-fiction love story, with a bit of sorcery thrown in. He even writes his own soundtrack, and adds his own canned laughter to the funny bits. So he really is an alien being from another planet. How else can he explain his mysteries to himself?

One of those mysteries is the humming noise. All through his late childhood and into his early teens he heard it. It was very loud, like a generator. It would wake him up at night, startling him out of his dreams with a throbbing, crazed insistence. And then he'd go searching for the source of the noise: in the walls, under the bed, out the window, in the hall. He'd go into the bathroom and look behind the cistern. And then downstairs to look in the kitchen. But he could never find the source of that mysterious noise. And on and on it would drone, like his house was on top of an underground UFO factory. Then he would get really frustrated with it, and he'd go and wake up his parents. 'Mam, Dad,' he'd say, shaking them awake. 'What is it that noise? Can you hear it? The noise. Surely you can hear it?' But they couldn't. Sometimes he'd wake his sister up too, trying to find the source of the noise. But no one but Steve ever heard if.

One night they were all out on the landing, Steve having woken them all up, and he was saying, 'Well surely you can hear it now, it's deafening.' But they didn't have the slightest idea what he was talking about.

'What noise?' they said.

And then he was shunted back to bed, his mother muttering about how he was having nightmares, even though he was fully awake. This had been going on for years.

Later, during the period we're dealing with in this book, he'd gone to live in a squat in London. As usual he was chasing some girl. He'd met her at the Windsor Free Festival in 1973, and she'd invited him to London to live with her in this squat. She had a blanket wrapped round her and a funny-looking Alsatian dog with a tattoo. Steve was drinking a pint of milk, and he offered her some. She told him she'd been done for dope-smuggling – it had been in all the papers – and that her parents had disowned her. Then she'd fallen over a cliff on acid. Her arm was all smashed up, and she had gangrene in her wrist. She had a dressing on, which she was supposed to change every day, but she didn't bother. And she'd make her money by busking the one and only song she knew: 'Don't Think Twice, It's All Right', by Bob Dylan. She could earn quite a bit of money doing that, owing less to the fact that she performed it particularly well (she didn't) than to the fact that she got people's sympathy. Injured girl with a scrawny dog. It was a sure-fire money-spinner. She was making about ten pounds a session. This was a lot of money in 1973.

So – as usual – Steve fell for her. And she suggested that, once the festival was over, he should try living in a squat with her in Camden.

He went back to Cardiff after the festival, to pick up his things, and, with another friend, also called Steve, he headed for London. When he got there the girl wasn't even there. She'd gone off hop-picking in Kent with some other guy.

Well – what else could they do? – they stayed in the squat.

It was as repulsive a place as you can imagine. Winos and dossers downstairs, actual turds on the floors and tables, doors all smashed in – they'd been used for firewood – windows broken, no water, no electricity, no gas, no lights. You used a candle if you needed a light. And the rules of the squat were quite simple. If you wanted to keep anything you had to hang on to it, otherwise it was anybody's property to do what they liked with. And if you needed to go to the toilet – assuming you could be bothered with the niceties, that is – you did it out of the window. The back garden was a stinking, steaming mess of shit, piss, cans, bottles, cardboard boxes, plastic containers, wrappers, discarded food, all sorts of rubbish which had been chucked out there, mouldering and festering and coming alive at night.

The floors were packed with people that night as every other night. And as Steve was going to sleep he felt something running over his leg. He jerked awake.

'What the fuck was that?' he said. 'Something just ran over my leg.'

Someone said, 'It's a rat. Don't worry about it man. There's loads of them here.'

Steve managed to spend a week and a half there, waiting for his girl to turn up. She never did turn up, and he never saw her again. In the end he couldn't handle any more.

One of the last days in the squat, he and the other Steve had come back from the pub. The squat was supposed to be haunted, and when they got back there was this icy cold feeling as they went in through the door. 'We both experienced that, what you call a cold spot,' he says. They went upstairs and crashed out. They were on downers, so it didn't matter that much. Steve said, 'Well it's a cold spot, so what?' and joined whoever else was on the floor and crashed out. But then he woke up, suddenly, and the other Steve woke up too. 'Droid,' he said, 'what the fuck is that?' He was hearing Steve's previously unheard humming noise, going groiugn-groiugn-groiugn-groiugn-groiugn, and pulsating all around the room like it used to do in Cardiff.

Steve said, 'I don't know, I really don't know, but I'm glad you can hear it too.' And he told him about how he'd been hearing this noise for a long period of his life. Finally the noise faded out, and they both went back to sleep, and when Steve woke up the following morning he was feeling elated that at last somebody else had heard this noise. So he wasn't crazy after all. After that the noise never came back.

'But I always had that as a sort of a mystery,' he says now. 'So if I met anyone from psychic circles I used to talk to them about it. I've heard all sorts of explanations.'

V (a self-confessed male-female alien being from Andromeda who writes books on psychic transformation, and who Steve writes to regularly) says: 'Experiencing humming sounds, of which there are various kinds, is not unusual. Often enough they represent pre-initiation adjustments being made to certain parts of our etheric sheath, and/or to actual Chakric points, unfolding petals, which are a bit blocked or sluggish, etc.'

Jenny Randles (a famous UFO expert) says it is something called Huna Druzz, a psychic training exercise.

Me, I prefer to think it was Steve's alien friends trying to contact him. In which case, they gave up in 1973, in that squat in Camden, and they've never tried again since. Probably they were so disgusted at the way Earthlings chose to live, they decided not to bother to invade the planet after all.

Steve wasn't having a very good time. After the break up with Mandy he'd started taking downers, and drinking beer a lot. He was perennially in love with some girl or another, and always disappointed. The downers served two purposes in his life. Firstly they numbed the pain of his serial disappointment, and secondly they served as ballast for his unstable brain. He was always liable to float away, like a helium balloon in a high wind. He'd become incapable of taking psychoactive drugs. It wasn't just LSD. Even the mildest psychedelics would send him doolally.

One time he was in love with a girl called Philippa. She was very concerned about him. 'You take too many bad drugs,' she told him. 'Downers, beer, they're not good for you. You should smoke dope instead.'

So they were at a party. A joint passed by. Always eager to please and impress, Steve took a toke. Just one toke, one tiny little puff. Philippa smiled at him indulgently. All of a sudden he was overtaken by the munchies. He had this irresistible urge to put something into his mouth. He went into the kitchen. It was full, as is the way of parties, then as now. People were standing about and chatting, passing joints, drinking beer, all immersed in their own separate little worlds. Steve found a box of cornflakes, which he began to eat. He was shovelling them into his mouth by the handful, ramming them in, and watching as cornflakes fell from his lips and onto the hairs that poked from his unbuttoned shirt. Steve has a very hairy chest. He also has hairy arms and shoulders. He's a very hairy man.

So he started to think – this idea began to formulate in his brain – that the hair on his chest was there to store food for some future Ice Age, like a hamster stores food in its pouch.

So far, no one had noticed him. Maybe he'd caught one or two people's eye for the voracious way he was shovelling cornflakes into his mouth. But that's all. You see all sorts of things at a party.

Unfortunately Steve now decided he needed to explain things. He felt that everyone in the party ought to know what was going on. He began to address all the people in the kitchen. So he was talking very loudly about hamsters and Ice Ages and hairy chests, and how you store food in them, still chewing mouthfuls of corn-flakes – cornflakes flying out of his mouth in crumbled amber sprays, and falling into his beard and onto the floor – while rubbing further cornflakes onto his chest to demonstrate. He'd undone his shirt some more to improve the effect. He'd be grabbing handfuls from the box, and then rubbing them all over his chest. 'See? To store food in, see? In the Ice Age. Like hamsters. Look, see. The cornflakes stay there. So when the Ice Age comes, I'll be all right, see. I'll be all right. People without hairy chests won't be all right. Nowhere to store their food, see? But I will be, because I'm adapted to it. See? I'm adapted to the coming Ice Age.'

The room went quiet. Except for Steve, that is. There was a certain relentless logic pounding through his brain, which kind of forced its way out of his mouth. He had to explain. People started edging from the room, quietly backing away. Soon Steve found himself completely alone. The kitchen was suddenly deserted.

Realizing that things had gone badly wrong, yet again, Steve skulked off into the night. He was looking for a place to kip. Eventually he found a spot under a hedge near a park, where he dossed down. And the following day he was on his way home when he bumped into the lovely Philippa, accompanied by some other man.

'Oh God, Droid, it's you. Oh, I was wrong, I was wrong. What can I say? I told you to smoke dope 'cos it's good for you, and it's not good for you at all. And if you're ever going to take acid, let me know, 'cos I don't even want to be in the same town as you, let alone the same party.'

As he was telling me this story Steve was constantly breaking into his characteristic spluttering guffaws. If anyone guffaws, it's Steve. The laughter bursts out of him, huge, explosive, like lava from an erupting volcano. That's what it sounds like: volcanic laughter.

'I felt this big,' he said, indicating with the smallest gap between the thumb and forefinger. And then he guffawed again.

So he took downers instead. In the end he'd taken so many that he became addicted to them. And then one day he was at home at his mum and dad's house when he threw a fit. He'd run out of pills. His parents persuaded him to see a 'specialist'. A psychiatrist, in other words. A shrink.

Well, he wasn't mad. He was doolally. He was bonkers. He was off his trolley. But he was never insane. He was an alien being from another planet addicted to sleeping pills, crossed in love and often very depressed. But anyone with such an innate capacity to laugh at themselves and the world around them can't be mad. To me, this is the height of sanity. The psychiatrist did him no good whatsoever.

He was prescribed Valium and then he'd go to see the psychiatrist every six weeks or so. Often he'd have to wait in the waiting room for an hour before he could get in for his appointment. He'd be waiting around, tense, dying for a fag. But the nurses would come up to him to ask if he had any cigarettes spare, for the doctors. The doctors were in their consulting rooms smoking cigarettes that they'd bummed off the patients outside. And once in the consulting room with the psychiatrist, that's all the two of them would do too: smoke fags. Smoke endless fags – sometimes as many as twenty in a session – and argue. They didn't get on at all. In fact, the doctor told him categorically that he was only seeing Steve as a favour. 'I thought, oh God, here come the hippies again.' That's what the doctor told him he'd thought the first time Steve walked into the room. And the two of them would argue and the doctor would get very irate, to the point where he would be banging the table. The doctor told him to read Aldous Huxley's *Brave New World*. But Steve said, 'Well, all right. But if I read this, then you read *Doors of Perception* and *Heaven and Hell*.' These are books by Aldous Huxley extolling the virtues of psychedelics. The doctor had, in fact, taken many drugs, as part of his training. He'd taken speed and opiates and a variety of other things. But he'd never taken acid. And this was Steve's point. 'Well if you haven't taken acid you don't know what you're talking about, and you can't say what is real and what isn't real. You don't know if you haven't experienced it.'

'And then, at the end of all this, he was under stress, and I was under stress, and I was going there because I was under stress and I was leaving there feeling I'd had even more stress,' says Steve now. 'And he appeared to be quite crazy. And all he ever said was, "We've got to make an appointment, Steve. See you in six weeks, and keep taking the tablets."'

Actually, he did say a lot more than this. He was trying to

encourage Steve to an academic career. Steve didn't want to go, but he applied for a place anyway, just to keep the doctor happy. He got a place at Lampeter University. And the last time he saw the doctor was just before he was due to go.

The doctor said, 'So, Steve, are you all ready to go to University?'

'Well no,' said Steve, 'I've changed my mind, I don't want to go, and I'm not going.'

The doctor's face dropped at this. It was the one thing he'd set his heart on. *His* heart, note, not Steve's. It was never a question of what was best for Steve. It was so the doctor felt better, that's all.

There's a postscript to this story. Many, many years later, Steve was back at the mental hospital. But this time it had nothing to do with him. It was Susan, his common-law wife, who had suffered a nervous breakdown due to postnatal depression. And Steve used to sit and wait for her there, while she was in seeing the psychiatrist. One day the head consultant came up to him. This was the other doctor's superior, so he knew about Steve's case.

'Ah, Steve,' the doctor said, while Steve was sitting there waiting, 'you've come to see me.'

'No I haven't,' said Steve.

'Yes, yes, you have,' said the doctor. 'I'm the doctor, and I know that you've come to see me.'

'No I haven't,' said Steve, 'I haven't come to see you.'

'Steve, I know perfectly well why you are here, so don't deny it. You've come to see me.'

'No, no, I haven't. I haven't come to see you. I'm just trying to sit here waiting. I'm waiting for my girlfriend who's in there seeing one of your colleagues.'

'No, no, no, I'm the doctor, I know you've come to see me. You can't deny it, Steve. Stop trying to deny that you've come to see me.'

'You've got it all wrong . . .'

And on like this, both of them absolutely convinced of their position, until Steve, exasperated, jumped up. 'All right,' he said, 'look, can we just . . . we'll go in there and we'll sort this out.'

So he banged on the door, and the two of them broke into the consultation the other doctor was having with Susan.

'I'm sorry to disturb you,' said Steve, 'But your colleague here is insisting that I've come to see him. So can you tell him that I'm not here to see him, but that I'm waiting outside while you're seeing Susan.'

'Well yes,' the other doctor said, 'that's right.'

'I rest my case,' said Steve. 'I am not here to see you. See? I am not here to see you.'

'Oh right, then,' said the consultant. 'You are not here to see me.'

'Well perhaps you can go back outside now,' said the other doctor, 'while I continue with the consultation.'

And Steve went back outside to resume his waiting, while the consultant went on his way.

Which makes you wonder who was sane and who was not. As Steve puts it now, 'I just thought it was so crazy that this top mental doctor was insisting something was real which was totally unreal. I always used to think that these psychiatrists were equally as crazy as the people they were supposed to be sorting out. It never made any sense to me.'

But the consequence of all of this is that Steve ended up as a Valium addict. Months of consultation, argument, fierce debate. Thousands of pounds in fees. Hours of bureaucracy, paperwork, forms to fill in, appointments to be made. Discussions between colleagues, meetings, case studies. A whole industry beavering madly away to turn one addiction into another. It's what they do to heroin addicts too. They turn them into methadone addicts.

The reason that Steve didn't want to go to university is that he had other plans. He wanted to be a rock star.

Just before he'd left school one of the teachers had come up to talk to him.

'So, boy,' he said, 'have you decided what you want to do?'

'I want to be a rock star,' said Steve.

'No, seriously, what would you like to do?'

'I want to be a rock star.'

'You've got to be joking. You've no chance of doing that. I mean a serious job, a proper job.'

'That is a serious job. I want to be a rock star.'

And that was the end of that conversation. And it's a homage to Steve's enduring optimism that it's still what he wants to be to this day. Well why not? Surely the world has room for one more balding, greying, forty-something-year-old rock star?

The trouble was he had no idea how to go about it. He just thought it would happen, that it would come to him as of right.

He had a few songs. One of them was called 'Extracting the Latex from a Rubber Ducky'. It came to him one night when he was sitting with a friend of his who was schizophrenic. The guy would mutter 'rubber ducky, rubber ducky' to himself endlessly. So Steve thought he could write a song about it. He said to his friend, 'Paul, I could write a song called "Extracting the Latex from a Rubber Ducky".'

Paul said, 'Yeah, well, you know, go for it.' And then immersed himself in his 'rubber ducky' chant once more.

So Steve went home and wrote the song. Here are the lyrics to the first verse:

> 'Extracting the latex from a rubber ducky,
> gets you in a mess, yes, very mucky,
> we'll give you all a try if you're very lucky,
> extracting the latex from a rubber ducky.'

It wasn't exactly meaningful. But he put a couple of chords to it, and there you are: Steve's first composition.

He started performing at the Chapter Arts Centre in Cardiff. He did 'Extracting the Latex from a Rubber Ducky', and a couple of other compositions, including 'He Left His Head in Acapulco', and 'Pippin the Pigeon'. It was all nonsense. Also he did cover versions. The trouble was, he couldn't really play guitar all that well. He could just about strum a few chords, that's all. And one night he was playing in the Arts Centre, doing a cover version of Bob Dylan's 'A Hard Rain's A-Gonna Fall', when two of the strings on his guitar broke. So he put on this voice. 'Actually this is the Brian Ferry version,' he said, and started hamming it up to cover the jangling cacophony of his strangulated guitar. It went down a storm. People loved him. They thought he was a comic genius.

'And then I got stuck doing Brian Ferry versions of everything. So I was doing this stupid Rubber Ducky song, and Brian Ferry voices for covers of other things, and all this rubbish people seemed to be, like, really into.'

One time he was at the Windsor Free Festival, with a couple of friends of his, off his head on downers as usual. He decided he wanted to play. He borrowed a guitar from someone and started hassling the organizers for a slot. He was probably drawling, and almost certainly incapable of listening to reason. In the end the organizers agreed, just to get rid of him. This was on the main stage, just after Hawkwind. So he was headlining for Hawkwind on this occasion. And he had this little yellow rubber duck with him, and he and his two friends got up on stage before this massive crowd, with a beat up old guitar and a kazoo and a rubber duck, and started playing the rubber ducky song. The crowd went wild. He had an encore for it.

'I just couldn't relate to it, 'cos there were all these thousands and thousands of hippie people out there in the field, all going wild about this rubbish.'

Some months later he was in London, on his way to a Van Morrison concert. And before the gig he went to a pub to get himself a drink. This was in Finsbury Park, an ordinary little pub at the end of a terraced street. So he was at the bar, relaxing with his drink, when this stranger came up to him.

'Oh, man,' the bloke said, boiling with enthusiasm, 'man, man, it's you. You're the guy who does the song about a rubber duck. You're from Wales. Oh, this is too much. There's all these people over here who've heard all about you. Come over and meet my friends. Far out, man! Too much.'

So Steve was getting his wish. He was actually, without even trying, becoming a rock star. The trouble was, he didn't really like that rubber ducky song.

'I played that song so much that one day I had to kill the rubber ducky. One night, in the Chapter bar in Cardiff, I rearranged some of the lyrics to include the death of the duck, and with some help I stabbed and stamped it into a shoe-box coffin. We even dressed a guy up as an undertaker. Of course, that wasn't the end of the bloody duck. I got calls to do the re-incarnation of the duck. I did it a couple of times, I'm sorry to say. But that time we killed the duck was wild. There were people in the crowd actually crying!'

*

But it wasn't to be. Steve wasn't going to be a rock star just yet. He was too depressed all the time, too involved with his continuing love quest. Steve's whole life has been a love quest.

He was involved with this student girl called Jo for a while. She was living in one of the halls of residence by the University, and he used to go and see her there. He went out with her a few times and would meet her at parties. But then the Christmas holidays came, and she went home to see her parents. She'd given Steve her address, so Steve decided to go and visit her. The address was somewhere in North Wales. So he hitchhiked all the way up there, a long and gruelling journey. It was very cold, frosty, first thing in the morning. And he arrived in the town only to discover that there was a new town and an old town, and that the address she'd given him didn't specify which. He looked it up in the telephone book, and there were several places listed with the same name. Also, her surname was Davis, which is a common Welsh name. There were literally thousands of entries under the name. So finding her was going to be more difficult than he expected.

He needed a place to stay. He looked in a post office window, and there was an advert saying: 'Are you seeking Truth? Peace? Spiritual Enlightenment?' He recognized the tone. It was the Divine Light Mission, Guru Maharaji's outfit, very in vogue at the time. So he went round to visit them.

'Do you know about Guru Maharaji?' they asked.

'Well, yes, I do. I know a lot about Guru Maharaji, actually, and, to be honest, although I can respect what you're into and that you believe in all this stuff, I'm not. But what I wanted, I just want somewhere to crash, and I'm looking for a girl who lives up here somewhere, and is it all right if I stay here?'

They agreed. So Steve stayed there for a few days, while he got on with the business of trying to find this girl.

Finally he managed to track down the house. It was a large, detached house on an expensive, new housing estate: very smart, very upper middle class. Steve was overjoyed. He thought, *At last, I've found the place.* He had a picture with him that he'd made for her. It was a black piece of board with autumn leaves of different colours glued onto it, which he'd varnished and stuck in a frame. It was his gift.

He got to the door and rang the bell. She answered the door, and Steve handed her his gift.

'Oh my god, Droid, what . . . what are you doing here?' she said.

'Jo, you said come up, and I've come up to see you,' he said. 'Aren't you pleased to see me?'

But it was obvious she was not. She was just taken aback at seeing him there so unexpectedly.

'Oh God,' she said, 'well I suppose you'd better come in.' And then, noticing the gift which he'd placed in her hands, she said, 'and what's this?'

'It's a present,' he said.

'My mother will like it,' she said.

And Steve thought, *Oh well, I made it for you, but your mother will like it. Fine.*

'You can't stay long,' she continued as she showed him into the house, 'because my parents have just gone shopping and they'll be back soon. You're gonna have to go. But would you like an orange or an apple or something? And a cup of coffee?'

So she gave him an apple and a cup of coffee, and then, when he'd finished these, she said, 'Well, you're gonna have to go now Steve, 'cos my parents will be coming back any minute now, and they'll freak out if they find you here. I'm sorry, like. That's it. I'll see you back in Cardiff.'

So he left, crestfallen. And as he walked away he was thinking, *Yes, fine, fine, I've come all this way, I've hitchhiked up from Cardiff in the middle of winter, I've spent nearly a whole week trying to find you, I've wandered around this twin town, the old town and the new town, I've asked everyone I've met whether they knew you or not, and then finally I've found you, and all I got was an apple and a cup of coffee. And now I've got to go all the way back to Cardiff. Yes, fine.*

So he started hitching back. He got a lift from one bloke who took him back to his farmhouse and gave him a smoke, and who then returned him to the main road. And then he was waiting by the road, and another car pulled in. *Great!* thought Steve, *I'm doing all right here. I've got another lift.* And he got in the car.

The driver said, 'I'm a plain-clothed policeman. We're doing a routine investigation. Would you mind coming to the station to answer a few questions?'

Steve thought, *Oh well, it's not such a good lift after all. But at least it's a lift.* And he agreed. 'Yeah, yeah, sure,' he said.

So he went to the police station with the officer. And then they started asking him questions. Like: 'Where were you at half past two in the morning on Tuesday the 6th July?'

'I don't know,' said Steve.

'What were you wearing at half-past two in the morning on Tuesday the 6th July?

'I don't know,' said Steve.

They kept asking him the same questions over and over again. And then they were talking in Welsh about him, and laughing. They were calling him Jesus Christ in Welsh. And the questions were getting more and more absurd.

'What kind of trousers are you wearing now?'

'I have on a pair of brown velour trousers.'

'And what kind of brown is that?'

'Rusty brown.'

'And what kind of shirt do you have on now?'

It was patently absurd, asking him all sorts of questions that they could answer themselves, and then writing it all down and laughing.

After a while they took him into the courthouse.

'You realize what this is?'

'Yes, it's a courthouse.'

'You realize you could end up in here?'

'What for?'

But they wouldn't say. They just started asking him the same old stupid questions, over and over again. It was several hours later that they finally told him what it as all about. They were looking for a vagrant who had murdered some man with a pitchfork several months before, and who had then set light to a barn. It clearly had nothing to do with Steve. The whole thing was put on, to have a go at the hippie. And then they said, 'Well you can go now.' They led him to the door, showed him out, and then said, 'Well that's it, you're free to go.'

It was cold and dark by now. They'd kept him in the place all day on purpose, to stop him getting a lift. It wasn't till the following day that he finally made it back to Cardiff.

And that's it. The perfect metaphor for Steve's life. Another failed love quest, an apple and a cup of coffee. And a bunch of hick Welsh policemen taking the piss out of him for looking like a hippie.

No wonder he was depressed.

8 'Enlicenment'

'Take not a maiden who, when she sees a man of bronze,
Loses possession of herself.
Nothing furthers.'

The I Ching, Hexagram 4, 'Youthful Folly'

Things weren't going all that well for me either.

I'd moved into a shared house in Colum Road. It was one of those 'houses of multiple occupation' that at the time might have been considered a hippie pad. The fact that such places still exist, whether or not there are any hippies living in them, is testimony to the enduring need for cheap accommodation for young people in every age. These days they might be student pads, or Goth pads, or punk pads, or ravers' pads, or whatever. Or postmodernists' pads. I don't care. It's all padding for the book.

But it was a hippie pad to me. What follows is the story of the one and only time when I genuinely fell into the category of 'hippie'.

I look back over my life now, and I can see, with an almost painful clarity, that though there have been times when I was

99

reasonably intelligent, there have been other times when I've been exceedingly dumb. These times have followed each other in routine succession, like a constantly turning wheel. You imagine that you grow up in a straight line, from childhood into adulthood, from youth into old age. But it's not like that at all. Twentynine is not necessarily more adult than nineteen, say, or even nine. At nine I was bright. At nineteen I still had some residual intelligence left. But by the time I'd moved into Colum Road, at the age of twenty, I was just awesomely dumb.

I shared the house with a variety of mainly young men like myself. Dave the communist lived there for a while. As did Alan, the man who gave me the Worthy Farm sign for my van. And Sumbo, a Nigerian film-maker. And Bob and Allison. And Tim. And a number of other people who were just passing through. And Cliff Pilchard. I'll tell you more about Cliff Pilchard later. Add to this the fact that there were always people visiting us, day and night, and crashing there, and eating there, or just hanging out with us, and you can see that it was a scruffy, friendly, often lively place to be.

But it was at this time that my love-life began to go downhill. All the way downhill, as it happens. My sins had come back to haunt me.

I went out briefly with a young hairdresser named Bernadette. When she packed me up I threw a wobbly. My reaction was out of all proportion to what I actually felt about her, or to the length of time we'd been going out. I've since realized that it was Beverley I was grieving for.

After that there were a couple of other girls. I had sex with one girl while we were sharing a nest of mattresses with two other blokes. One of them was Cliff Pilchard. The three of them had been tripping, and I'd kind of moved in on them. They were all huddled up under a blanket round a drug dealer's house, and they asked me to put on a record. I put on Berlin by Lou Reed. 'They're taking my children away,' followed by the sounds of a distressed baby screaming: 'Mommy, mommy, mommy!' I'm sure it put them all at their ease. The girl kept looking at me out of the corner of her eye. Later we went back to Cliff's place to sleep, and lay down on these mattresses. I'd manœuvred it so I was next to the girl. I touched her, and she moved towards me, achingly aroused. We didn't say a single word. She rolled into my arms as if by silent command. The day after, the two men were looking at me strangely.

One day Cliff and I were tripping. We met this girl who told me that she'd met me at a party a couple of years before. That was in my 'free-love' period. She said she'd often thought about me since. She liked the way I talked. She was living in Newport now, just down the road from Cardiff. It was in Newport that she'd met Gaynor, the girl I'd slept with two or three times the year before. Gaynor still talked about me too. That was what the two girls had in common, that they both still thought about me. I slept with this girl too. We made love. And before she left she promised to put Gaynor in contact with me. Gaynor sent me a letter. It told me how much she wanted to see me again, and it contained a copy of Desiderata: 'Go placidly amid the noise and haste.' Gaynor said she'd seen this poem and thought of me. I never replied to the letter.

And then I was going out with Jane, who I met in a disco one night. She was very shapely, with a wild bush of curling, brown hair. Then I suddenly became bored, and I packed her up too. It was after this that the thought came into my head. It was possibly the last intelligent thought I had for more than a year. *I don't treat women very well, do I? I ought to stop going out with them for a while. I ought to give it a rest.* I felt that the next girl might be the right girl, the one I would fall in love with and stay with for the rest of my life, and that meanwhile I should learn to love them in other ways. It was five years before I had another proper girlfriend. I became increasingly, almost pathologically shy in women's company. As I said in Chapter 3: justice does really seem to exist.

I got into smoking dope instead. I smoked from morning till night for more than twelve months. It began to seem like years. Actually, that isn't all that accurate. I was never up in the morning, and I didn't go to bed at night. So I smoked dope from evening till morning, with occasional breaks down the pub. Not too often, as it happens, as no one ever had any money.

My hair was getting longer and longer, as was my beard. It was jet-black, unlike now. I looked like a turbanless Sikh. I never washed or ironed my clothes. I wore the same clothes every day.

101

It's probably my only saving grace, that during this time as an archetypal hippie I didn't actually wear flares. I had a pair of Wranglers, turned up at the ankle. And I wore a combat jacket and a black T-shirt, and baseball boots. That would be a Socialist Workers' Party costume now, all prepared to man the barricades. But it wasn't. I was trying to be a sadhu.

But this is all getting out of sequence. It didn't all happen overnight, or even in that order. It was a process.

The reason I can say – confidently – that I'd never been a proper hippie till this point, is that I didn't actually like hippie things. I didn't listen to rock music. I listened to electronic music and jazz. I'd skipped through *The Lord of the Rings*, but hadn't really liked it all that much. I preferred the works of Joyce and Pound and Beckett. I'd always considered myself – very arrogantly, on reflection (so maybe Simon had been right) – as an 'Artist'.

But it was as if I'd lost faith somewhere down the line. The truth is, I wasn't happy.

It was while I was staying with Richard and Jude that I'd started smoking dope with a vengeance. Richard was dealing the stuff. He had a huge lump of Moroccan hidden away in his wardrobe, very fragrant, very pure, at least a pound's weight. And he was caning it every night, and I was joining him and Jude in their nightly sessions.

While I was there I picked up a copy of *A Separate Reality* by Carlos Casteneda. In case you don't know it, it is one of a series of books that purport to be the autobiography of an apprentice to a modern sorcerer. Carlos Casteneda was an American academic of Spanish extraction who had gone to Mexico sometime in the sixties as an anthropologist to study the use of psychotropic plants amongst the Yaqui Indians. Don Juan, the sorcerer, had taken him on as his apprentice, and was teaching him his philosophy and his methods of magical transformation using a variety of substances, including magic mushrooms and the Peyote cactus. It was a cult hippie book.

I became entranced by it. I was drawn into it. I believed every word. It described, in an uncluttered, unembelleshed style, a world of such awesome power and mystery, that my own world seemed shallow by comparison: a sham, a superficial make-believe, a grey, ragged curtain shrouding out the light. I began to yearn for something better, something more authentic, more 'real'.

Then Bernadette had happened. Then I'd moved into Colum Road. Then I'd become depressed.

It was Cliff Pilchard's room I moved into. This was sometime after the four-in-a-bed episode. Cliff moved downstairs, into a little boxroom no bigger than his single mattress, which he festooned with blankets and tapestries, turning it into a little, warm, cosy womb. He said he liked rooms like that. Meanwhile I was trying to be a writer. I was sitting in my own, stark room – painted white, and decorated sparsely with choice pictures (including *The Canterbury Tales* by William Blake) – composing drivel. I knew it was drivel even while I was writing it. It was full of tedious angst. It was sometime in late autumn, and I knew that the leaves would be falling from the trees in the green spaces around the Museum. I wanted to take a walk under the trees, and to hear the wind brushing through them, and to kick up the fallen leaves to hear that dry, rustling sound. But I didn't. I just sat there composing angst about how I would like to be somewhere else. I knew that if I did go out I'd feel better instantly. I knew it and yet I was almost savouring the sorry feeling I was building up, imagining the leaves out there, and yet resolutely refusing to go out and kick about amongst them. I was punishing myself with the leaves. It was my first depression – a play-acting depression, as I can see now – brought on by the autumn leaves. How poetic. (How pathetic!)

It was after this that I started hanging round with Pilchard a lot.

Cliff Pilchard. That's not his real name of course. I made it up. But it suits him. There was certainly something fishy about him, not to say vertiginous. He considered himself to be a high spiritual being, a guru. And it's a mark of how stupid I was becoming by then that I took him at his word.

We took a lot of LSD together, and smoked a lot of dope. Sumbo, the Nigerian film-maker, who was over here doing a course, called us White Rastas. And he was right, in a way. We didn't say 'Jah!' as we blew on a chillum: we said, 'Bom Shankar!'

and then put the chillum to our foreheads before taking in a lungful of the biting smoke and collapsing into fits of . . . of dry coughing. I would have said, 'before collapsing into fits of giggles', except we didn't. We didn't laugh much. We took our dope very, very seriously.

To be fair to Cliff, I probably did him as much damage as he did to me in the end. To have his spiritual credentials accepted like that, without the slightest criticism: it couldn't have helped his ego much, puffing it up to a dangerous degree. And megalomania is always a much more fragile state than false modesty. At least the disingenuously modest person can feign delighted surprise when someone points out something decent about his character. The megalomaniac, on the other hand, can't allow anything about himself but utter perfection. The merest hint of the awful truth – that you're just a boring little fart like anyone else – and the balloon is burst. Pop! No more ego.

So maybe I wasn't so dumb after all. I'd tucked away my pride for the time being. But it was still there when I needed it.

Cliff had this wild shock of electric black hair that weaved and bobbed about his head like a sixth sense. It was like he was feeling his way round with it, as if psychokinetic forces were controlling it, and he was using it as his antennae. Which was useful in a way, because he was virtually blind.

He wore these incredibly thick octagonal glasses that made him look like Phineas of the Fabulous Furry Freak Brothers. He loved the Fabulous Furry Freak Brothers. I think he would have cast me in the role of Freewheelin' Franklin, though I was more like Fat Freddy. I was easily as dumb as Fat Freddy – and I had a cat – but I was the wrong shape and size.

On our first trip together we started off in his tiny little room, next to Tim's. Tim was shagging yet another ex-girlfriend of mine, Sue. We could hear them grunting and groaning and humping away in there. I said, 'Embarrassment is pink and warm,' which we both thought was incredibly profound. Afterwards we went for a walk, and Cliff was trying to persuade me that the world didn't exist. He was looping about my logic with these strange, fractal meanderings. It all sounded very deep. I guess this was when I took him on as my guru. He obviously knew something I didn't.

As the night wore on we took on these roles. I became Carlos Casteneda, dumbly rational. And he was Don Juan, tricking me up the psychic garden path with subversive rhetoric, guiding me into the crazy acceptance of this strange new proposition. The world doesn't exist. We don't exist. The trees and the leaves and the grass and the birds, emerging into the dawn light as they now were, they don't exist either. And the sky above and the earth beneath: none of it is actually real.

And I believed him! And I went on believing him.

Tell me: what's the difference between LSD and alcohol? With alcohol you get off your face and talk loads of shit, and then wake up the following day feeling guilty and ashamed. LSD users, on the other hand, get off their face and talk loads of shit, and then wake up the following day still believing it.

So Cliff took me under his wing to guide me spiritually into this strange new non-world of his.

I've thought about it since. If the world doesn't exist – and to be fair to Cliff once more, he meant that it was some sort of spiritual emanation from the mind of God – if the world doesn't actually exist, then nothing matters. And if nothing matters, then you don't have to care. And if you don't have to care, then you don't have to do anything. It's the psychic equivalent of a shot of heroin. Nothing matters. You can sit around all day looking at your shoe and call it a spiritual quest. Which is exactly what we did. We sat around all day, doing nothing.

Nothing exists. Fleas don't exist, lice don't exist. Dust doesn't exist. Fag-ash doesn't exist. Clothes don't exist, carpets don't exist. So carpets don't need sweeping then; clothes don't need washing. Bedding doesn't need changing; ashtrays don't need emptying. And fleas can hop about non-existently all over the place and use your cup of tea for a nice hot swimming-bath, doing the backstroke as practice for the flea Olympics. All life is sacred, man. Let the lice live!

I remember the first time I looked into Cliff's hair and saw them. He must have invited me to do so. I can't imagine it was something that happened in the course of a normal day's entertainment. And there they were. It was like a jungle. Not just one or two: hundreds. And not just spindly little things: great fat lobsters crawling about behind his ears, every hair sprinkled with nits, like the sparkly decorations on a Christmas tree.

'Cliff!' I said. 'You've got fucking lice. You've got millions of fucking lice all over your fucking head!'

And, of course, I'd got lice by then as well.

That was just the beginning of our troubles. My cat had had kittens. So we had about half a dozen cats running about the place. On top of that, it was a long, hot summer. We got fleas. The whole of Cardiff was suffering a flea epidemic that year. It probably started in our flat.

So we had lice and we had fleas, and we had dust and we had fag-ash, and we had grimy clothes and stained bedding, and we had stinking feet from the half-rotten baseballs boots we all chose to wear; and we had long hair and we had drugs, and we had all sorts of weird philosophies, and we had mattresses on the floor and we had tapestries on the wall, and we had all-night sessions listening to rock music while off our heads on LSD; and we blew chillums and we said, 'Bom Shankar', and we had bangles and beads and patchouli oil, and we said 'man' and 'suss' and 'far out', and we called women 'chicks' and men 'guys', and we philosophized and read books about spiritual enlightenment; and we lived off raw vegetables we bought down the market once a week, and no one cooked and no one cleaned, and no one did anything much at all, except maybe scratch our heads and then our ankles, and then fish the fleas out of our tea, before rolling another spliff and saying, 'Far out, man, fuckin' good gear that!'

I'd made it at last! I'd become a hippie.

There were many memorable nights, usually tripping. One night we were listening to Jimi Hendrix, and his guitar seemed to be going 'Nyah, nyah, nyah, you can't keep up with me.' He was thumbing his nose at the world. I had this magic tooth. I could feel the energy flow through me as I brought my upper and lower jaw into the correct alignment. Later – years later – the tooth shattered. I'd ground it into oblivion.

Dave the communist was living with us. He was tripping that night too. He got up to go to bed. He was walking like a mannequin, all arms and legs and stiff-necked inhibition. He was walking very slowly, creaking across the room as if he was encased in some horrible, tortuous contraption, as if every slight move had to be guarded against the evil that was out there. I went over to him. 'Dave, man. Are you all right?' He kind of half-looked at me, shiftily, as if by acknowledging my presence whatever evil it was would find him out. 'Dave, it's me, Chris. Can't you talk to me?' He shrugged me off and made his clumsy, slow deliberate way across the room. His eyes were seething with pain and confused fear.

It took him about six weeks to be normal again. He moved out soon after that. He never took another trip again.

It was around this time that he had a dream. In it he was on a spiral staircase, heading up. And above him, headed down, there was this fascist. They were shouting accusations across to each other. And in between there was this blinding white light.

'I suppose you'll think it's spiritual,' he said, grumpily.

'Of course,' I said.

Another night I had a cold. We were tripping again. A dew-drop formed on the end of my nose and I found myself looking at it, cross-eyed. I was caught in a moment of contemplation observing the world through a glittering dew-drop on the end of my nose. It was the Dew-Drop of All Eternity, radiating pure, blissful energy from the end of my nose.

There was this dealer-bloke we used to see. It's how we scored our dope. He had a wonderful vocabulary. 'What? Far out. Yeah. Too much, man. I mean, yeah. Peakin' man, peakin'. Far out. Right on. Yeah.' It was great. He never actually said anything.

Piss-Off Pete would visit occasionally. He was still sane in those days. I was in guru-mode by now, sitting cross-legged reading spiritual textbooks, studying for a Masters degree in Karma Mechanics. I often think it might have been me who encouraged him to his later excesses, by talking to him about it. Well it wasn't me who made him mad, of course. But I encouraged him with the script.

Steve used to come and see us too. I was sharing a room with Alan at the time. Steve was 'stompin'' as he called it, off his head on downers and booze. He crashed out on the floor and then, later, he got up again to have a piss. He started pissing in the fire-place. It was pouring out all over the floor, steaming. Alan screamed at him. 'Droid, you cunt, what the fuck do you think you're doing?' And he chucked him out.

'I thought I was in the park,' said Steve, by way of explanation. 'I thought I was pissing against a tree.'

Another time he came round and he was blathering and guffawing and raving on. I said, 'Droid, you're becoming a parody of yourself.' So that was one more intelligent thought I had that year. It was true.

Steve used to come and see Bob and Allison too, in the upstairs back room. It was the room that had first of all been Cliff's, and then mine. Steve couldn't cope with all the parasites. He was blocked out on downers, but even he had more sensibility than us. He refused to sit down anywhere. Bob said, 'It's all right, Steve, you can crash in our room, we haven't got any of these things.' Bob was Steve's guru, a kind of down-to-earth, trustworthy bloke. It was one of Steve's mantras. 'Bob! Bob!' he used to say, as if the name was resonant with some deeper meaning. So Steve believed him. And he fell asleep, and when he woke up there was a flea hopping about on his cushion.

'Bob! Bob!' said Steve. 'There's a fucking flea. I just . . . you told me that you didn't have anything in this room. And look: there's a flea.'

'No Steve, what I meant was, we've got a few fleas. But we haven't got anything else.'

Bob was an interesting bloke. I believe he had integrity. He was writing a book, about an albino who comes to visit a strange town. He knew every inch of that imaginary town, and every person who lived there. I don't know if he ever finished his book or not. He was a good friend of mine. He'd see me and he'd leap across the room and pick me up in a bear-hug. 'Chris!' he'd say. He seemed to like me.

He decided I needed a fuck. He was probably right. He took me off to darkest Wales to meet some friends of his who liked that sort of thing. We all got very, very pissed. I had women coming to my tent, but I was so out of it I fell asleep.

Allison was this very, very pretty, slim girl with long brown hair that went down to her bum. She was proud of her hair. She used to comb it for hours every night. One day she went into hysterics. She was so upset with all the lice. Bob told her it was good for her to experience this side of life. It was like purgatory, he said. She should keep it in her memory.

Cliff Pilchard had this philosophy. Well, it was a sort of non-philosophy, really, like the non-world he inhabited. 'I like to imagine my cranium's opening up, like something out of Monty Python, and all my brains are splurging out . . .' he said, and he'd make this squelching noise, 'Squish!' And he lived that. He was trying to get rid of his brains.

Cliff believed that the ego should be abolished. That was the essence of his philosophy. He used to say it a lot. 'Abolish the ego.' Which is funny, on reflection. He believed he was a higher spiritual being. In other words: he was an egomaniac. And that was characteristic of that whole era, a bunch of egotists declaiming against the ego. Almost everyone I knew was an egomaniac in one form or another, including me. Piss-Off Pete was an egomaniac, who believed he was the singular reason for the creation of the Universe, hence his self-proclaimed title, 'Creation Number One'. Cliff Pilchard was an egomaniac who believed he was one of the saints, a higher spiritual being. Steve was an egomaniac who thought he was destined to become an International Superstar (though – typical Steve – this was a relatively innocent form of egomania). I was a self-deprecating egomaniac with a secret urge to have sex with all of womankind, but who only fell in love with men. Dave the communist was the only person I knew who wasn't a full-blown egomaniac. At least he believed in something outside of himself.

It was the most egotistical period in human history.

Cliff didn't have a sense of humour either, which is one of the marks of the confirmed egotist. He thought humour was cruel. The only jokes he made were childish puns, which he would giggle at hysterically. Otherwise he never laughed. And, once again, I find myself reflecting on this. Piss-Off Pete could not laugh. Syd Barret could not laugh. Peter Green could not laugh. Brian Wilson could not laugh. And all of them went mad. Except Cliff Pilchard, that is. He became an antiques dealer instead, which probably amounts to the same thing.

One night we were tripping, yet again, and I took a puff on a joint. 'Where does the smoke go?' asked Cliff.

I had no idea. At the time it seemed like a revelation. Now it seems like a joke.

And another time he'd been sitting there meditating, when he suddenly burst into tears. He'd been in this secret place, a kind of desert, with the Buddha and the Christ, he told me. They'd welcomed him there and he knew it was the place he belonged. And then he'd been cast out, back into this grey, lice-ridden world of ours. He was never the same after that.

Finally I decided I would have to take action against the lice. I used to douse my hair religiously, and force Cliff to do the same. And one day I was combing my hair, as I had done for many months, over the sink with the fine-tooth comb, when a little black thing fell out. Usually there were two or three wriggling and kicking their little legs about. This time it was just one. I looked at it, and it was still. I flicked it with the comb. It moved, but then was still. I flicked it again. Again it moved, and again it was still. It was no more than a fleck of dust. I looked into my hair, and all the little white bits were no more than dried skin. I nearly jumped for joy. I no longer had lice.

Do you believe in genocide? I do. I like to slaughter lice.

The household ground slowly on to its inevitable, humiliating end. First of all the landlord wanted to move his son and a friend into the premises. The rest of us were all squeezed into the downstairs rooms, while the landlord's son and his friend took the attic flat.

Then we were busted. A policeman came round to check out a complaint about a stolen camera. There was all this drug paraphernalia clearly on display: chillums and hash pipes and ripped Rizla packets. Maybe even a lump of hash or two and a bag of grass. The policeman didn't say anything, and we just shrugged it off and got on with our lives. A couple of weeks later we were raided. They broke down the front door, even though it was always kept on the latch. We were done for 'Allowing Premises . . .'

The policeman who'd come round that first time had been promoted to the drug's squad. He said, 'What were you thinking of? I gave you two whole weeks to clear up.'

Another policeman said, 'How come druggies' flats always look the same? Mattresses on the floor. I don't know how you could live like this.'

At our trial I took the stand. I was asked a few meaningless questions. 'Are you Christopher James Stone of Colum Road, Cardiff?' Stuff like that. And then I stepped down again.

The solicitor then read from the policeman's statement: '"I asked Mr Stone if the drugs belonged to him, and he smiled." I'd like the court to take note,' he said, 'that Mr Stone is always smiling.'

We were all found guilty and given a £40 fine. Summing up, the magistrate said, 'It's all very well claiming to show us a new way to live, and a new society. But to do it while signing on the dole is merely a form of parasitism.'

In other words he was fining us, not for taking drugs, but for signing on while we were doing it.

Then a French woman named Allyette moved in with us. This might have been before or after the bust: I have no idea now. She made the most gorgeous fried potatoes with herbs. She had no money, so Cliff and I kept her with our dole money. She made a play for me, but I was excruciatingly shy by now. She ended up sleeping with Cliff instead. Sometime after that he moved out with her. I found out later that she was slagging me off around the town. 'Cliff Pilchard's buddy-pal,' she called me. I was hurt because, after all, I'd made a contribution to her keep for all those months.

I'd become known as 'the happy hippie' by then, because I was always smiling. I felt that I was happy. I'd catch a glimpse of myself in a mirror smiling and think that I must be happy. But it was a vacuous form of happiness. It was a smile I'd learned to hide behind. I'd been on holiday from myself. I was soon to learn that you cannot find real happiness by denying yourself. When my intelligence returned, it did so with a vengeance. I'd begun to hate what I'd become.

I've just had a letter from Dave. I sent him a copy of all the things I've written about him so far. What follows is a transcript of his letter, word for word:

Dear Chris,

Got your letter this morning – thanks, and for all the stuff from your book – I laughed a lot. Don't worry about anything you write about me, my vanity exceeds my paranoia a thousand fold, and like all vain people I'd probably be flattered by a complete character assassination if it was published.

A couple of corrections which you can incorporate or ignore as you feel fit.

The famous leather trousers I got on Kensington Market, not Camden. I don't know if you ever went there but Kensington Market (indoors actually, and not much of a market) was the Mecca of high hippiedom in the late sixties and early seventies. I used to buy my loons there, remember loons? Twenty-six-inch waist I could get into then, two pound fifty a pair.

On the acid thing, there's probably too much that I could write, but I actually did take it again after that bum trip – about a year later when I was living in Pennylan Road with Richard. It was a sort of challenge, and it was nothing special. I went into my job on the adventure playground the next day and found it rather difficult to communicate with the kids, that was all.

Now comes the boring bit, which may or may not be worth reading. I can remember the bit you're writing about much too clearly. We were all in the back room at Colum Road. It was in its end phase, we'd stopped paying the rent, and I think Cliff's incessant spirituality was getting to me. We were about twenty minutes into the trip, when someone who was just visiting us who wasn't normally around started laughing and cracking jokes or something, and Pilchard, who'd been sitting in the lotus position, blew up and started shouting at him. Something like, 'You've fucking blown it, I was trying to achieve white light, and now you've blown it!' That's when I got up to leave the room. I remember thinking, that's it, the trip's over, which it wasn't, of course. But I went upstairs to go to sleep, which is not a terribly good idea when you're tripping, and woke up in the middle of a dream where I was something like a sweating beast in hell, which was like the bottom of a long lift shaft, and there was this god-like figure up the top accusing me of wasting my life and telling me that all that learning was a total waste of time. I remember seeing myself as a sort of donkey without a brain and thinking, this is the long night of the soul, when it's always three o'clock in the morning – which is a line from the *Crack Up* that Scott Fitzgerald lifted from some medieval cleric – except I was taking it literally and thinking it would stay three o'clock, which is more or less what it did for a very long time.

When I actually did come down in the morning, you lot were in the back room by the kitchen still and looked at me really worried. I remember trying to make coffee and not being able to work out whether the water in the kettle was hot or cold or whether the kettle had been turned on or thinking I could make it hot myself without plugging it in – which is something I think a lot of people get sometime or other on acid. Anyway, I remember you telling me later that I made the coffee with cold water, and you were all so scared of freaking me out any more that you all sat there and drank it . . . Yeah, great coffee. Thanks Dave.

The problem after that was that I could hardly sleep for weeks and there were all sorts of people having conversations in my head – Pilchard, you, everyone, except I kept thinking I couldn't hear my own voice.

I didn't get back to anywhere near normal until I got out of Colum Road and hitched up to my uncle's in the Midlands – throwing up in a café in Birmingham New Street Station on the way. I thought I was being followed by heroin-pushing Christians. I think I must have been suffering nicotine-withdrawal symptoms then even though I didn't smoke straights, because every time I smelt cigarette smoke the paranoia got particularly bad.

The only good thing was that getting out meant I missed the bust. And I also discovered that I could dance, which I'd been too inhibited to do before. Nice twist that one, don't you think?

That's it for now. I admit to being grievously embarrassed by some aspects of my former self, mainly in relation to women, but what can you do? That's what we were like. Incidentally I remember you coming into my room in

Mackintosh Place the morning after your first night with Val and saying: Dave, quick, what's her name? I can't remember her name!

Anyway, keep writing the book, I look forward to reading it,

All the best,

Dave.

Dave went on to edit the only communist paper in Britain to wholeheartedly support the Soviet Union. It had a readership of about three and a half people. I went to see him during the Solidarność days in Poland. We were sitting in a park in Southall, which is where he was living at the time, on one of those picnic benches. I said, 'Dave, if communism's so good, how come the Poles don't want it?'

'What Poland needs is more socialism, not less socialism,' he said, banging the table with his fist in his characteristic way. Then he went into a three-hour rant about it, which made me laugh. That's what I liked about Dave: he was always funny, even when he wasn't trying to be. These days he lives in Austria, with his girlfriend and their child, where he nurses his little disappointments – such as the fall of communism, for instance – with quantities of Austrian beer. He's a part-time translator and a teacher of English. Who knows? I might even ask him to translate this book. He can add several inches to his height and make himself into a dashing hero.

As for Cliff Pilchard: he got more and more spiritual.

One day we were all around at Richard and Jude's place. This was sometime after we'd all gone our separate ways. There was me and Dave and Bob and Allison, and Cliff, of course, and Richard and Jude. He'd started to get into Divine Light by now, and he was saying, breathlessly pious, 'Look at that cloud: it is like the Goddess Shakti in all her glorious splendour.' Something like that. Dave said, 'Cliff, you obviously see yourself as some sort of spiritual ombudsman.'

He blinked at that, but carried on, lecturing Bob, half closing his eyes as if exploring the inner landscape of his mind. 'You know, Bob,' he was saying, 'I can see so well with my third eye now that I hardly need these glasses. In fact, I can see better without them.'

Bob was perched on a chair in front of him. He leaned forwards and snatched the glasses from Cliff's face. And then, leaning back a bit, he held up three fingers at arm's length behind him.

'OK Cliff. How many fingers?'

'Four,' said Cliff, blinking slightly.

Bob fell about laughing and gave him his glasses back.

'It was three, Cliff. Three fingers.'

'No it wasn't. It was four.'

'It was three, Cliff.'

'Bob, I know it was four fingers. You're just bullshitting me, man. You're always bullshitting. Why can't you stop bullshitting. It was four fingers.' And he went off into one of his characteristic self-righteous spiritual rants.

The last time I saw Cliff Pilchard he wasn't wearing glasses. His Third Eye hadn't opened, however. He had contact lenses instead. This was around 1979, after Thatcher, after the punk explosion, but he looked exactly the same, his hair still bobbing around in a Jimi Hendrix puff-ball frizz. I said, 'My God, Cliff, you look like you never left San Francisco. What year do you think it is, 1956 or something?'

'You mean 1966, don't you?' he said.

'Do I?' I said.

He'd been a heroin addict, he told me, but now he was an antiques dealer. He said, 'I need at least a hundred and fifty quid a week to survive.' He was into money now. That kind of says it all. The man had declared against materialism in all its forms. He'd said, 'Abolish the ego,' but now he needed at least a hundred and fifty quid to survive. From spiritual guru, to heroin addict, to greedy antiques dealer, in the space of less than a decade. From Love-child to Thatcher's child, the spirit of the times.

9 Not an Earth Mother *or* Nasturtiums in Barbed Wire

Des lives on the Windmill Hill council estate in Glastonbury. He was the man I met at the solstice, on the traffic island just outside Amesbury. I loved the Windmill Hill estate the minute I saw it. That's all it is, a common-or-garden council estate, with all the usual four-square, straight-up-and-down, belt-and-braces architecture, with the usual front gardens, lovingly tended, with neat privet hedges bordering the pavement, where men wash and polish their cars weekly, and where women wash their net curtains and polish their windows till they gleam. It could be anywhere. Except you look up to see those spectacular views across the Levels to the Mendips, the air is clear and fresh, and the quality of the light, at least on certain days, seems to add a shimmer to the very brickwork. There's a Spar shop on the estate, selling all the usual things: magazines, newspapers, groceries, green-groceries, fresh meat and cooked meat, cans of beans and packets of biscuits, cigarettes and tobacco, beers, wines and spirits. There's even a post office in there. What makes it unusual is its position. You approach it from a certain direction, and there it is, in all its mystical splendour, floating spiritually above that plain, ordinary, down-to-earth shop: Glastonbury Tor, topped with the mysterious tower of St Michael's chapel. I like the Windmill estate better than any other part of Glastonbury for precisely this reason: that the Tor still exerts its strange fascination, despite the ordinariness of the surroundings. Or perhaps because of them.

Actually, it's not such an ordinary council estate really. It's full of hippies.

I was parked up in Des's parking space (he has no car) in a car park backed by houses and skirted by garages. It seemed a fine place to be. No New Age Traveller ever had a better park-up. It was while I was there that I started writing this book.

I was there for a few days, getting to know Des. He was, after all, my very first unadulterated, up-front, totally unashamed hippie-subject. At the time of writing he was forty-seven years old, with a lined, craggy face that looks as if it has the mark of tragedy upon it. Which it has, though we won't go into that here. He has long, red-tinted hair, a full beard and a deep, rumbling laugh. He's very thin, muscular and wiry, with a kind of prowling masculinity about him. When I arrived he was dressed in a pair of obscenely short shorts. There was a phone call. He was talking on the phone while doing these strange t'ai chi exercises, bending and stretching and playing with his testicles, growling as he talked. He lives in a bungalow with his nine-year-old daughter, Angelina. He's a lone parent, living off benefits.

Angelina. Well, Angelina is something else. She's very bright, but with a hint of mischief about her, and an occasional fuming temper. Des is very hard on her. Not at all like a hippie. Sometimes, it seemed to me, he was too hard.

We went shopping one day. Des had a few things in his basket. I noticed a fine bottle of Chardonnay, Darjeeling tea and venison steaks.

'Do you always buy these things, Des?' I asked, astounded.
'Whenever I can.'
'How can you afford it?' I asked.

'I can't,' he growled, 'but you have to live well.'

He smokes the largest roll-ups I've ever seen: great fat cones like chillums, or like Bob Marley spliffs, from which he takes two or three huge lungfuls before crushing the thing out. I soon learned that I could save on tobacco money by smoking his dog-ends. One of Des's dog-ends was usually enough for one of my cigarettes.

Des and the High Priest had made arrangements to get me into the Pilton Pop Festival for the duration. That's what the festival is called locally: the Pilton Pop Festival. To the rest of the world it's the 'Glastonbury Performing Arts Festival', or something equally long-winded and pretentious. It's gone through several name changes over the years. But locally it's still called what it always was called: the Pilton Pop Festival.

Where better to continue my researches?

Meanwhile I'd agreed to take one or two people and a few things in with me. So on the day we were going to start out for the festival (it was several days at least before the festival itself was due to start) we drove around town to pick up a few bits and pieces. Des was performing there, so it was mike stands and amplifiers and drum kits we were collecting. Plus, at one point we pulled off the road, and someone called Sally arrived with two cellos, which were packed away in the compartment above the driving cab, and wrapped up very carefully, in my Afghan carpet, which I happen to carry for just such an occasion. We were due to pick Sally up later. Then I left Des with the van, while I went off to see Jude. He agreed to come and pick me up at six o'clock.

Jude is my old friend from Cardiff. In Glastonbury she's known as Willow. She's a practising witch.

I asked her if she remembered Piss-Off Pete.

'Who?' she said.

Earlier in the book I described her as a 'hippie Earth Mother type'. This is entirely untrue. It was short-hand, meaning she's big and blonde, kind of Scandinavian looking. That's where all the Earth Mothers come from: from Scandinavia. Well she may have been a hippie, and she may well also worship the Earth, but she's not in the slightest bit motherly. When she read it she was very offended. 'I'm not the Earth Mother type, am I? Is that how you see me, as an Earth Mother? Well,' she sighed. She was going round to all her friends complaining. 'Have you heard what Chris is calling me? An Earth Mother. You don't think I'm an Earth Mother, do you?'

'Of course not Willow,' her friends would say, 'you're nothing like an Earth Mother.

'Can't you call me an Earth-worshipper type? I just don't like that word, "mother",' she said to me one day.

'No, listen,' I started to say . . .

'Because I'm not in the slightest bit like an Earth Mother.'

'No Jude, what I'll do is . . .'

'I can't see how you can call me an Earth Mother, I really can't.'

'No, but . . .'

'I've never had the slightest inclination to have children, so you just can't use that word "mother", can you?'

'No, but . . .'

'Calling me an Earth Mother. It just doesn't suit me.'

And on like this.

'You don't listen, do you, Jude?' I said in the end, becoming exasperated.

'No. I never do,' she agreed. And that's when I told her of my plan, to leave the description in the book, but to add a disclaimer. Which is what I've done.

But all of this is a long time after the day I went round to see her, before going on to Pilton. I hadn't even written the words 'Earth Mother' then. Maybe I wish I never had. I just thought I'd better get it in now, while we're talking about Jude. Jude is not an Earth Mother. She has never been an Earth Mother. And she has no intentions of ever becoming an Earth Mother either.

There you are, Jude. Task accomplished.

The last time I'd been in contact with her, we hadn't got on all that well. This was in the early eighties. We were poles apart in our lifestyles and beliefs then. She was living in a commune in a blind Welsh valley, and was on a spiritual path. I was a hard-core Marxist and confirmed atheist. So when she asked me if I wanted to hear a lecture by some spiritual guru, I'd refused. Also, I had a child. I'd gone 'straight'. Egg and chips down the caff, trips to the seaside, a pint with the lads, that sort of thing. But Jude was still resolutely a hippie. It was a philosophy I'd come to despise. I guess I was a little rude. But both of us have changed dramatically since then. Age mellows even the hardest of hard-core Marxists, and – I've had to admit – that atheism is itself only a belief. I'm not so sure of anything any more. Besides which, I happen to like her.

She's not a hippie, at least not to look at. She dresses conservatively, a bit like a nursery-school teacher. (Not that I'm accusing her of being a nursery-school teacher, you understand. I think you know by now that she does not like children. I thought I'd better make that clear too. Jude is not a nursery-school teacher either.)

Actually, she has the air of a 1930s Bohemian artist. Smokes endless cigarettes with a deep-inhaling, clenched-teeth grimace of satisfaction. She likes her cigarettes. She also likes TV, and her favourite reading matter is the *Radio Times*. But she has a knowledge of folklore, and of ancient history, of the practice of magic, of traditional beliefs, of witchcraft, of Egyptology, of the cabbala, of the spiritual practices of the West and the East, of the psychology of dreams, of the symbolism of the tarot, which borders on the encyclopaedic. Also she is an artist. She painted her own tarot deck.

On this particular day, somewhere in June, we sat in her garden and drank tea. This is always what we've done, as long as I've known her. Drink tea. Jude has a wonderful garden, crowded with plants and with a pond over which a stone Buddha presides, contemplating. Like all the best gardens, there are sculptures nestling in amongst the foliage: pagan sculptures and spiritual sculptures, as well as chimes and crystals and bits of mirror and stone, and twisty bits of dried wood. It's a work of art, Jude's garden.

Jude was telling me about her life, and all the things that had happened to her since I'd seen her. She'd done the whole hippie thing, from top to bottom. She'd lived in a commune and then been a traveller. She said, 'I used to believe that we could make the wastelands grow. We'd move onto a rubbish dump, say, and we'd be able to make it flourish. We'd plant it and nurture it and tend it till it became a paradise. And then when people drove passed they'd say, "Look at what the hippies have done!" So I had these nasturtiums in a pot. I carried them everywhere we went. And everywhere we stopped, I got out the nasturtiums, and put them down beside the van, as a symbol. The trouble is, I'd not thought about the kids and the dogs. Kids play, and they make a mess. And dogs rip up the plastic rubbish bags. So every night the dogs would come, and rip open the plastic sacks, and every morning I'd get up and put it all away again. And you couldn't talk to the owners. "Fuck off you bitch, what's it got to do with you?" Pointing. That's all you'd get. So I'd back off. And then these types would come round, to score dope. "Hey, Charley, got any fuckin' dope, man?" And they'd tread on the nasturtiums. And the kids would play with the nasturtiums. And the dogs would piss on the nasturtiums. So I had to put wire netting round the pot, to stop people ruining them. And that was how that idea ended up, from making the wastelands grow, to those sad little nasturtiums, in a pot, surrounded by barbed wire – well, wire netting really, but that's what it felt like – sitting there amid all the filth and squalor in whatever decrepit site we ended up on at the time. Pathetic.'

'Why nasturtiums?' I asked.

'Because they're easy to grow.'

One time, in the throes of a failed love affair, she had let go of her life by agreeing to everything. She would say 'Whatever' and go along with whatever anyone suggested.

'Would you like some speed?'

'Whatever.'

'Some acid?'

'Whatever.'

'Come to London with me.'

'Whatever.'

But something was protecting her. She was round at some dealer's house who offered her heroin. 'Whatever,' she said, and she took it. It was beautiful beyond belief. She was out there amongst the stars, her mind clear and focused, free of all the emotional baggage that had always held her back before. And the following day she was sitting there, when she had this vision. An owl flew out of one wall, across the room, and through the other wall. Then a man walked in. A very handsome man, elegantly dressed in a smart suit.

'Hello,' he said. 'I'm a heroin addict.'

'Oh yes?' she said.

'Yes. I'm here to score. Have you taken any yourself?'

'Well yes, as it happens. I had some last night.'

'I expect you enjoyed it.'

'Yes I did.'

'I expect your mind was clear and focused in a way you've never known before.'

'Yes, it was.'

'And I expect you will want to take some more tonight.'

'Yes. I probably will.'

'Then let me tell you,' he said. 'I used to be like you. I'd take my heroin and be there, out amongst the stars. But then you need more and more to get you there. And then it stops affecting you so much. Then it stops affecting you at all. And then you find you need to take it just to stay normal, and that if you don't take it you get very, very sick. And that's how you end up like me, a heroin addict, coming round to places like this to beg for heroin just to keep you alive. So, if I were you, I would never take it again.'

She didn't say 'Whatever' this time, she told me. And she never did take heroin again.

Glastonbury is the hippie capital of the world. People have been coming here, seeking enlightenment and whatever, since the late sixties. But it's grown and grown, as more and more people have turned up in waves. Jude is personally responsible for one such influx, which caused chaos in the town for several months, possibly even years. She was in a truck at the time, with Charley Barley. Charley Barley is the archetypal hippie, with long, silver-grey hair and dreadlocks in his beard. He looks like Fagin. They were on their way to the Peace Camp at Molesworth, but heard that it was about to be evicted. So they came to Glastonbury instead. It was still a quiet little market town in those days, with just a few hippie-mystical types hanging round. This was in the spring of '85, just before the battle of the beanfield. They were at one farm, but there was trouble and they had to leave. Then she heard about another local farm. She met German Ben, who told her it was all right to come and stay. It was run by this dippy Christian woman with a taste for the drink. Ben said, 'Wave a fiver at her and she'll let you in.' So that's what they did. They got to the gate, and the woman said, 'You can't come in here,' and Charley flashed a fiver at her, and she said, 'You can park down there, in the orchard.'

The convoy, meanwhile, had been evicted from Molesworth, and then brutally attacked by the police on its way to the Stonehenge Free Festival. I've told that story in another book. The police went berserk, beating up women and children, pregnant women, smashing everyone's vans in, even setting light to them. It was an atrocity, no less. The Pilton Festival was on, and Michael Eavis opened the gates for the battered remains of the convoy to come in, and lick its wounds. They were in a real state, battered and bemused. Frightened. Jude and Charley had gone to festival, and they met their friends there, and told them about the farm. 'Just wave a fiver at her and she'll let you in.'

And so more of the travellers moved on to the farm, all waving fivers. And then more came. And then more and more. And then the Brew Crew moved on too, kids who had been pouring out of the cities all this time, buying buses and going on the road. Many of them had no idea how to go about it. They'd just get pissed and stoned all the time. Their favourite drink was Special Brew, hence the name Brew Crew. Another name for them was drongos. Every group in society has its drongos. Really it refers to ignorant people. Jude was considered a 'middle-class wanker' because she read books.

And someone arrived who had hepatitis, and there was an outbreak. Jude caught it, and she was forced into burning her shit, as there was no toilet. She would wait until Charley had gone to bed, and then shit on a newspaper, then wrap it up and put it on the fire.

Someone went wild with an axe in Victoria Wine, and hippies were banned from the town. All the pubs and shops had signs up saying NO HIPPIES. One of the locals organized what was called a hippie-wrecker, a big vehicle to move and to wreck the travellers' vehicles. It was open warfare in the town. Vicious newspaper headlines, every week. Questions in the council chamber. Lies and distortion. Vigilantes with pickaxe handles, smashing up anyone who looked a bit different. Gangs of kids beating up homeless people. It still happens.

'It was beautiful in that orchard when we got there, full of apple blossom,' said Jude. 'But you should have seen how it ended up.

Supermarket trolleys dumped in the hedgerows. Empty cans of Special Brew. Mud and slime and filth.'

Jude finished with Charley Barley. 'I was fed up with his infidelities, and with fronting out his theatrics all the time.'

She started going out with Chris, her present partner. He's a carpenter, a big, awkward, quietly astute man, who had also been a traveller. They had a plot of land on Dragon Hill, a travellers' community which is still going. There was a sign. TREAD LIGHTLY UPON THE EARTH, it said.

Jude laughed when she told me this. She has an infectious laugh, deep and scornfully expressive.

'It was embarrassing,' said Jude, 'stuck behind this stupid, pretentious sign.'

And there was an argument about shit. Chris ate fish. One of the other residents said, 'Can you not put your shit on the compost, please. We are vegans.'

'It was a case of, "My shit is better than your shit",' said Jude laughing again. They moved out.

After that they moved to West Wales. But all anyone wanted to talk about was dogs and children. Jude has a need for intellectual challenge. She wants to talk about all the really big things – the gods of ancient Egypt, the pathways of the cabbala – not dogs and children. They were lonely and bored. So they came back to Glastonbury. It was like Glastonbury wouldn't let go. They lived in a bender in the woods for about three years. Jude would make wicker baskets. They lived a near Neolithic lifestyle.

She said, 'When I came into a house with electricity, I could feel it, in the air. And the walls were hard and ungiving. It would feel like they were closing in on you. I couldn't wait to get out. In a bender the walls are soft, and they flap in the wind. You feel you are part of the elements, not separate from them.'

But then something happened. She'd avoided the twentieth century for so many years. Suddenly she wanted it again. A washing machine. A fridge. A vac. A TV. She wanted it all. Comfort. Nice food. A clean house. A garden she could tend. Walls on which to hang her paintings. It must have been age catching up with her. They moved back into the town, which is where they've been ever since.

After this her parents died, within four days of each other.

First of all it was her dad, and then her mum. Her mum must have died of loneliness or a broken heart. They only had each other. So it was one Christmas, and Jude was loading all their effects into a skip – their slippers, their pyjamas, their ornaments, their pictures, the accumulated detritus of an ordinary life – and she just thought, *Is this all there is? Just this?* It was devastating. It wasn't only the loss of her parents, whom she had adored. It was that their death had brought into question all of her beliefs. She had always believed in reincarnation, in the idea that the soul survived. She had even remembered some of her past lives in incredible material detail. But now she began to question it all. Maybe it had all been a fantasy. Maybe all of this was an elaborate way of avoiding the awful truth, that there's nothing there, and this is all that will be left over of us in the end: these few, meaningless knick-knacks, these accidental fragments, these pathetic remains, to be cast into a skip when the time comes. To be born, and then forgotten.

She was an only child. She had no other family.

She became a recluse, comforting herself with the Soaps and with cheap comedy, crabby and – I'm sure she won't mind me saying this – at times misanthropic. It was like, 'What's the point?' If that's all there is to it, that lonely feeling as she loaded all these familiar things into a skip at Christmas, if this is all it amounts to in the end, then why bother? A profound emptiness. And this is where I come into the picture, maybe. It had been like this for a few years. But I was a familiar face out of her past arriving unexpectedly. Familiar. Like family. I came from another time. We're from the same era. We understand each other. Even though the interpretations have been different, we've had similar experiences. She's since told me that she feels at ease with me, that she can be herself when I'm around. That's because I feel the same.

So we were still drinking tea out there in Jude's heavenly garden, as the sun slanted in from the west through the trees, as dappled, warm light flickered and danced, and the birds chattering playfully, while her cats lounged around the pond, and my thoughts lounged around my head. I was thinking, *I've missed you.*

I said, 'It's nice to talk to you again, Jude.'

She said, 'I like to hear you call me Jude. Everyone calls me Willow. But I like Jude. It's the name my parents gave me.'

It was getting late by now. I was still waiting for Des to turn up. Eventually I gave him a ring.

'So what's happening Des. It's past seven o'clock.'

'Sorry mate,' he rumbled. 'We've had a bit of an emergency. There's an American woman here who's going through a crisis. We've been trying to calm her down. I'll be down in ten minutes.'

Jude asked me if I'd like to eat, but I refused. Des had said that he was cooking. So I waited. I waited and waited. Still no Des. I rang him up again.

'Des, we're supposed to be going over to Pilton tonight. We've got a lot to do. I wanted to go shopping before we went.'

'Sorry mate, sorry. I'll get a lift sorted out right now.'

Eventually the lift came. It was Susanna (who'd also been at Stonehenge) and Colleen, the American woman, driving Colleen's hired car. We went shopping. Colleen was talking all the time, about the Tor, and what had happened to her.

'It was like, I could see the Tor up there, and there was this incredible energy running through my body, and I was thinking, *I can't do it, I can't do it*. I had to steel myself, take deep breaths, and then run up it. I'd never have made it otherwise. And then, when I got there, there was this rush coming down on me through my head. It was, like, amazing.' She was going on and on like this, in a breathless rush of enthusiasm. She was being mystical and enthusiastic at the same time, in that typical American way.

'I don't know what you're talking about,' I said.

We got back to Des's and the place was full. There was Susanna and her daughter, Poppy. And Angelina. And Des, of course. And Colleen. A man called Dicken, from Stourbridge in the Black Country, down on his motorbike. Des kept calling him Dylan. And a Brummie called Tom. And someone else, I can't remember his name. We'll call him Toilet Man, for reasons which will become obvious later.

The food wasn't cooked. Des gave me instructions, and I made pizzas, which went into the oven. There were two small pizzas between all of these people.

While we were eating we were discussing the line-up. Neil

Young had been booked to play, but he'd cancelled due to a cut finger. Various people had been rumoured to be taking his place.

'I've heard one name, which would be completely awesome,' said Des, looking round at everyone with the air of someone in-the-know. 'I was told that the Rolling Stones might turn up.'

I said, 'What's so awesome about watching a bunch of super-annuated showbiz has-beens prancing about?'

The room went silent. All eyes fixed on me in disbelief. It was like I'd just committed the ultimate blasphemy, the ultimate sin. And then all voices started up at once.

'You can't say that.'

'That's bollocks.'

'Mick might be showbiz, but Keef is still the ultimate rock'n'roller.'

'They're still a great band, you know.'

'Look, the Stones are just the biggest band in the world,' etc., etc.

In the end they didn't play, so we were all none the wiser. I still think they're a bunch of superannuated showbiz has-beens, however.

The van wasn't loaded yet. There were still all sorts of things to get in there. Susanna and I loaded all her stuff, and then Dicken loaded all of his. Des hadn't even started to pack yet. Toilet Man was helping. We were piling more and more stuff into the van. It was piled high, floor to ceiling. Des was barking orders at every-one.

'Dylan, take this amp out.'

'The name's Dicken.'

'Yeah. Just take this amp out.'

And then, 'Dylan, there's a bass guitar here, and an acoustic.'

'Dicken, Des; Dicken.'

'What?'

'My name is Dicken, not Dylan.'

'Oh, yeah, yeah. Sorry. Anyway, this bass guitar . . .' etc., etc.

By now it was getting late, and we were still not moving. Angelina was stropping about, not getting on with her packing.

'Angelina, have you packed your stuff yet?' said Des.

'I can't find my yellow bag.'

'Well where did you last see it?'

'I don't know.'

'Look, just put it in another bag.'

'Oh-h-h-h-h-h . . .' she wailed.

'Angelina! I'm warning you. Put your stuff in another bag. Now!' he roared.

Des and I had obtained wristbands a couple of days before. But he was working, so there was a pass waiting for him at the gate. He wanted to give Dicken his wristband. They're little rubbery wristbands, sealed together with a couple of studs. Once they're on you can't take them off. So Des got me to cut his off at an angle. 'See, you can tuck it round here, and it'll stay on,' he said. 'I've done it before, and it works.' So then he was fiddling about with Dicken's wrist, trying to get the thing to stay on. 'Hold still, Dylan, I can't get it on while you're moving about.'

'The name's Dicken, Des, not Dylan.'

'Yeah, yeah, anyway, just try to stay still.'

By this time, Toilet Man was already on board. That's because we'd actually loaded the stuff in around him. He was in the toilet-cubicle, sitting on the plastic bucket which is my chemical loo. Hence 'Toilet Man'. I went out and revved up the engine. Other people got on board too. There was hardly any room for anyone. People were piled in there with things on their laps, with things beneath their feet, leaning on things. I drove out of the car park and onto the road. Almost everyone was on board who was going with us. All except Colleen, that is, who was staying at Des's house for the duration; and Tom, who was only here to see us off. But Des and Dicken still hadn't arrived. I was sitting there, the engine running, waiting to see them from my rear-view mirror. I waited five minutes. I waited ten minutes. I waited for a quarter of an hour. Eventually I lost my temper, and stormed into the house.

'I'm losing it, honest. How much longer have we got to wait for you to get things sorted? This has been going on all fucking night.'

'It's Dylan's wristband. It won't stay on.'

'I wish you'd stop calling me Dylan.'

'What?'

'It's Dicken, Des. My name is Dicken.'

Apparently Dicken was refusing to move until the wristband

was fixed. He was completely paralysed, fearful he might get caught with the dodgy wristband. So they'd been sticking it with glue and trying to sew it on, and all sorts. He had Des and Colleen and Tom fluttering around him, trying to fix his wristband. He was refusing to move until it was completely secure. And it was still falling off.

'Well I'm getting pissed off,' I said. 'I can't cope with this. I thought we were leaving hours ago.'

'Go with the flow. Goddess time,' said Colleen, launching herself at me, with arms outstretched, trying to give me a TLC-type hug. She's not just American. She's Californian. 'We're into Goddess time now,' she said.

'Goddess time? Goddess time? What the fuck is Goddess time?' I shrieked, starting to get hysterical. 'I don't believe in the fucking Goddess.'

And there's Colleen, this big, bountiful, uninhibited Californian woman, joyously bearing down on me with her bosom heaving, to wrap me in her tender loving, outstretched arms; while I'm stumbling backward over the telephone table towards the open front door, trying to get away from her. I'm from Birmingham. We just don't do things like that.

'Are you a city boy?' she said.

'Yes I am.'

'Thought so. City boys are always in a hurry.'

'Well I'm going to sit back outside. So can you please ask them to hurry up now?' I said. And I ran back to the safety of the van.

Fifteen minutes later they came over to the van. Dicken was still fiddling with his wristband. It fell off again.

So. We've got Dicken in there, with his accordions and his tent. Susanna and Poppy, with all their things. Angelina. A man in the toilet. Me and Des, and all our camping and other equipment. Plus we've got about half a ton of musical gear: amps and drum kits and guitars and bass guitars and two cellos, and leads and mikes and mike stands, and God knows what else. 'Are we ready to go?' I asked.

'Yeah,' said Des. 'Just one more person to pick up.'

We drove down to the town, and parked up on the pavement, in a fairly dangerous spot, while Des went across to get Sally. It was the place where the cellos had arrived from earlier in the day.

And then there was more stuff arriving. Boxes of tomatoes, boxes of courgettes, boxes of fruit, sailing across the road and in through the passenger side door, and into the already overcrowded back. Boxes and boxes. Kitchen equipment, pots and pans, and cutlery and crockery, all sorts. And then something arrived, and I thought I was going to have a nervous breakdown. The most inappropriate object I have ever seen. A vacuum cleaner.

'A vacuum cleaner?' I screamed. 'I can't believe it. A fucking vacuum cleaner now. What on earth can you do with a vacuum cleaner in Pilton?'

Well I know now, of course. They're used for Druid ceremonies.

Finally Sally got in, followed by Des. 'Thanks,' she said, and then we were off.

We were halfway to Pilton when Dicken said, 'I've left my inhaler in my helmet on my bike. We'll have to go back.'

'What?'

'We'll have to go back.'

'We can't go back.'

'Look, I can't do without my inhaler. We must go back.'

'Dicken,' I said, 'we're on our way now, and there's no way I'm turning round to go back. You'll just have to do without.'

'But . . .'

But we didn't. I didn't care about anything any more. I didn't care about Dicken's inhaler. I didn't care about anyone in the van. I never wanted to see Glastonbury again at that moment, not ever. I just wasn't going to turn around for any reason, barring, maybe, an all-out nuclear attack.

'You'll have to do without,' I said again. And I put my foot down.

It was God knows what time by now: eleven, or even later. We'd heard rumours that there were two-mile queues. As it happens the queue was much shorter, and we got in fairly easily. Maybe there is such a thing as 'Goddess time' after all. The security men wanted to see our wristbands, and we all waved at them. Dicken waved with both hands. Then they were looking in the back to see if we had any extra passengers on board. They were looking suspiciously at the toilet cubicle. But it was piled high with stuff all around. You could see they didn't want to go to all the bother of unloading it. Des explained the situation, that we were taking in equipment, and they waved us through. 'It's late,' they said. 'We just want to get home.' And eventually we were in. Everyone cheered.

It was raining by now, a steady persistent drizzle, and the site was turning to a muddy slush. We had to drive across the site, to the sacred field. There were hundreds of vehicles moving in every direction, and several delays. Various traffic-control types were shouting at us. We had to wait for at least ten minutes at one point while Des went into a Portakabin to massage someone's back. The sacred field was a slimy, dark pit, along a narrow lane defined by poles. But we got there in the end and let Susanna, Poppy and the Toilet Man off. Toilet Man said, 'Thank God I'm not claustrophobic.' He'd been drinking whisky in there. Someone came up to us complaining that no vehicles were allowed on the sacred field. 'Green security,' he said, as if it meant anything. Everyone seemed to be wanting to tell us what to do. We explained that we were just unloading things. Susanna and Poppy and Toilet Man unloaded all their stuff, which was a time-consuming operation in the pitch-dark. They had to disentangle all their things from all of everybody else's things. It took ages.

Then we drove back over the other side of the site to where we were to be located, in the litter-pickers field. The rain was getting heavier and heavier. We had to go up a steep hill, and the path was already streaming. At the bottom of the slope was a churned-up sea of slimy, dark mud and the wheels skidded and the engine squealed as I put my foot down to make it through. The back end slid left and right. But we got up in the end. And then we unloaded all of Sally's stuff in the dripping rain. Boxes of courgettes and boxes of tomatoes and kitchen equipment and all the rest. Plus the vacuum cleaner and the cellos. Sally wanted us to deliver some of it to another part of the site, but Des lost his temper. 'This is as far as we're going. This will have to do.' Then we unloaded the musical equipment into a tent. Des found somewhere for Angelina to sleep, Dicken put up his tent, and then the van was my own again.

The marquee in the litter-pickers field was selling beer. Stella at £1.50 a can. It was lovely. I began to feel quite at ease, for the first time in about six hours. It was one o'clock in the morning by now.

Sally said, 'I hear you're writing a book. What's it about?'

'Hippies,' I said.

'What's a hippie?'

'I don't know,' I said. 'But if Des is anything to go by, it's some-one who lives on a council estate, drinks Chardonnay and eats venison steaks.'

Which is about as good a definition as I've come up with so far.

10 The Rules of Sensible Driving

I implied that I didn't have any relationships while I was living in Colum Road. Actually there was one. It was with my wife.

Her name was Lois. I'd known her for a couple of years, since my student days. We had both worked in the cloakroom in the Students' Union. I remember her standing on the cloakroom desk and stretching herself like a cat. I didn't actually fancy her. She was a pale, funny little thing, skinny and bedraggled-looking with lank, off-coloured hair and shabby clothes. But she kind of grew on me.

I used to go and see her a lot. We had good conversations. And she'd visit me in Colum Road too. She was with us the day we got raided, and was busted too, despite the fact that she didn't live there.

The marriage was a marriage of convenience. She was Rhodesian, and wanted a British passport. I was just doing her a favour, that's all. I didn't believe in marriage. But then something happened. I fell in love with her.

I can't say how it happened now. It happened slowly, bit by bit. It took months, years even. It started to happen after we got wed.

How we came to get married. She was telling me about her predicament, how she needed this passport to stay in the country to continue her education. She didn't want to go back to Rhodesia. She told me that someone had offered to marry her, but he wanted something in return. Maybe it was money, maybe it was sex; I can't remember now.

I said, 'I'll marry you, Lois.'

'Would you Chris?'

'Yeah. Why not? It'll be a good excuse for a party.'

So that was it. We were getting married because it would be a good excuse for a party. Marriage as an institution was dead, and we were dancing on its grave.

We got married. Dave the communist was there. And Graham, my friend from Brum who had gone out with Rose after me. Maybe Steve, though he doesn't remember it, and some of the others from Colum Road. I only had a combat jacket, so someone lent me a smart jacket to wear. That might have been Steve. I was woken up in the morning with a bottle of whisky and a spliff, and then we kind of ambled off to Lois's house. We passed a TV shop on the way, and there was a Marx Brothers film showing on one of the channels. It was *Marx Brothers Go West*. It was the bit where Groucho is holding two carriages of the train together, and everyone is walking over him. The film speeds up and Groucho's arms and legs are stretched like elastic. We went into the shop to watch more of it. The shop assistant was only vaguely amused.

That kind of says it. We were being zany and wacky in the way of an old Marx Brothers movie. That was our attitude to life. It was my attitude to this marriage thing. We were kids, really.

We got to Lois's place, and there were more spliffs and more slugs of whisky. Lois had decked her place out with flowers, and had flowers in her hair. She was very pretty.

Then we went to the Registry Office to do the deed, and later we threw a party at a friend's house.

Dave was my best man. He made a speech. 'Cunts, bastards, wankers,' he said, before he was drowned out by the blare of the party.

At a certain point I was blowing chillums out in the back room with all the ultra-cool hip dope-smoker dudes. Very stoned. I was sitting cross-legged on the floor. Lois came up and, crouching down behind me, put her arms around my chest. She was pressing herself against my back, in that cat-like way of hers. 'Do you want to come upstairs and consummate the marriage?' she asked.

Well I was very stoned and embarrassed at her forthrightness. Everyone was looking at me. I was the centre of attention. Also, I was confused at the implications. There weren't supposed to be any strings attached in this arrangement. I wasn't marrying her because I wanted to get her into bed. I was doing it because I was the all-round good guy, the happy hippie. I was in full-blown spiritual mode by now. I'd given up sex. I was chasing enlightenment. I didn't want her, or anyone else, to think that I'd only been after sex. I was above such things. That was the way I'd been before. I wasn't like that now. Airily I rejected her offer.

Steve turned up after the pubs had closed. He was stomping as usual, larger than life, gibbering and guffawing and waving his arms about. He'd bought the entire pub with him. This was a small terraced house, and it was already full. Now it was difficult to even breath in there.

Suddenly there were screams. The owner of the house was throwing a complete hysterical fit. She was scuttling round on all fours screaming at everyone: 'Get out, fucking get out, who are all these people, I don't even know you?'

It was after the marriage that the process of falling in love began.

There were a couple of things at first, little signs.

One day we were walking down the road and Lois was talking. She was asthmatic and smoked heavily. Consequently she had this husky voice. It was very sexy. I could feel her voice melting my insides. She sounded so womanly. And then I looked at her and there was just this funny little girl skipping down the road beside me.

Another time we were sitting in her flat (I think we'd been talking about crockery for some reason) and she said, 'We'll always know each other, Chris. I expect we'll still know each other when we're old.' The statement made me breathless. It seemed to be a statement about our marriage. It was as if the marriage, so blithely, so mischievously undertaken, had suddenly started to become real.

And then it happened. We went tripping together. You always fall in love with the woman you trip with. Well, I do anyway. Well, I did on this occasion.

She came round to Colum Road one morning. She'd been up all night, she told me, tripping with this character she'd just met. He'd talked at her solidly throughout the trip. She said it was as if her whole world had collapsed, like he was undermining her in some way. She wanted to do a trip with me, to sort her head out. I was her natural choice, her husband.

We went out to the park. We dropped the acid. It was fine at first. It was a lovely sunny day. We took off our shoes and socks and rolled up our trousers and were playing in the weir with all the kids. It was fun. The water took on this oily, thick quality. It had weight and substance as it oozed around the rocks and danced over the weir, forming bubbles. The bubbles bobbed about playfully on the surface before they popped.

After that we walked to Llandaff Cathedral. The cathedral bells were sounding. Lois said, 'Listen: aren't they lovely?'

But they weren't lovely. They weren't lovely at all. There was a snarling growl in the heavy drone as it hung in the air. It got worse and worse as we approached the cathedral. The shuddering bells seemed to resonate with some dark presence. And inside the cathedral it was dingy and inhospitable and the building seemed to groan under the weight of some nameless, ancient Thing. I can remember staring into the darkness, trying to see what was there. I was trying to contact something. I was trying to pray, I guess. But nothing answered but the shuddering bells and the nameless evil hidden in the darkness.

Something was eating at me. Lois said, 'I know how it feels. It's how I felt last night. As if your whole world was being undermined.'

So there was some sort of exchange happening here. Lois had felt undermined the night before, and she'd come round to see me to sort herself out. And now it was me who was carrying the weight of that vacuity, that emptiness. Somehow she'd displaced it onto me.

We started walking again. We were walking along and I suddenly wanted to kiss her. Maybe I did kiss her and she pushed me away. I said, 'What's sex for, Lois?'

'It makes the world go round,' she said, and laughed.

I guided her back to Colum Road. People could see I was freaked out. I was in a terrible state and didn't dare look anyone in the eye. I put on a record. It was my favourite record at the time, by Jerry Garcia. It starts with some meandering electronics, before breaking into the first song. 'To lay me down.' I used to hear it as 'To lay ME down,' meaning: to lay down the burdens of responsibility for myself. To lay down the ego. But I couldn't wait for the song. The electronics had that same note of snarling emptiness the bells had had earlier. I snatched it off the deck.

Lois put on a record instead. It was 'White Bird' by the Incredible String Band. It was very gentle, very soothing.

'Relax,' Lois said, 'relax.' And she began to stroke my brow.

I closed my eyes. And that's when it happened.

I could see Lois's silhouette behind my eyes, glowing. She had one foot tucked up beneath her and the other stretched out behind. Her back was straight. There was a topknot on her head. She was the goddess. I could see all her chakras, like a lacework pattern of light, shimmering up and down her body. And there, in her loins, pulsating with a special red light, was the chakra that joined her to me. We were joined in that place, god and goddess, eternal creatures on our journey through time, two parts of the same being. We were man and wife. We had always been man and wife. We would always be, for ever. For ever and ever. Amen.

The record finished, and she got up to leave. It was very sudden. 'See you later,' she said blithely, and left. I guess she was bored with ministering to me. It was like a part of myself being wrenched away. I slammed my fist into the door as she left and let out an involuntary sob. Then I watched from the window as she disappeared down the street. I was crying.

Dave came over. He was concerned about me. He pointed at a pot plant and said, by way of conversation, 'What's that look like to you.'

'Euch!' I said. I could see the decay inherent in the roots, the way the roots seemed to be rotting into the soil. It looked like death.

He decided he was going to take me to the pub. We went to the Park Lane Bar, the place where Mandy had rejected Steve. It was a very plain and down-to-earth place. We drank Guinness.

Someone put 'Rock Your Baby' by George McCrae on the juke-box. They were putting it on over and over, again and again and again. It had just been released. 'Woman, take me in your arms and rock your baby.' They must have played it twenty times that night. It was my song for Lois.

I've thought about this since. What was that quality in the bells I was so afraid of? What was the presence that so horrified me?

It was myself, the part of me I'd banished in order to be a good hippie. It was my sexuality, hidden in the darkness. It was my own mind.

There have to be rules. That seems clear to me now. Often the rules are arbitrary, such as which side of the road you drive on. In continental Europe they drive on the right, and in Britain on the left. It doesn't matter either way, as long as everyone agrees to drive on one side or the other. It doesn't matter whether green means stop, or green means go, as long as we all agree. These are the rules of sensible driving. And it's no use arguing with them. It's no use being an anarchist for a day and deciding that, actually, you want to drive on the other side for a change, or that you should be allowed to jump the red light. That would be stupid. It would be suicidal. It would mean death.

The rules of sex and love aren't quite the same. Sometimes they're just arbitrary, sometimes they're there to keep the peace, to stop people bumping into each other. But there are also rules that are oppressive, and these need to be got rid of. If the rules of sensible driving included such things as black people having to give way to white people, or women having to pull over to allow men to overtake, or homosexuals not being allowed to drive at all, then these rules would – naturally – have to be resisted.

Some societies are polyandrous, others polygamous. In some men hold hands with each other and show affection publicly, and in others they are not allowed to. In some older men use young girls as currency, and young men are not allowed to marry at all. In others free love is permitted, but usually only at certain times of the year. In Afghanistan the rules are very strict. If you hand your lover a rose it means you want to marry them. In France it was considered the civilized thing to do to have (or to be) a mistress. The ancient Greeks considered homosexuality a graceful form of relationship. The rules of sex and love vary greatly. Some of these rules are arbitrary, like the rules of sensible driving, and some are merely oppressive.

For many people for much of the time, the rules of sex and love in England had been OK. The model of common decency was the family, and it had generally worked out. Men had power, but they showed deference and respect to their women. They stood up when a woman entered the room. They opened doors for her. They took her coat. That was how my Granddad treated my Nan. It was how my Uncle George would treat my Auntie Elsie. But there were anomalies. For homosexuals, in particular, the rules needed changing. For women too, though it should always be remembered that not all women believed all of the feminist rhetoric all the time. And in confronting the rules as they had appeared to us, in the realization of their arbitrariness, we had decided to throw all of them out. Everything was to be permitted, everything allowed. We saw the rules – all rules – as tools of oppression, rather than as tools of convenience. We got rid of the rules. And then we had no rules left to live by. No guidance. No good sense.

Imagine getting rid of the rules of sensible driving, even for a day. The red light no longer means stop. The green light no longer means go. You can do what you want. You can drive the wrong way up a one-way street, drive on any side of the road, on the pavement if you like. Speed up at zebra crossings, ignore road signs, overtake on the inside lane. Anything. There would be some serious accidents, and then everything would grind to a halt.

And that's exactly what did happen. There were some serious accidents, and then everything ground to a halt.

Actually, I'm not really speaking generally here, I'm speaking personally. Other people can tell their own stories. But for me,

Lois was a serious accident. And after that everything ground to a halt.

She moved in with Brian. Brian was the guy who had talked to her all night and undermined her world. So that's where my goddess went, she went to live with the man who had undermined her world. He gave her a necklace which she wore. It said 'Wil', a contraction of her maiden name. That seemed like a statement to me, a denial that she'd changed her last name at all, a denial that she was – actually – my wife.

So I was the other man in a triangle, yet again. Only this time I was the husband, and it was someone else in bed with my wife.

One day I was round her house. Brian was out somewhere. We were both very stoned. But something seemed to be building up between us. It was something in the air, like an undercurrent, a tension. It was palpable, heavy, like the weight of destiny. I had no idea what it was. There was something constricting my movements, a kind of wooden body-armour, a coffin-like structure holding me in. The hours stretched out with this strange tension. I could feel her pulling me towards her, but I couldn't move. We were talking about something meaningless, and the meaning was all in our minds. And then, suddenly, I broke out. I dived across the room and was kissing her, and the next thing I knew, we were fucking, on the floor in front of the fire.

I came. And then Brian walked in. Just like that, in the same second. It was fate. The whole day had that ring of fate to it, like something welling up from the depths.

We were barely undressed. It had happened so quickly. Lois had her trousers off, and mine were around my ankles. I was on top of her. We were stretched out on the floor in front of the fire, entangled in this lonely, strange embrace. Brian stood at the door, silently. I jerked up, wanting to move. Lois pulled me to her. She pulled my head down so that it lay on her shoulder. She was holding on to me like I was her life-raft and she was drowning. But I was weak. I couldn't cope. Brian was just standing there in the doorway, looking at us. I got up and, dressing quickly, slid out through the door, ducking past Brian and apologizing. Lois cried.

I guess that's when I lost her. But the love just got stronger and stronger.

We did a lot of trips together. I was always in awe of her and she always seemed scornful of me.

Once we went for a holiday together. We hitched to the south coast and slept in a bus shelter. The early morning sun seemed to drag the clouds into a luminous embrace. We dropped a trip. We were sitting in a field on the cliff-top, and I could see the waves down below, flexing and heaving like rippling muscles. The sea was alive, like a huge, dangerous, bountiful god. I could really feel his presence there. I pointed it out to Lois and she said, 'I don't believe in all that mystical stuff.' The weather was shifting constantly, from sun, to cloud, to bright wind, to rain. The wind seemed to be blowing all the colours around. There were tiny black insects nuzzling around in the grass.

We went to get something to eat. I was a vegetarian, but Lois had a pork pie. She said, 'Go on, have a bite. You know you want to.' I had my combat jacket on and a shirt with pockets and a pair of jeans. I had too many pockets. I was looking for my tobacco, going through all of these pockets and not being able to find it. Lois laughed.

We walked through the town, and there was a peculiar notice in a grubby, dark little window, like a seventeenth-century tract. And, on the beach, a strange, pink blubbery-looking thing.

'What is it? What is it? It's strange. I wonder what it is?' I was saying. I was going on and on about it.

'Why can't you just leave the mystery, Chris?' she said. 'Why do you always have to know what something is?'

We walked along the harbour wall where kids were fishing. Lois was chatting to them, very relaxed. One child showed her a crab he'd caught. The sea bosomed up against the sea wall sending salt spray into the air. You could smell the tang of saltiness in the air.

We met some people and went back to their house. They had a young child, no more than a toddler. The toddler looked into the airing cupboard and saw a spider. He cried. 'Mummy, there's a spider in there!'

The woman took the child in her arms. 'Yes there is, isn't there?' she said, going to take a look. She didn't make a fuss about it, and the child became relaxed. Later Lois said, 'I liked the way she dealt with the spider.'

We'd heard there was a Victorian rubbish dump and we went off to find it. We were sifting through all this rubbish, finding antique glass bottles, pale green, with a soft, lustrous sheen, like jewels. Lois picked all the biggest ones, and I had all the smallest.

We went to a pub in the evening. There were two blokes playing darts. They just threw the darts and didn't say a word, taking it in turns. It was a form of language.

I'd had this dream since I was a child. It was about love. In the earliest version I was on the back of a white swan with my sweetheart at the time, Rosie. We were flying high, exhilarated, breathless, seeing the toy-town world spread out below us, the roads like pale ribbons trailing across the countryside. And there, in the distance, was a mountain. I could see it from where we sat. It was my mountain. And high, high up, along a dusty trail, there was a jewelled stone, which is where I would one day go. It was the place of my heart.

The dream became a recurring one. Always I would see the mountain, and know that somewhere in its heights was my destiny. But the mountain was becoming more distant. In one dream I was in a pub with Simon, playing pinball, and everyone was jabbering senselessly. I could see the mountain out of the window. In another it rose up, ghostlike, behind the desolation of some inner-city slum.

I was saving up to go to India by now. I'd left Colum Road and was living in a bedsit on my own. I was working in the steelworks again, as a Sampler's Assistant. We would collect coal from various points around the factory and grind it up and dry it, to test its carbon content. The factory was like a scene from a Hieronymous Bosch painting of Hell, with grinding contraptions and dark, satanic-mill-like buildings lit up by a backdrop of raging fire. Sulphurous yellow smoke belched from the coke ovens.

I'd given up dope by now. Just packed it up. Or rather, I was only smoking it intermittently.

One day I was pushing my barrow to collect a load. And suddenly I had this vision. It was myself, etched in coloured light, seething with anger. It was my banished self rising up before me, seeking revenge.

I had this dream. Once more I was on my way to find that

mountain of mine, walking through the darkness. I knew I was heading in the right direction. And then I passed a discotheque. There was a purple swirling light and the thud of a bass. Lois was in the lobby. She called me in. I went in, and then, some hours later, found myself sitting by a glass wall. I was bored to death. Lois passed by. Suddenly I was consumed by a vicious anger. 'It's your fault,' I screamed, as I leapt across the room with a knife in my hand. And then the dream switched. It was me being attacked, by two men with paper bags over their heads, on which were drawn the crude semblance's of human faces. They were stabbing at me with their knives. They were not human. They were the Un-Men.

I travelled to India with a bloke called Pete. It was his idea, and he'd picked me because, as he said, I was the happy hippie. He bullied me all the way. I hadn't been all that successful at saving my money. I only managed to get enough by claiming a tax rebate. We put all our money together, in true hippie style. But he had more money than me and kept the extra back for treats for himself, and would quibble whenever I wanted to spend any. He was fussy and neurotic and would only eat English food.

The whole thing was a farce. We spent half of our money on paying someone to drive us there. There were six of us in a Volkswagen Combi: two New Zealand girls, the couple who owned the van, and Pete and I, who slept in a tent on the top. We were squabbling all the way.

It was morning somewhere in the wild, desert flatlands in Turkey or Iran. In the distance there were these hazy mountains shimmering like crumbling castles in the ruddy morning light. I was writing Lois a letter. I was trying to describe the scene. 'I can see red mountains in the distance,' I wrote. I felt a fraud. Here was I, still pretending to be a writer, and the only adjective I could find to describe these mountains was 'red'. It still is.

Later we were in the desert in Afghanistan. It was night, utterly dark, utterly clear; a night like you never see in the West, the sky a vast pagoda of stars stretching into infinity. A shooting star burnt its way across the night sky. Pete was wittering on. 'Cor, look. A shooting star! Far out, brilliant. Wow!' He was going on and on, enthusing endlessly. He was getting on my nerves. Suddenly this thought crossed my mind. I thought, *It doesn't matter how far you travel, you can never get away from yourself.*

We finally arrived in Nepal, where we were dropped off. Pete and I went on a trek, in the Anapurna range of mountains. It was very cold first thing in the morning, but got warm once you were toiling up the mountains. We stopped for a cup of tea one morning, and I took off my jacket. I had my passport and all my traveller's cheques in a pouch around my neck, and I took this off too. And then I carried on. It was about half an hour later that I realized I'd left my pouch behind. I rushed back down the mountain, but the pouch with all my money in, my passport and traveller's cheques, was gone.

It's times like this you know who your friends are. Pete left me behind in Nepal, without a penny, while he continued his journey. I was glad. The rest of the people on the trek – strangers – clubbed together to give me enough money to get back to Kathmandu. After that I had to work, in restaurants mainly, waiting on people. I still have the replacement passport. Where it says 'occupation' I'd written 'WRITER' in capital letters. But the R is slightly misshapen. It looks like an A.

I was in Nepal for about three months, before I set off for home. On the way back I stopped with an acquaintance in Afghanistan. His name was David. He was the brother of Richard, the mad scientist who lived with Jude before she became Willow. We spent a lot of time blowing that mind-numbingly strong Afghan black, and talking about love. He was having a romance with an Afghan girl. He was having to learn all the rules of lovemaking in that country, which were very strict. They were chaperoned when they went out together. He was puzzling whether to hand her a single red rose. This formal act had symbolic meaning. It took the lovemaking to the next stage of development. It meant 'I love you'.

One day we were listening to *Blood on the Tracks* by Bob Dylan, 'Shelter From the Storm':

> *'Suddenly I turned around and she was standing there*
> *With silver bracelets on her wrists and flowers in her hair,*
> *She walked up to me so gracefully and took my crown of thorns,*
> *Come in, she said, I'll give ya*
> *Shelter from the storm.'*

The song finished and David said, 'You're thinking about someone, aren't you? You're thinking about Lois.'

I burst into tears. It was true. Without realizing it myself even, I'd been thinking about her, how she'd soothed my brow when I was in such confusion, how she'd had flowers in her hair on our wedding day.

'How did you know?' I asked.

'It's all you've talked about all week.'

I wrote a letter to Lois explaining my feelings, how I'd come all this way, half way across the world, to discover that I did, indeed, love her. I'd bought a ring in Agra, a moonstone set in silver. I realized it was meant to be our wedding ring. And then I set out on the long journey home. I travelled by public transport from Kabul to Istanbul in seven days, non-stop. And then I hitched across Europe, which took ten more days, sleeping in the backs of the cars when I did sleep.

Piss-Off Pete was one of the first people I met when I got back to Cardiff. His flat backed on to Lois's. The shift from endearing eccentricity to downright madness must already have begun. I knocked at his door, and he let me in to his dark little flat. 'Pete!' I said. 'How're you doin', man?'

He said nothing. He began to get books down from his shelves and to open them at certain pages before laying them across his bed. There was the Tibetan *Book of the Dead* and the *Tao-te Ching*. There were books by Lobsang Rampa and Ramakrishna. There was the *Bhagavad-Gita* and the Buddhist sutras. I don't know, all these mystical and spiritual books that were current in our day: guide books to a spiritual country, repair manuals for the soul. And he said – and these were his only words, accompanied by a broad sweep of his hand across the array of books laid open on his bed – 'This is what I am.'

'How did the Villa do, Pete?' I asked. 'Did you see the match the other night? Fucking excellent goal.'

After that I called on Lois. I handed her the ring. She said, 'I liked the first letter you sent me, the one about the red mountains. But the other letters were . . . well . . .' And then she changed the subject.

I saw Lois, too, this year. It's been a year of meeting ex-lovers and

145

old friends again, to say nothing of ex-wives. She lives in a council flat with her young son. She's a single parent now. She looks the same, if a little older. Just as scruffy as she ever was. I had the feeling she was lonely, by herself. But what could I do about it now? Twenty years, it's a long time. We went out for a drink together. I said, 'You realize I was in love with you, don't you, Lois?'

'Were you?' she said, sounding surprised. 'I'm sorry. I didn't know what was going on half the time. I was just a kid.'

'You mean you didn't notice? How could you not notice? Why do you think I was always acting so strange? And those letters I sent you.'

'I was trying to live my life without the concept of love,' she said. 'I didn't believe in love.'

11 And Another Thing

'Childlike folly brings good fortune.'

The I Ching, Hexagram 4, 'Youthful Folly'

Why did I go to India? I guess I was searching for something, a guru perhaps. It was the thing to do. Well, I had one or two experiences that were enlightening in a way, but not in the mystical sense of the word. There were no gurus in India, or none that I met. There was a lot of mystic mumbo-jumbo of every description: but whatever enlightened beings there were must have been keeping themselves to themselves. I began to grow weary of the whole unedifying structure.

Somewhere, at some time, someone grabbed me by the hand. 'You want guru?' he said. 'Come, come, you meet enlightened being.' He was a little wiry man with a grubby turban, unshaven, some teeth missing, some rotten, and the rest stained red with betel-nut juice. He was chewing the nut and then occasionally gobbing out this blood-red fluid.

'No,' I told him, and tried to make some excuse.

But he was insisting. He wouldn't let go of my hand. 'Come, come. Come meet guru.'

I began to have this horrible sensation, like he was trying to sell me something tacky, the spiritual version of some off-the-shelf, factory-made souvenir, some gaudy trinket or meaningless bauble. In India, it seemed, enlightenment had become a holiday concept, a branch of the tourist industry, like native dances in Bali, or rides on an elephant to see the tribes in Thailand. It was like buying a work of native art in good faith, and then turning it over to find the words MADE IN TAIWÀN printed underneath. The whole thing had become nasty.

Well maybe that grubby little man was genuine, who knows? Maybe there was a guru waiting at the other end. In that case, I'd lost my chance at enlightenment. And then maybe my sensation that this was all part of some cheap scam was the truth. Certainly the man was desperate. He was holding my hand, refusing to let go, coming up close to me and breathing in my face. I was repulsed. I jerked my hand free and ran away, while he chased after me screaming 'Enlightenment, enlightenment, guru, guru,' like some kind of abuse. If this was enlightenment, I didn't want to know.

That wasn't the only experience I had in India. Some of the experiences were genuinely beautiful. But that was one of the ones that began to shake my faith. That one experience encapsulated something for me, gave birth to a new thought. It refocused my viewpoint. Here I was, God knows how many miles from home, half a world away, in a hot, dirty, insect-ridden, irritating, uncomfortably alien country, being threatened, almost, by the very thing I'd come out here to find. I began to yearn, quietly, for my own cool, polite, down-to-earth land, where there were no gurus, maybe, but where there was at least a sense of decorum. And if there was truth to be found, truth in some form, I was just as likely to find it in England, as in India, who knows?

I went to India in search of enlightenment. I came back gloriously cynical. Maybe cynicism is enlightenment in another form. It was certainly liberating for me. I was following in the footsteps of Richard Alpert, Timothy Leary's associate, who'd met an Indian guru and changed his name to Baba Ram Das. I was following in the footsteps of Allen Ginsburg, who had howled in the fifties, but had Ommed in the sixties. But I was wholly unprepared for such a momentous journey. I'd never been abroad. I'd never even been to Scotland, let alone Europe, let alone Asia. Travelling out there in the VW camper van with all the others: it was like taking England with us. Inside the van we were in England – eating English food, talking English, reading English books – while outside, through the windscreen, the world was a moving picture. It was like watching TV. From the lush affluence of Western Europe, through the grey broken cities of Yugoslavia and Bulgaria, into the out-of-date parody of the West that is Turkey. And on, into Asia. The vast plains of Iran. The ruggedness of Afghanistan. And down the Khyber pass into Pakistan, all heat and bustle. And then into India itself: exotic India, mysterious India, peculiar India, where people would stare at you like you were the man-in-the-moon, and ask you endless questions. 'What is your name, please? What country do you come from? Ah, England, yes. I have a cousin who lives in Nottingham, England. Do you know him?'

The man who owned the van was an ex-professional photographer who'd had a nervous breakdown. There was something desperately constrained about him. He held his lips like they were two lumps of undigested meat stuck to his face. One day he said, 'Look at this,' indicating his wife. She was peeling an apple with a knife. She peeled and peeled, the apple skin coming away in a delicate, spiralling curve, without breaking. 'She always peels apples that way. It's her speciality. She can do potatoes too.'

In Turkey we stayed with some students. There was a picture of Jimi Hendrix on the wall of their flat. 'Oh,' I said, by way of conversation, 'you like Jimi Hendrix then?'

'No,' they replied, decisively. 'It's a cover. We are revolutionaries.'

They all had beards. 'Revolutionaries have beards,' they told us. 'Fascists have moustaches.'

The chief revolutionary had a picture of himself training with the PLO. 'There, see, it's me,' he said, pointing to one figure, head swathed in a Palestinian-style scarf, holding a Kalashnikov. All the other people in the photograph were wearing Palestinian-style headscarves too, and holding Kalashnikovs. You couldn't tell one from another.

The chief revolutionary never drank or smoked. 'We revolutionaries must always be alert for the revolution,' he told me. Then we had a peanut-throwing competition. We had to throw the peanuts in the air and catch them in our mouths. First he threw one, and then I did. We were throwing them higher and higher, almost to the ceiling. Then he threw one which bounced off the ceiling, and missed it. I threw the next one. It also bounced off the ceiling, but I caught it. Everyone laughed and clapped me on the back. 'You are a true revolutionary,' they said.

In Afghanistan Pete and I stayed with Richard's brother, David, and his friends. This was on the way out, before the return journey when I'd stayed with David by myself and discussed love, life and Lois with him. There were four of them, all working for the British Council, teaching English as a foreign language. They earned so much money they had a servant. I found this deeply embarrassing, to be sitting on high-backed, colonial chairs, round a dinner table, being waited on by a servant. I expressed my discomfort. 'But it gives them employment,' they told me, as if they were doing him a favour.

'Why don't you just give him the money, if you want to help? Why make him wait on you?'

'It's how they like it. Anyway, we're busy people.'

They weren't hippies. But they looked like hippies. They had long hair and they smoked dope. Everyone looked like a hippie in those days, every young person, that is. It was hard to tell who was a hippie and who was not. It was the era of the mistaken identity.

One night we were all smoking Afghan black. It was so strong it made your limbs judder. Suddenly one of the British Council crew said, 'Let's make a tape for our students.'

We were all supposed to read from a prepared text. When it came to my bit I put on this cheerful chappie Cockney accent. It was dreadful. Everyone cracked up laughing. But then the dope was so strong it was like being placed in body-armour. I became horribly self-conscious, and had to run away. This was the second time I'd had that reaction from dope. The first time was in Lois's flat. It's how I've felt about it ever since.

In Pakistan we stayed with a wealthy middle-class family. We were there for over a week. They were very hospitable.

They had two daughters who would wait on us sometimes. They were beautiful, graceful, with long black hair and shimmeringly dark eyes. The father of the household would make his girls froth the coffee for us. They made coffee the way we make cocoa, mixing it with milk and sugar and stirring it into a paste. The process took about fifteen minutes, and the result was delicious. One of the girls made coffee for Pete, while the other one made it for me. I had this sudden feeling that the father was trying to marry them off to us.

One evening I expressed an interest in the Sufis, a mysterious Islamic sect. 'They're just tramps,' I was told. Nevertheless I was driven out to meet a colony of them, who lived by a mosque. I don't know if they were real Sufis or not. They did look like tramps, with ragged greatcoats and shabby beards. They were smoking heaps of pot and giggling.

Then, in India, I met my guru at last. This was in Agra, near the Taj Mahal. He was a Baba, a follower of Siva. He wore only a loincloth, with a piece of sackcloth round his shoulders. So he was a Baba in other ways too. The loincloth looked like a nappy. He was the same age as me, with long hair and a beard, like an Indian hippie. I had a blim of hash with me, which he made into a chillum. 'Bom Shankar,' he said, as he raised the chillum to his forehead, and then took a long pull. And then he passed it to me. 'Bom Shankar,' I should have said, but I didn't. How many times had I said it in England? How often had I invoked the god Siva? And yet, here I was, in Siva's country, with a Siva follower before me, in the shadow of the great Taj Mahal, and I just couldn't say it. 'Bom Shankar!' All hail to Siva. It would have sounded false in my mouth. They were not my words any more. This was not my world.

The Baba offered me a banana, but I refused. He pressed me to take a piece, and as I gripped the end, he deftly broke it off with a flick of the wrist, leaving me with the largest portion. Then he laughed. After that he lit a cigarette. Really he wanted more dope, but I didn't have the cash. So he smoked his cigarette and then, when he'd finished it, he flicked it derisively into the night air. It arced and span, leaving a trail of sparks. It seemed like a statement, somehow, resonant with meaning. 'Here, this is my mortal coil, my life. See how I flick it off. See how little I care for it.'

The Baba spoke French, but only halting English. My French was equally halting. So the conversation ground to many awkward silences. About the only sense I managed to get from him was that he was a Baba because he didn't like work. That's what he said. He was on a spiritual quest, and spiritual quests were incompatible with work.

Was he my guru? Not really. But I could identify with him. Had he been a Westerner, he would certainly have been a hippie. Hippies don't like work either. As it was, he was a Baba instead.

Finally we got to Nepal, where Pete and I left our travelling companions, and we were on our own, two kids out of England, in this strange, exotic world. We met the King of Bhutan. It was like this. There were a bunch of us looking around a museum of Nepalese brassware in Kathmandu. We'd paid good money to get in, so when the attendant started trying to hustle us out, we ignored him. We stayed on in that museum, looking at all the brass gods and the brass Buddhas, until the attendants were getting really frantic. In the end we relented and left. And on the stairs we passed a peculiar entourage. 'Namaste,' we said, in proper Nepalese style, holding our hands in the attitude of prayer and bowing, 'Namaste.' There were a couple of Buddhist monks and three or four other people. 'Namaste,' we said, as each of them passed. 'Namaste,' they said in reply. And then the last two came up the stairs, laughing. It was a young couple. The man was dressed in a kind of kilt with stack-heeled shoes and long socks and what appeared to be a Marks & Spencer's golf-sweater with a diamond pattern across the chest, while the woman was wearing Eastern clothes. 'Namaste,' we said. 'And a good morning to you too,' they said, in perfect Oxford English accents, laughing at the surprised looks on our faces. We went out into the courtyard, and through the gates into the street. There was a crowd there, and a couple of Rolls Royces. 'What's happening?' we asked. 'It's the King of Bhutan on a state visit,' we were told. Well, I don't know which one was the King of Bhutan. I've since found out he is the same age as me. So I like to imagine it was that young man at the end, with his Marks & Sparks sweater and his Oxbridge accent, and his laughing 'Good

Morning'. I like to think that because it suits me to think that. Many years later I wrote him a letter. He never replied.

It was after this that I began to have my doubts about what was happening over there. I began to realize that we, the hippies, were just the first wave of a movement that was going to destroy their way of life. We thought we were travellers. Really we were tourists.

I'd lost my money and my passport by now, and I was stuck in Kathmandu, working. I worked for one man who was a high-caste brahmin. He spoke perfect English. He told me that he'd tried to visit England once, but they'd refused him entry. He was a wealthy man, and it was a holiday, that's all. But the immigration officers had decided he was trying to enter the country illegally, as an immigrant. 'Why would I do that?' he said. 'My business is in Nepal. They were letting German people and Italian people in for their holidays, but not me, an Indian. They said, "Why do you want to come here?" I said, "Because this is England, because I speak English. Because I have grown up hearing about England. All my life I have heard about how wonderful and liberal and free you English are. What should I think about it now?" It was my black face, that's all. They didn't like my black face.'

But that Brahmin treated me like dirt. He had me in his power and he knew it. I was working for nothing, for food and board, and he fed me only the poorest food. He watched me like a hawk to make sure I never ate the food on the counter but only the workers' food. Dhal and rice with yoghurt, every day. Twelve hours a day, for a plate of dhal. All the Nepalese workers felt sorry for me, and would feed me titbits once in a while. It was very humiliating. I left to work in another restaurant, where I became known as the English Waiter. Lots of people came to visit me, and the trade went up accordingly. It got too busy for the cooks and they became unhappy with my presence. They asked me to leave. They had a servant. He was a little boy who slept in a hole under the stairs, on a pile of rags.

The whole of Kathmandu was like that. Little boys sleeping on rags in holes beneath the stairs. People shitting in the streets. Grimy cafés full of out-of-it hippies.

I met a man who'd been in Kathmandu ten years before. He

was crying. 'They've spoilt it,' he said. 'Ten years ago it was the most beautiful city on earth. Now look at it.'

I was becoming depressed. I was in Nepal, but I was depressed. I was staying in a hotel. At night, as I settled down to sleep, I could hear the sounds of rats scuffling in the roof space. I could hear them scratching around up there, keeping me awake. And in the morning I was woken up by the sound of cooing doves. Doves in the morning, rats at night. It was symbolic. Except that, as I later realized, they were not rats scuffling in the roof at all. It was the doves, settling down to sleep, that's all, just as I was.

In a conversation one evening, the manager of the hotel said, 'We Nepalese want money. We want progress. We want all the things you Westerners have. Cars, washing machines, everything.'

I said, 'Why? It won't make you happy. We Westerners have all the material things, but we are not happy. You live in the most beautiful country in the world, isn't that enough?'

'Ah,' he said, 'but you can't eat scenery.'

And then my money and my passport came through and I moved over to the west of the country, near the Anapurna range, where there was a lake with hotels on the shore. It was very quiet, very peaceful. And all the hippies would sit around in the restaurants and hotels smoking dope.

One hotel played Elton John tapes, all day long. An Australian hippie said to the manager, 'You like Elton, don't you? You're always playing that record.'

'No I don't,' he said. 'I just put it on because I know you hippies like to hear music.' And there was this look of terrible weariness in his eyes, as if he could see the rest of his life measured out in Elton John tapes and endless pancakes served to ignorant tourists off their heads on dope-cake. Forever more. It was a kind of hell.

On my way home, I stopped off in New Delhi briefly. I was in a park in the centre of the city, with a friend. A man came up to us, a soothsayer. He wanted to read my fortune. I told him to go away. He was asking for money, certainly, and I was hanging on to mine. But then he played a trick on my companion.

'You write name. You write name of someone you know,' he said, and handed my friend a pen and a piece of paper. My friend did as he was asked, folding the paper, as he was instructed to do, and then handing it over. The soothsayer took the folded piece of paper and then palmed it. He then proceeded to write a name himself on another piece of paper. On presenting it, it turned out to be the same name my friend had written.

'It's a trick,' I said.

'No trick. I read your fortune. Very cheap.'

'It's a trick, and I haven't got any money.'

'Your friend. I read his fortune?'

'We've got to go.'

'No, please. I can read fortunes. No tricks, honest.'

'So you admit it was a trick?'

'No. Yes. Maybe. But I can read fortunes.'

'I haven't got any money.'

'Please, please. I read your fortune. I read your friend's fortune. Listen, listen, I tell you something, for free. Then you know. Then you let me read friend's fortune. OK?'

'OK.'

'You are looking for something,' he said. 'You are looking for something, here in India. But you will not find it. Not here. You will find it somewhere else, somewhere many miles from here, where it is very, very cold.'

Suddenly he appeared to be telling the truth. It was a formula, perhaps, a trick, like the trick with the bit of paper (though I'm no longer so sure that was a trick either); but it carried some truth with it; and I knew then that the man was sincere, that he really did have something to tell us. But I was hardened by then, by India, by my experiences, by a growing cynicism. I brushed him aside and dragged my friend away. That's when he cursed me.

I have no idea what he said. He gave me this look and pointed and screamed something at me, and I knew it was a curse.

Actually, before Pete and I set out on our journey to India, we'd stopped off in London briefly, to get visas and inoculations and to pick up traveller's cheques and all the rest. We were staying with a friend of Pete's who'd recently moved there from Cardiff. And we met this bloke.

I can't remember where, exactly, we met him. I can't remember what he looked like. I have some vague impression of cropped hair and jeans, though I may be projecting that.

'I don't know what you're going to India for,' he said. 'It's a waste of time. Why go all that way? You should stay here. London is the place. London is where it's happening now. Great music everywhere. Loads of bands, loads of venues. London is where it's at. There's something in the air.'

Well I don't remember his exact words either. Something like that. But I've realized since that he was referring to the London pub-rock scene at the time, the precursor of punk. This was late summer, 1975.

If you listened to Malcolm McLaren, of course, you'd be forgiven for thinking that he invented punk. But punk was happening long before it acquired that name. It was down to an attitude, and a growing cynicism. People were becoming increasingly unhappy with the airy pretensions of progressive rock. All those interminable guitar solos, that overblown, overproduced, overplayed posturing with pretensions to classicism, as far away from raw, earthy rock'n'roll as you can get. Well a long guitar solo is all right, if the guitarist is talented and inventive enough. Jimi Hendrix could play solos that wheeled about in the air like flocks of wild-bird notes at sunrise. But then again, Jimi Hendrix could actually play the guitar. Many of the others couldn't. You remember Ten Years After? There's a performance by them in the Woodstock Movie. The same four or five tuneless notes played over and over again, very fast. Well Alvin Lee only had one lick, it's just that he practised it so often he could play it at this ridiculous speed, twiddly-dee, twiddly-dee, twiddly-dee, over and over again. And then, finally, he's got no notes left to play. So he pants into the microphone instead, repeating the same phrase over and over again. It's like he's masturbating in front of you. On and on. Grinding repetition. Pointless posturing, devoid of originality or thought, stretching out a vain parody of a twelve-bar blues until it nearly breaks under the strain. On and on and on. 'I'm goin' home, to my baby.' Yawn!

So it's no wonder punk happened. Punk stripped music down to the bare essentials again. It was raw and expressive and in-your-face alive. No guitar solos because – unlike Alvin Lee – no one was pretending they could play guitar solos. It was just fast, and furiously angry.

But it's also wrong to think of punk as separate from hippie. It's not separate at all. It was part of the same thing. Many punks had been hippies, before they cut their hair. Many punks became hippies again. They were engaged in the same cultural processes. The hippie squatting scene in the early seventies gave way to the punk squatting scene in the later seventies. The hippie travelling scene of the early seventies gave way to the punk travelling scene of the later seventies. The punks followed the hippies out onto the road. Finally, the hippie festival scene of the early seventies gave way to the punk festival scene of the later seventies. It was a continuum. The only difference was the hairstyle. The only difference was the cut of your jeans. The only difference, really, was that punk was angry.

And this, too, was a natural progression. The hippies had believed in peace and love. But successive confrontations with various aspects of the establishment over the years had begun to make them angry.

There were drug busts and attacks on squats. Sometimes physical force was used. Sometimes people got hurt. Many people were gaoled. Finally there was the attack on the last of the Windsor Free Festivals.

The Windsor Free had been going since 1972, in Windsor Great Park. It was called by Bill 'Ubi' Dwyer, on the basis of an acid vision he'd had. The first year was quiet, just a few hundred hippies hidden in a copse. The second year had got bigger. And by the third year – 300,000 leaflets having been distributed, BR laying on extra trains for the occasion, with 300 bands offering their services, six main stages each with six stage managers – it was massive. It was an act of breathtaking defiance, taking on the establishment at its very heart, on land owned by the Royal Family. But, as usual, the defiance was playful. The Queen was invited, but sent a letter politely declining. The fact that she wrote at all was taken as a positive sign.

The festival had already been going on for five days when, on the morning of 29 August 1974, up to eight hundred police stormed the festival site. People were woken up and ordered to leave, and then, when some of them refused, were attacked. The police went out of control. There were scenes of violence that were later reported in the newspapers. Wally Hope saw a pregnant woman being kicked in the belly, and a young boy being punched in the face. Ubi Dwyer was gaoled, for 'Incitement to Cause a Public Nuisance'.

Wally Hope. The name comes up again. I've written about him before, in my previous book. But you just can't investigate hippies without reference to Wally Hope. All through my research the name kept coming up, again and again. I began to think I was going to have to do a rewrite of the first book. Wally Hope was the hippie martyr. Incidentally, there's a pamphlet about him, written by the anarcho-punk band, Crass. It's called 'The Last of the Hippies'. Just like this book.

His real name was Phil Russell, and it was he who had called the first Stonehenge Free Festival, in the same year that the Windsor Free had been attacked. A year later he was dead. It's not possible to go into the full story here. Perhaps no one will ever know what really happened. All we can say is that he was arrested and held on a drugs charge, put into mental hospital where he was fed psychiatric drugs, and that, later, he died in mysterious circumstances. But if there is a source to the hippie anger it is here. Phil Russell's death brought it home to everyone. This was serious stuff, not playful any more. The British establishment, so civilized, so quaint, with their costumes and their pageantry, their wigs, their rituals, their playacting: all of this actually hides a dangerous intent.

At the heart of the hippie movement lies the question of property rights. Who owns what? The slogan of the Windsor Free was 'Pay No Rent'. Windsor Great Park had been 'enclosed' by George III, to make way for his private hunt. Prior to that it had been common land. In other words, it had been stolen. The Windsor Free was an attempt to 'borrow' it back, for the people. The other name for both the Windsor Festival, and the Stonehenge Festival (as well as the one or two others, at Watchfield in 1975 and Seasalter in 1976) was the People's Free Festival. Squatting, travelling, free-festival organization, all of these question the historical validity of the rights of the property-owning establishment.

It's just that the property-owning establishment weren't open to questioning. And they were not opposed to using violence when necessary.

By late summer 1975, while I was starting out for India, the hippies were becoming angry. And by 1976, when I got back, the punk explosion had started. Two sides of the same thing.

Trouble is, I got stuck, straight smack bang in the middle. Too young to be a hippie, too old to be a punk. It's been the bane of my life ever since.

So. Back in England. Rejected by my wife. Having rejected my spiritual hopes. Having begun to reject dope. Having begun to question the whole hippie edifice. Becoming increasingly estranged from my peers. Becoming increasingly cynical and angry. Seething with some barely suppressed anger most of the time, but not knowing what, exactly, I was angry about. Having lost my direction and my faith and my sense of well-being. Having lost faith in the hippie dream, but not knowing what to replace it with. Not knowing what to do with my life. Not knowing where to go or who to be any more. What could I do? I moved to Hull.

Why Hull? Because the road to Hull was paved with good intentions. Because Graham was there. Graham was the bloke Rose, my first girlfriend, had left me for. I went up for a weekend and stayed in the area for five years. It might have been a case of 'out of the frying pan, into the fire', except it wasn't nearly as exciting as that. More like, 'out of the pig trough, into the mire'. From one desperately unfashionable British city to another.

Actually, it's not all that bad. Quite nice really, in a grand, Victorian, seedy sort of way. It was built on the wealth of the fishing industry, now grinding into slow decline. The docks were deserted, with a certain melancholy calm. It smelled of fish. Also, being on the east coast, it could be very, very cold. Not the year I arrived, however. Nineteen seventy-six saw a ruthless, blazing summer.

Graham was going through a hiatus in his life. So was I. We did a lot of drinking. We got stoned too, occasionally. But I was still being hauled into this self-conscious straitjacket by it. Actually that's not quite accurate. A straitjacket implies some external bondage. Whatever it was that was holding me in, it was holding me in from the inside.

I took to drinking instead. Graham and I got jobs on an archaeological site – £8 a week on top of our dole money – and we'd go over to the pub every lunchtime. We'd go to the pub in the evenings too, when we could afford it. Sometimes it was a question of, 'Shall we eat tonight, or go out for a drink?' So we'd compromise. We'd drink Guinness.

One day I decided I needed a proper job, a career. Hull is a merchant port, and my dad was in the Navy. I decided I wanted to be a merchant seaman. I was having delicious visions of a life at sea. All those exotic ports, all those strange countries. I think I was probably thinking more of all the brothels in those exotic ports and those strange countries. So I went to the Merchant Navy office in the town to sign up.

'How old are you?' they asked.

'Twenty-three.'

'You're too old. You have to sign up when you're seventeen.'

So there you are. Twenty-three years old, and already passed it.

And then, on Bonfire Night that year, Graham met an old friend of his from Birmingham: Steve. Steve was working for the RSPB in Bridlington, further up the coast. He invited us to come up and share his flat.

It was a one-bedroomed flat, with a kitchen and a living room. Graham lived in a cubby-hole under the stairs, while I slept on the settee. Only Steve had any privacy. But my life had taken a strange turn by now. It was like I was drifting aimlessly, blown about by the wind. Nothing was making any sense any more.

I'd lost my sense of humour. I couldn't take a joke. People would crack a joke and I'd see it as an affront. What had happened to Piss-Off Pete at first, and then to Cliff Pilchard, was now happening to me. All the humour was gone, and it's humour that keeps us sane.

Things came to a head at Christmas that year. I was shopping for Christmas presents for my Mom and Dad. I was outside Woolworth's one bright, sharp winter's day, trying to think what to buy. And then something came to me. I can't say 'suddenly' because that would sound too dramatic. It was quiet, furtive, strange. It crept into my belly like some lonely creature crawling into a hole. It was just a feeling, there in that prosaic shop doorway, at this festive time of the year. The feeling was that life was meaningless, empty. It was a profound sense of emptiness, like a hole opening up inside me. Life was a sham, a show, with nothing inside. The whole world seemed dismal and strange, like a soap opera without a script, a book without feeling, a meal without company. I thought, *If things don't get better by this time next year, I'm going to top myself.*

I got back to the flat and Graham said, 'What's up with you?'

'Nothing. Why?'

'I just had this feeling. You kept coming into my thoughts. And then the radio said your name.'

'What do you mean, the radio said my name?'

'I don't know. It said your name, that's all. Someone on the radio said your name.'

Actually, that's what Graham and I had really talked about when we met in that pub in Birmingham this year. We talked about depression. Not the sort of depression I had playacted with in Colum Road. Not the occasional feeling of exhaustion or emptiness we all feel at times. No, real, grim, grey, grimy depression, the debilitating kind. Industrial-strength depression, to score out your insides. Graham had had a bout recently, while my worst attack had come that day in Bridlington, outside Woolworth's. I've had attacks since, but never like that. It was evil. I told him about it, about how I'd been feeling when we shared that flat, how desperate and lonely I'd felt.

'I hadn't noticed,' he said. 'I was too busy meditating.'

I moved out of Bridlington in the Spring. Graham stayed and got a job selling candyfloss. I was back in Hull for a while. I got stoned one night, and then realized I was about to be caught in that straitjacket again. So I went for a walk. I was just walking, walking, going nowhere, wandering the half-familiar streets in a kind of dream. At one point there was a woman walking ahead of me, and I noticed that she had suddenly speeded up as she heard my footsteps approaching. And then I found myself in a part of the city I'd never been before. There were decrepit factories behind broken fences. I looked into one factory and thought, *Give me work.* It was work I wanted, even then. There was a disused railway line with an empty station. Crooked streets and blackened churches. (The churches seemed to harbour evil to me.) It was a strange, deserted landscape. There was a canal with a bridge over it. I went down, underneath the bridge. Then I heard voices and started. I could hear them above me, muttering and mumbling. It was so unexpected, so sudden, I wanted to run away. They must have crept up on me without my knowing, and now they were descending the stairs to join me under the bridge. I rushed up the stairs on the other side to get away, and then sneaked back down to take a look, positive I would see someone, hearing the voices all the way down.

What were they saying? Nothing. There was no one there. It was in my imagination, that's all. I was all alone.

It was after that I began to feel liberated.

I came to a patch of waste ground, over a railway track, on which a colony of cooling towers sprouted, like peculiar mushrooms. It was a huge space, like a private playground. I climbed the rickety staircase up the side of one of the cooling towers. The wind was buffeting the structure, threatening to shake me off. So I came down. It had started to drizzle, a cool spring rain. I lifted up my face and the rain felt like soft points of electricity against my skin. The city was a circle of orange lights around me. Suddenly (and it's not too dramatic a word this time) I felt alive again. That thought I'd had on the threshold at Woolworth's came back to me. Only now it felt good. I was glad that life was empty. I was glad it was meaningless. No God. No Siva. No Krishna. No Buddha. No Jesus. No need to chant and *Om*. No need to pray. There was nothing there, nothing between me and the stars. Nothing. Just the sky above and the earth beneath, the electric rain, and those weird industrial sculptures rising up in a kind of defiance against the clouds. It was a moment of complete calm, alone with myself, knowing I was alone, knowing it didn't matter. I was safe. I was free. I wasn't a hippie any more. I was myself.

Well it wasn't exactly cold, as the soothsayer had predicted. But it was cold compared to India.

Rain.

Rain, rain, rain, rattling on the roof of the van, falling in waves, washing down the hillside in muddy streams, gathering in pools: relentless, driving rain, hissing and shifting and blustering about. Rain.

And then mud. Streams of mud. Rivers of mud. Oceans of dark, slimy, greasy, sticky mud. Mud up to your ankles when you walked. Mud splashing your trouser legs and up over your coat. Mud on the toilet seats in the awful festival toilets, looking like shit. Mud to stand up in and mud to sit down in. Mud.

That was Pilton that year. Rain. And then mud.

The reason we were on the litter-pickers field is that Des was organizing the stage there. It was high up on the hillside, overlooking the site. I wasn't working on the field. I was there as part

163

of the entertainment crew. But I liked the idea of serving the lit-ter-pickers. The litter-pickers are the working class of the Pilton Festival. They're there to work, picking up litter. Mind you, they don't get paid very much. They have to buy their tickets. And then, when the Festival is over, if they've done all of their shifts to their supervisor's satisfaction, they get their ticket money back. That's all they get, the chance to come to the Pilton Festival and then work for nothing. It seemed like a raw deal to me.

They also get fed. Unfortunately for them, the food franchise has gone out to a couple of sloppy vegans. So that's what they get to eat: vegan slop. Bowls of vegetables in a runny sauce. The same thing every day. Working hard all day, in the pouring rain, for a bowl of vegetables. But the organizers were well organized. They'd put out a couple of franchises for vegetarian burger stalls. Not that the burgers were free: the litter-pickers had to pay for them. And being hungry (and unable to face any more bowls of unpeeled potatoes in various bland sauces), they were flocking to them. One of the vegetarian burger stalls was run by the orga-nizers themselves (or by their children, rather). And this was the cause of my first wobbly at the Pilton Festival.

It was getting late into the first day, and we hadn't eaten all day. We'd delivered all of that food and all of that equipment for them – including their poxy vacuum cleaner – but no one was offering to feed us. I was hungry. All I'd had to eat in the last two days was a flimsy slice of pizza. Des didn't seem to be worried about it. He was in his 'go with the flow' festival phase. 'Some-thing will turn up,' he grumbled. I was too hungry to wait. Instead I offered to buy Des and Angelina some food. So Des was right. Something did turn up. I did.

I went to the vegetarian burger stall run by the organizers' children and ordered burger and chips three times. The burgers were £1.50 each, £2 with salad. So I ordered three burgers with salad, and stood back to watch. It was appalling. There were a bunch of kids in there, aged between about eight and fourteen, running around amid all that hot fat and cooking equipment, and they had no idea what they were doing. Not one of them could cook. There were flames leaping and fat sizzling, and a bunch of kids squabbling, and people queuing up, waiting, and I was starving and Angelina was starving, and the kids – who knew Angelina – were taunting her. 'Nyer, nyer, nyer Angelina,' they were saying in that sing-song way that kids use to effect derision. I was steadily losing my temper, not just with the kids: with the adults who'd put them here. And we were just waiting and waiting while this was going on.

But eventually the food came.

'You said salad, didn't you?' the kid asked.

'Yes,' I said.

And he put one slice of cucumber and a bit of lettuce into the bun with the burger. One slice of cucumber.

'What's this?' I asked.

'Salad,' the kid said.

'Salad? Salad? One slice of cucumber for 50p. You call that salad?'

'I'm sorry,' he said, 'it's what I was told to do.'

I stormed back to the van.

'I'm fed up,' I said. 'I'm pissed off. One slice of cucumber for 50p. And the chips are inedible. And it took fifteen minutes to get served. And none of them know what they're doing. I'd be surprised if there wasn't fire in there. It's fucking dangerous. I hate festivals, I really do.'

Later Susanna was talking to the organizer of the litter-pickers field. He was moaning on about how hard the work was, how spiritually unrewarding.

'So why do you do it?' she asked.

He paused. And then, enunciating his words very carefully, he named a five-figure sum.

The first Pilton Festival took place on 19 September 1970, after the young Michael Eavis had visited the Bath Blues Festival earlier in the summer. He was suitably impressed. He decided he wanted one of his own.

Perhaps the only mystery is how a person like Michael Eavis came to be at the Bath Blues Festival in the first place. He was a churchgoer, a Methodist. He was also a dairy farmer, working the land that had been worked by his family since 1894. I imagine that his background had been severe; or strict, at least. I imagine that he would have been a cautious man – cautious and practical – being from hardy, hardworking yeoman stock. So how come he was at this festival? That's easy. He hopped the fence.

Well no, he didn't really hop the fence. But the fences had come down, and he walked in for free. I only wanted to say that because it became a feature of my stay at Pilton this year, watching the countless hordes hopping over the fences. It was nice to think that – though he didn't actually hop the fence himself – Michael Eavis had actually blagged his way into his first festival.

He was thirty-five years old.

Anyway, he came away from this festival in love with the whole thing. The light and colour of the scene must have impressed him, probably because it did contrast so severely with his own background. He'd never seen hippies before. He'd never seen clothes like that before. Here we have a bunch of people having fun. A bunch of people ideologically opposed to the very work ethic he'd been brought up to worship, dressed in flowing robes, with patchwork clothes and dangly hairdos. Many of them would have been dancing. Some of them, indeed, may have been dancing naked. Dancing naked was the thing to do if you were a hippie. On top of which, he loved the music. Actually he'd always loved the music. He played Radio One to his cows, and had made a record himself many years before: a 78, which he refuses to let anyone hear. But it crossed his mind that here might be a way of making money, to supplement the income from the farm. So he set out to recreate some of the ingredients on his own land. He booked the Kinks to headline the show, in September that year. In the end they backed out, and Marc Bolan and T. Rex played instead.

The show was not a great success. Only 2,500 people turned up. And Jimi Hendrix had just died, so there was a kind of gloom over the event, an atmosphere of mourning. But Eavis provided free milk, and the proceedings must have gone smoothly enough for him to think that it wasn't such an unmitigated disaster. He must have thought that, since he was to host a similar event the following year. And that subsequent event has since become a legend.

According to the official programme of the 1997 festival, it was called the Glastonbury Fayre, and held over the solstice period in June 1971. I said it was a similar event. It was similar in that

166

bands played and hippies attended. But in every other way it was entirely dissimilar. It was one of the earliest free festivals.

This second festival was Andrew Kerr's idea. Kerr had been the personal assistant of Randolph Churchill from 1959 until his death in 1968. After that he became a free spirit, a hippie. I met him. He came to visit me in my van. He's a dapper little chap, not much younger than my Dad, but a Universe away in terms of his attitudes. Very sprightly, very sparkly, very alive.

He isn't 'little' really. He's five foot ten. I only said that because he reminds me of my Dad, and my Dad is little. And also because 'dapper little chap' as a phrase suits him. Anyway, it sounds better than 'a dapper medium-sized chap'.

We met up so that he could correct some of the errors that have accumulated around the event over the years. There's been a number of official histories written. Not one of the writers took the trouble to consult with Andrew Kerr.

The first thing he told me was that the spelling was wrong. All the books I consulted spelled it the same way: as 'Glastonbury Fayre'.

'It was Fair,' he said to me: 'F-A-I-R. Glastonbury Fair.'

He'd gone to the Isle of Wight Festival in 1970, he told me, and had been appalled at the rank commercialism of the event. It was in his Rover driving back that it had occurred to him that he wanted to create a festival of his own. The car was full of people, and he started telling them of his idea. He said, 'Well it's definitely not going to be like the other festivals. We've got to have a festival that's not a hype, that is a celebration of life and gives respect to the environment.'

He'd come by what he described as 'a little money'. I expect it was quite a large sum of money by my standards, but a little money by the standards of those circles he moved around in. He'd been reading the New Testament. 'Give all that you have and follow me,' it said. So he decided to do that. He decided to give his money away in the form of a free festival.

'Something was kind of inside me over this period,' he says to me now, 'and I will definitely not say that it was to do with drugs.'

So, together with Arabella Churchill (Randolph's daughter) and a number of other people, he formed Solstice Capers Ltd., in

167

order to execute his fantasy. That's when the festival was planned to take place: summer solstice the following year.

Well I was interested in this. I was interested in how the ancient celebration of the solstice came to be revived. I mean, it's such a commonplace now. Almost a whole generation have grown up to recognize its significance. It has become something of a tradition. But back then, when Andrew Kerr was planning his event, there was no such tradition. I was hoping for some mystical revelation, of the kind that Ubi Dwyer had had, before the Windsor Free, or Wally Hope before Stonehenge. But actually he'd read it in a book. It was *The View Over Atlantis* by John Michell, a very influential book amongst the hippies at the time. But it was definitely revelations he was looking for.

And his first thought, in fact, had been to hold it at Stonehenge, on a round stage. It was only later, in the wake of Michael Eavis's mini-festival, that he considered Pilton and opted for the pyramid.

Jimi Hendrix was asked to play. 'I'll be there,' he said. But, of course, he never lived to fulfil that promise. However, the world premiere of *Rainbow Bridge*, Hendrix's film, took place at the festival. So perhaps he was there in other ways.

By now someone had suggested that Kerr approach Michael Eavis, and an appointment was made. The day before, however, Kerr climbed Glastonbury Tor, along with the usual carload of people. They spent the night there. Someone offered him an oat cake. That was Bill Harkin, later to design the pyramid stage. He stayed up all night – 'the excitement of the occasion prevented me from sleeping' – and in the morning he went over to visit Eavis.

There was no rainbow, note. This is one of the myths that he wanted me to clear up. He did not see a rainbow over Worthy Farm from Glastonbury Tor, as previous histories have stated it. The rainbow came later.

So, arriving in Pilton Village, and parking up, he met Michael Eavis for the first time.

His first impression was that Eavis's face was shining. 'Open, genuine, blazing, outgoing': these were the adjectives he used to describe the young Michael Eavis that day.

Kerr told the farmer of his plan, and offered to pay for the use of the land. 'We don't have much money, but we'll pay what we can,' he said.

And Eavis didn't even think about it. He just said yes.

'It was the most blessed thing in my life,' says Kerr now. 'The chance to live out a dream, a really crazy dream.'

I met Michael Eavis too, a little before I met Andrew Kerr. It was Michael Eavis who gave me Kerr's address. I interviewed him at Worthy Farm, in his office: the same office from which he runs the festival every year. It's tiny, not much bigger than your average toilet, and packed with files, as well as a desk and two chairs, a computer, telephones, notice boards, all crammed in there, like a pile of junk stuffed precariously into a cupboard. It seemed extraordinary to think that, year after year, that huge event has emerged from this tiny space.

What puzzled me was why Eavis had gone along with Kerr's idea. He wasn't exactly going to make his fortune. He was a straight-laced Somerset farmer, and a Christian to boot. He didn't even drink or smoke cigarettes, let alone go along with the excesses of the hippies who came with Andrew Kerr to invade his farmhouse that year.

'That's a good question,' Eavis said. 'I'm puzzled about this as well. But I had an affinity with the hippies. I mean, I can always talk to hippies, anywhere I go. Maybe it's that I get more of a dialogue with these people than I do with a lot of other people. But it was all very romantic at the time. It was a very romantic thing to be doing, all lovey-dovey, and I was in love.'

Des told me a good story. He said he was driving around the back lanes near Pilton one year, just after the festival, when he came across Michael Eavis, carrying a plastic bag, and scouring around the hedgerows.

'What are you up to, Michael?' he asked.

And Michael showed him what was in the bag. It was human excrement. Apparently one of the local farmers had told him that he would object to the festival unless Michael did this: unless he went round the hedgerows himself to collect the shit. He was not allowed to get contractors in to do the work. He had to do it himself. And such was his dedication to the festival that he had actually agreed. Maybe it was the same spirit that had urged him to accept Andrew Kerr's proposal all those years before.

Anyway, whatever the reason, Worthy Farm soon became the stomping ground for the countercultural elite of the time. Kerr sold up his house on the Thames at Chiswick and moved into the farmhouse. And it was while he was entering the farm gates that first time that he saw the rainbow spanning the house.

All sorts of people were coming and going during the nine months leading up to the festival. Hawkwind practised in the barn, as did the Pink Fairies. The cast of Hair turned up. Members of the Grateful Dead. Friends of John Lennon. Some thieves and plenty of phoneys. Even a guru or two. Some of them had peculiar aliases, like Zee and Toad. It was the Beautiful People, hair and floral dresses wafting in the breeze, odorous with patchouli oil. Headbands and sandals. Flappy flares. Waistcoats. Scarfs. Frilly shirts. The smell of hemp and garlic. I'm certain they would have indulged in late-night philosophical conversations under the influence of some high-grade stimulants. Eavis was just tending his herd, letting them get on with it. But there they were, in all their full-blown hippie splendour, talking heaven down from the stars, the Lords and Ladies of the revolution.

What the local people thought about this hippie invasion in the months preceding the festival is not on record. The police were fairly sanguine about it, however. Kerr had to speak to them to make arrangements about traffic flow and access and the rest, and a number of officers came to see him at the farmhouse. In order to get to Kerr's room they had to pass through Bill Harkin's room, which was full of people sitting on the floor blowing chillums. So they tiptoed gingerly through that, like it was an obstacle course. As Kerr stood up from his desk to greet them, he glanced out of the window. He was confronted with the sight of a naked female draped against the wheel of a cart which was parked in the middle of the lawn outside. And there, in front of her, 'with a lazy-lob on' (it's a naval term), dancing and wobbling his buttocks about, completely naked, performing what looked like some sort of magical sex rite, was the High Priest. Yes, the High Priest: the same High Priest we've met before. Kerr was embarrassed. He didn't know what to do. The policemen just leaned over to get a better view through the window, and spluttered with laughter. After that they had to pick their way back through the chillum obstacle course in Bill Harkin's room again. No one had moved an inch.

Later they said, 'We know they're all smoking pot. But we're not interested in you lot. It's the big boys we're after.' They were West Country policemen. A different breed in those days.

The actual festival, the following year, was a high-camp hippie to-do. Kerr had planned it 'in the medieval tradition, with music, dance, poetry, theatre, lights and the opportunity for spontaneous entertainment'. When he introduced the bands to the audience, he said:

'Glastonbury is a place far too beautiful for yet another rock festival. If the festival has a specific intention it is to create an increase of awareness in the power of the Universe, a heightening of consciousness and a recognition of our place in the function of this our tired and molested planet. We have spent too long telling the Universe to shut up; we must search for the humility to listen. The Earth is groaning for contact with our ears and eyes. Universal awareness touches gently at our shoulders. We are creators being created and we must prove our worth.'

Bill Harkin designed the Pyramid stage, one-tenth the size of the Great Pyramid itself. It was built out of scaffolding covered with expanded metal and plastic sheeting, and placed on a blind spring, near the so-called Michael line that joins Glastonbury to Stonehenge, in a natural amphitheatre. Kerr dowsed the spot himself. It was certainly a spectacular structure. Officially the festival ran from the 20th to the 24th of June, but what with early arrivals, and late departures, actually managed to stretch out for over a week. The acts were Hawkwind, Traffic, Melanie, Fairport Convention and David Bowie. The Grateful Dead were supposed to have turned up, but never did. Between 12,000 and 15,000 people attended.

So far, so good. A fairly typical rock festival at the time. But it was also a celebration of this peculiar new culture. And that's where things seemed to get a little crazy.

I used the expression 'high camp' to describe it earlier. That's because I've seen the photographs. There's something theatrical about the whole event. People are decidedly in costume. The usual things: flowery robes and Afghan coats and bangles and beads and dodgy-looking hairdos. But there's an air of playacting about the scenes that are presented to you, a feeling of 'Look at me!'. One oft-used photograph shows a bunch of people worshipping the rising solstice sun. Their hands are all raised in the air, and one or two are kneeling. Is it ecstasy? Or just amateur dramatics?

Well why not? By 1971 the media were all-powerful, as they are now. Why not play them at their own game by adopting costumes – or no clothing at all – and posing in order to set your own agenda?

The photographer was a freelance at the time, working for various West Country publications. He's virtually made a living out of recycling festival memorabilia ever since. He just happened to turn up at the festival. His name is Brian Walker. There's another photograph of his which appears regularly, and which he has resold many times. The magazines always pick the same sets of photographs it seems. It's of three men in a naked embrace, with a Gay Liberation Front poster beside them. 'Right On!' the poster says. But the picture editors usually crop the picture. In the full version there's a heterosexual couple looking at them. And their eyes are a picture: a mixture of surprise and distaste. You forget that so much of this was actually very new at the time.

One day Kerr was talking to the men from the Milk Marketing Board. They were running a milk stall on site. Suddenly someone called Gyp turned the corner. He was this classically beautiful man, with a profusion of hair, shrouded in a cape, with a top hat and high boots. Kerr considered him a nuisance and was hoping he wouldn't come over to talk. But he did.

'Hi,' he said. 'Do you like my clothes? But they are wonderful.'

At which point he raised the cape above his head to reveal that he was only wearing the boots and a shirt underneath.

'Go away, Gyp,' said Kerr.

But it broke the ice with the Milk Marketing Board men. They were cackling with laughter. They couldn't contain themselves.

That night Gyp went into the village and picked someone's prize gladioli. Then he rang on the door.

'Look,' he said, when the woman answered it, 'I've brought you these beautiful flowers.'

So there was some suspicion among the villagers, naturally. Most of them had no idea what to make of it at all. One farm manager accused the hippies of trampling crops, damaging hedges and turning a field into an open lavatory. People were kept awake by the noise, and complained to the local vicar. The vicar's wife said, 'But what can he do about controlling pop music which continues into the early hours?' Eavis tried to impose a twelve o'clock curfew, but the hippies always managed to stretch things out. On one occasion he could clearly be seen through the back-lit plastic sheeting chasing the stage manager about, trying to get the music turned off. And the police warned the festival-goers not to walk around naked in public places. Chief Inspector Lewis Clark said, 'If people were trying to get into a place with no clothes on we would send them back because it could annoy the residents.' And then he added, darkly, 'There are laws concerning nude persons in a public place.'

The *Sun*'s account is the best. LOVE IN THE MUD ORGY, says the headline. And then it goes on to describe a twenty-year-old woman making love to a series of men in a mud pool:

> A police spokesman said, 'It was an amazing sight. Our men saw this girl making love in the mud with one man, then several others joined in.
> 'About a thousand people stood by and watched.
> 'We're not interested in that sort of thing – they weren't annoying anyone or causing any offence as far as we know.'
> Later, 'Magic Michael', a twenty-four-year-old hippie from a Welsh commune, danced naked on stage for an hour to the accompaniment of bongo drums and frenzied squeals.

Which begs the question, really, of why the police didn't arrest 'Magic Michael'?

So, here I am, more than a quarter of a century later, enjoying – if that's the word – the legacy of that first free festival. And I've got a hand-painted WORTHY FARM sign from that era in my van, and a map of Glastonbury on my wall. It must mean something.

I'd told Des that I hated festivals. This is true. I can't see the point, really, of leaving the cities to come into the countryside, only to camp out in another, rudimentary, dirty, uncomfortable city like the Pilton Pop Festival.

But I was trapped here, so I had to make the best of it. I'm only telling you this so you know what privations I went through in order to deliver you this little entertainment. An artist must suffer for his work.

And I did suffer. I suffered all that rain and all that mud. I suffered plates of vegan slop. I suffered listening to Des and Dicken's interminable arguments.

'Dylan, concentrate will you. You're not playing it right.'

'The name's Dicken, Des, Dicken. Dickendickendickendicken. Dicken!'

'What?'

'DICKEN!'

And then I suffered sleepless nights because of all those people coming over the wall. It was a concrete wall this year, about nine feet high. I didn't mind them coming over the wall, myself, as long as they did it quietly. It was the security guards chasing and screaming abuse at them that got to me. 'I can see you there. Fuck off. Fuck off. Get back. D'ya hear me? Fuck off. If you come over, I'll phone through, and someone will pick you up.'

The following day I was talking about it to a friend, when someone overheard me.

'Fucking security guards,' I was saying, 'keeping me awake. I'd rather people got in for nothing than to have to put up with all that ranting.'

'Well I think they're doing a good job,' this other person said. 'It's the blaggers that are ruining it for all the rest.'

'What do you expect?' I said. 'Most people can't afford the ticket prices.'

'Then they should stay away.'

'But the fact is, they're not going to stay away, are they? They'll come whether you want them to or not. It's inevitable. If they like the bands, but they haven't got the money, then they'll hop the fence. I even think that Eavis caters for them. He expects them to come.'

'Then they should work, like me. I'm a litter-picker supervisor. I've done it every year since the festival began.'

'For what? For your ticket money back? Most people aren't that stupid. Anyway, maybe they haven't got the money up-front to pay for the ticket in the first place.'

'Then they should come before the wall goes up and find some work to do. It only goes up a month before the festival starts.'

'So what you're saying is that you expect people to come a month in advance in order to sit around in a field, waiting for a couple of days worth of festival. And that's all right, but hopping the wall isn't. You're off your trolley,' I said. 'And anyway,' I added, triumphantly, 'Michael Eavis blagged his way into his first festival. Did you know that?'

I later heard that the main injuries at the festival that year were spinal injuries, some very serious, from landing badly after leaping the wall. One woman I know broke her spine. The other complaint was trench foot.

Well I had some adventures there, and I'm not complaining. Occasionally I'd even venture out from the litter-pickers field. This was usually so I could get some proper food inside me. I went over to the sacred field, to visit the Druids a couple of times. The first time Ellie was there, but by the second she'd disappeared. Ellie had been in my van on the solstice, the day of the ceremony on the traffic island. 'Where's Ellie?' I asked.

'She's not here.'

Susanna and Denny told me that the High Priest had banished her from the field. He'd told her 'in no uncertain terms' that had she been Queen Guinevere in a previous life she would have been dragged out by her hair and called a whore and a harlot. This was the first time I became aware that all was not Love and Peace in the hippie camp. I happen to like Ellie.

Susanna told me a story. There were look-out posts all along the top of the wall, manned by security guards. They were like metal cages. Suddenly one of the cages began to collapse, and the security guard was falling. People clapped and cheered.

'He broke his leg,' said Susanna. 'So the last thing he heard before he broke his leg was a lot of people clapping and cheering. I wonder what he made of that?'

But most of the time was spent in my van in the litter-pickers field, avoiding the rain. Lots of people spent lots of time in my van, avoiding the rain. It became the resource centre for all the musicians. They were practising in there. And in the evenings it became the pub. We'd buy beers from the marquee and bring them back to the van to drink. It's always been an ambition of mine, to own a pub. And now here I was, in a pub with wheels.

Des was having trouble setting up the stage in the marquee. A stage was supposed to be arriving, but it never turned up. So I lent him my Afghan carpet – which I carry for just such an occasion – and that became the stage instead. People had to take their boots off to step on the carpet. That was my only proviso. All the musicians played in their socks, which made them feel very homely, very laid back. It's a surprise that they weren't playing country and western all the time, so laid back were they. So, in this muddy marquee, in this muddy field, in this muddy festival, in this muddy county, in this muddy country, in this muddy June, there was one little patch that never got muddy at all: my Afghan carpet.

There was a musician friend of Des's, a big, gangly, hunched man with a lined face, grey hair, and a little Krishna bob at the back of his head. He had a friend, a dour, sullen, sour-faced woman. She was one of those people who can bully you quietly. She doesn't have to say anything. You can sense her disapproval, like waves in an ocean of toxic waste, washing over you. And she could genuinely psyche you out. She genuinely psyched me out.

I was talking about this woman with a friend of mine, many months after.

'What was her name again?' I asked.

'Er . . . J . . . J . . . J . . . something. Joy was it?'

'No. Misery more like.'

So we'll call her Misery.

One day I was doing a reading. It was all part of the entertainment. I was going to read a story I'd written years ago, called 'Off the Grails', about the first time I'd met the High Priest. Misery saw the title.

'Do you believe that I have the Holy Grail,' she said.

'Hmmm,' I said, noncommittally, 'have you?'

'Yes. Do you believe the Holy Grail could be a stone?'

I hadn't considered this. 'No.' But I showed her the last line of the story. 'In my story it says that the Holy Grail is a cup of tea.'

She huffed angrily and stared. I'd said the wrong thing.

'Look,' I added, 'maybe the Holy Grail is having a sense of humour, don't you think?'

But she just huffed again and ground her teeth. After that she never took her eyes off me.

I got up on stage (well, onto my Afghan carpet) and started reading the story. I've read it a few times, and it usually raises a few laughs. But Misery was staring at me. I could feel the cold points of her eyes needling into me. So much for the Krishna ideal. I got to one of the lines which usually raises a laugh. Nothing. Not a murmur. Not a titter. Not even a smile. It was awful. And Misery just stared and stared. It was like there was only me and her in the room, and those steely eyes, psyching me out. I read out the next joke, and got the same response.

'It doesn't seem to be going down too well,' I said.

I said, 'Well if no one's going to laugh, I might as well read out a miserable story.' Which I did. It didn't raise any laughs either. But then again, it wasn't meant to.

Later, Des's friend said, 'You did well there, to keep going. You know she was psyching you out, don't you?'

'Was she?' I said. 'I hadn't noticed.'

And then, on the Thursday, I was sitting in my van late at night drinking a beer, and watching all the brake lights winking on and off in a huge snake leading up to one of the gates. It went on for hours. The cars were shuffling forward slowly, and then stopping again, with the brake lights going on and off. And there were all these lights twinkling in the valley, and across the hillsides. Fires burning. Traders' lights along the main drag. Torches and headlights moving about. I was impressed. From a distance it all looked so beautiful. Like a constellation of stars in the deep night. And I imagined Michael Eavis sitting there in the farmhouse watching the same scene. Did I ask myself what he went to all this trouble for? I realized then that he would have been thinking, *I did this. This is mine.*

So the days were spent wandering between my van and the marquee, picking up a few beers now and then, and receiving visitors.

One day someone came to call on Des. She was an attractive young woman with hennaed hair and a kind-looking face. There was one rule in the van, too.

'Take your shoes off before you get in,' I called.

She got in and embraced Des, and Des introduced me. Then this man got on board. He was the most astounding sight. He didn't have any shoes on, so he couldn't take any shoes off. He

177

was dressed like an Indian sadhu, with a raggedy yellow robe wrapped over his shoulders. A cadaverously thin man, with tiny round glasses, and long, grey, dreadlocked hair: he was the very picture of an Indian saint.

Goodness, I thought, *I've got Mahatma Gandhi on board.*

'This is Swami Barmy,' the woman said. It was some such Indian-sounding name, even though he was clearly a Westerner.

And then he grinned.

'Grin' is simply not a big enough word. There's no word in the English language to describe the sheer extent of his grin. He beamed. He broadcast. He projected that grin, like an anti-aircraft spotlight into the night sky. It stretched from ear to ear. It threatened to split his face in two. It showed all his teeth like a row of tombstones. He grinned at Des and he grinned at me. He grinned so widely and so persistently that I was forced to count his teeth. What else could I do? It was all I could see. Grin, grin, grin. It was most disconcerting. And then he sat down cross-legged on the bench seat and, still grinning, began to rub his feet. He was rubbing the mud off. He rubbed the mud into little balls which he collected in his hand. And once he'd rubbed it all off, he threw it out of the door.

He said a few things, always with that grin on his face. I couldn't tell where his accent came from. It was a cross between mid-Atlantic and Indian. I thought he might have been an American. So I asked him where he was from.

'Basildon,' he said.

I almost cracked up.

'So you're a hippie then?' I asked, stifling my laughter.

'Last of the pure spirit,' he said, grinning some more. 'Went to India in '73. Never came back.'

I went to find him later. He was part of the Rainbow Gathering, a circle of hippies meeting in various parts of the world to pray and meditate and visualize for world peace. They were going to Greece next, he told me. I thought I might try and follow them, as part of this project. But no matter where I looked I could never find him again. Obviously he'd raised his vibrational level and ascended into a higher dimension. Either that, or he'd given me the wrong directions.

I have to say that I took an instant and total dislike to the man, though I'm sure he didn't deserve it. His grin got on my nerves. He seemed to be wearing his bliss like a badge. His clothes got on my nerves. I was thinking, *Oh, it's enlightenment as a fashion statement, is it?* His Indian accent got on my nerves. *It's Basil from Basildon pretending to be a guru*, I thought.

But I never could explain why, exactly, I disliked him so much. Actually he'd been totally inoffensive. Polite even. He'd taken the trouble not to dirty my floor with his feet. It's true, there were peculiar moments. At one point I'd been trying to talk to him outside, trying to get directions for the Rainbow Gathering circle. And he'd bent himself back as I was talking, almost bending himself double so that his hands touched the floor behind him. It was odd. But he was harmless enough.

It took me months to realize why I disliked him. In fact, I only realized today, as I sat down to write this. He was me as I had wanted to be. He had fulfilled exactly the dreams I'd had. He'd gone to India and stayed. He was the happy hippie I might have been. It wasn't him I disliked, at all, it was me. The hippie me.

13 The Trouble with Hippies

'In punishing folly
It does not further one
To commit transgressions.
The only thing that furthers
Is to prevent transgressions.'

The I Ching, Hexagram 4, 'Youthful Folly'

The trouble with hippies is that many of them haven't grown up yet. It was a conscious decision and determined by their own rhetoric. They were, if you remember, the party of youth in rebellion against the forces of age and conservatism. Except that none of them is youthful any longer and the rebellion belongs to another generation. But they had a massive agenda. They were going to change the world. They never did change the world, however, or only in certain ways. The world just moved on and left them behind.

I was on my way to the Big Green Gathering, a few weeks after Pilton. This is another of those summer festivals, a real hard-core hippie affair. Pilton isn't really a hippie festival, although it's the hippies who run the infrastructure. It's laid on by hippies in order to make money out of the punters. But the Big Green Gathering is a pure hippie do, even down to the technology. It's a showcase for alternative technology. No generators are allowed on site.

I didn't really want to go. Another week sitting in some field somewhere, out of touch with real life, no TV, miles from the nearest pub, surrounded by hippies. It didn't really appeal. But I girded my loins, as it were, strapped on my armour and, armed with five gallons of best Somerset cider, set out to do my authorial duty.

I had Tim with me. I like Tim. He's the most completely useless person I have ever met. Every time he puts up a tent, it falls down. If he has a drink he spills it. If he flicks his ash at the ashtray, the ashtray goes on the floor. Then he'll tread in it too. He used to be in a cult hippie band back in the seventies. They were called Gryphon, and played hippie music with medieval instruments. Tim was the lyricist. They made their last album in the same studios as the Sex Pistols, when they were making *Never Mind the Bollocks*. He became fascinated by the Sex Pistols and the whole punk movement. He wanted his own band to sound like that too. Punk music played on medieval instruments. It doesn't bear thinking about.

Actually I'd said that to him at the time. I'd said that he was the most completely useless person I'd ever met. We were sitting in the van at the Big Green Gathering, Tim and I, with a pint of that potent cider in front of each of us, smoking fags and chatting, when Tim flicked his cigarette at the ashtray. The ashtray was already surrounded by fag-butts and ash where he's missed it previously. He missed it again, but caught it with his knuckle in the process, and the ashtray went on the floor. He lent over to pick it up, and knocked his drink over. I said, 'Tim, you're the most completely useless person I've ever met.' And he laughed his booming great laugh.

So that was Tim, Doing His Own Thing. Knocking over ashtrays.

He's a veteran of the Stonehenge Free Festival, an ex-Wally, and an Archdruid to boot.

The Wallies were followers of Wally Hope, members of the Wally Tribe, who started the Stonehenge Free Festival. They were all called Wally. It's a badge-of-honour among festival-goers to be able to say you were one of the Wallies.

As an Archdruid he heads the Secular Order of Druids, based in Bath. The reason he's an Archdruid is that there's no one to oppose him. The Secular Order of Druids consists of Tim and various of his drinking cronies when he can persuade them to leave the pub. Mostly he can't. He's generally the only member, so there's no one else to challenge his Druidic qualifications. He's fifty years old, with a healthy-looking beer belly, long, curling hair and the air of an overgrown schoolboy. Fifty years old, and still signing on. It's a record he's proud of.

He told me that he thought the hippie movement was like the Romantic movement of the early nineteenth century. And that's what Tim is really: an old Romantic.

We drove over to Glastonbury to pick up Des, Angelina, Susanna and Poppy, and a young man named Andy, who was playing bass in Des's band. I'd met Andy at Pilton, where he'd hopped the fence. He's another of these young hippies who are such a mystery to me, with cascading dreadlocks and a baggy jumper. I mean, why would anyone want to be a hippie in this day and age? It would be like me wearing Teddy-boy suits and listening to Elvis. You'd think it was time they made up their own fashions. But, then again, this is the age of the pick'n'mix philosophy and the pick'n'mix fashion statement. You can buy all your hippie gear down at Oxfam these days. It's cheaper than Marks & Spencers.

Des was nowhere near ready as usual, but Susanna was waiting by the car park with all her tat. I told Des that I wasn't willing to wait for him this time, that I wanted to get a move on. So he agreed to take a later lift. And we set out for Warminster, where the festival was taking place.

Once again I got in for free. I was there as part of the Stonehenge exhibition in the Druid circle.

Andy didn't have a ticket so I had to drop him off before we got to the gates. He ambled about a bit, and then slipped through when no one was looking.

We drove over to the Druid circle. The Druid circle consisted of a couple of yurts joined together with a tarpaulin canopy, and a circle of tents with a fire in the middle. Under the canopy was a photographic history of the Stonehenge Free Festival, on boards.

This was the Stonehenge exhibition. A yurt, by the way, is a Tibetan portable round-house, made of curved wooden slats covered in tarpaulin. Or is that Mongolian?

Someone helped me to park. I had to pull in as close as possible to the stall next door, so that I fitted exactly into the circle. The guy was giving me inch-by-inch directions. 'Back, back, back, back another inch, another inch. That's it. Stop! Now pull in as close as you can. Over there. As close as you can.' I didn't pull in close enough, and the guy told me off. 'See that? He's parked in exactly the same place. He's not pulled it in at all. We'll have to start again now.' He was talking about me as if I wasn't there. You could hear the exasperation in his voice. But he was also loving the power of it. 'Back, back, back. Stop! Now forward. That's it, that's it, over there, another inch, yes, yes, OK,' slamming his hand hard against the van. It was my first meeting with the Druid circle control freaks.

This was Mick the Mouth, as I was later to find out, Doing His Own Thing, namely: ordering people about.

I don't know if they all had compound nicknames like this. But I liked to imagine they did. In which case there was Bob the Knob and Steve the Peeved, as well as Des Res, Denny la Rude, Tim the Dim and Chris the Piss. They were all ex-Stonehenge festival goers. Denny was the boss.

Susanna got out and put up her tent next to my van. Then she did a strange thing. She started tying all these bits of string and things between my van and her tent, bits of tarpaulin and plastic, in this weird, elaborate, woven structure. I had no idea what it was for. It served no apparent purpose.

I ought to tell you about Susanna. She's one of the mainstays of the road-protest movement. She was on the traffic island near Stonehenge with us, if you remember. Then she was in my van on the way to Pilton. And here she is again. She's in her late forties or early fifties, perhaps, and has four kids: Rainbow, Star, Sonny and Poppy. One day I suggested I'd like to talk to Rainbow, on the basis that I wanted her to tell me what it was like to have a hippie for a mum.

'I'm not a hippie,' said Susanna.

'Susanna, you've got one kid called Rainbow, and another called Star. How can you say you're not a hippie?'

'No, you see, while I was pregnant with Rainbow I had this dream. Rainbow came to me and told me she was to be called Rainbow. That's why she's called Rainbow. And Star is Star because she was born in Hollywood, you see.'

'Yes, I see,' I said. It sounded like a hippie explanation to me.

Another time there had been something wrong with the van. I forget what. There was always something wrong with the van. But Susanna suggested she could hold her pendulum over it to find out what was wrong. She thought she could dowse the fault.

'And you say you're not a hippie, Susanna?' I said. 'I think I'd rather have a mechanic, if you don't mind.'

The van was the pub. I wanted to call it 'The Druid Arms', but everyone else kept calling it 'C. J.'s'. This was Tim's idea. He thought he could sell the cider. 'It's all right,' he said, 'I'll do all the work. I'll sell it for you. I'll just have the odd pint now and then, you know, for my troubles.' I should have guessed what that really meant. In the end Tim and I (and one or two occasional guests) drank the cider between us.

Des turned up five or six hours later. He'd been Doing His Own Thing, taking his time, while I'd been lounging about in the sun, drinking cider and relaxing. 'I'm glad I didn't wait,' I told Susanna. 'I would have killed him by now.'

Later a young couple turned up. This was Rob and Emma, with their two kids. I'd met them at Pilton. Rob is an American with some exotic blood running through his veins. There's more than a touch of Native American about him. He was also to be the keyboard player in Des's band. Emma's a Somerset lass, pleasantly down to earth. They're a nice couple, quietly in love. Neither of them is a hippie.

In the evening we were all called round the fire by Denny, who was the Mistress of Ceremonies. There were about fifteen or twenty of us by now.

'First of all we should all get to know each other,' she said, Doing Her Own Thing. 'I want us to go round the circle and each of us say our names.'

So we did that. But it wasn't enough.

'Now I want us to go round the circle again, only this time I want you all to say your name in a silly voice.'

184

The High Priest said his name in a guttural growl, with grunts and squeaks. Someone else said their name in a high, Mickey Mouse voice. It was getting embarrassing.

Oh no, I thought, *it's a Boy Scout camp*.

And I ducked down out of sight behind Tim before Denny could cast her eye on me. Denny was the campfire Commandant, a hippie autocrat. Brown Owl in a party frock.

The first couple of days there were very pleasant. I loved having people in the van. One evening I had four people round the table, plus four or five along the bench seat down the side, plus two or three standing up in the back, all with drinks in their hand. I cast a warm, proprietorial glance over the space, just like a proper landlord. It was standing room only, just like a proper pub.

But then all these annoying little squabbles started happening. The Druid circle was next to the Rainbow circle, and there were border disputes. Each was always accusing the other of encroaching on their territory. The Rainbow circle had a matriarchal feel to it, even though there were men running it, whereas the Druid circle was decidedly patriarchal, despite Denny's leadership. It was the Matriarchs versus the Patriarchs.

'Excuse me, you can't put your tent there, this is the Druid circle.'

'No it's not. It's the Rainbow circle.'

'No it's not. The Rainbow circle is there, look.'

'That's only because you Druids pinched our space.'

'Well you can't put your tent there anyway.'

'Well I'm going to.'

'Well if you put your tent there, I'm going to pull it down again.'

'Well if you pull my tent down, I'll pull your tent down.'

'Well if you pull my tent down, I'll pull your tepee down.'

'Well if you pull my tepee down, I'll pull your yurt down.'

This went on for the whole week. It was a case of 'nyer, nyer, nyer', like the kids in the burger tent at Pilton.

'They're trying to take over,' Denny said.

'Take what over?' said Rob.

And everyone wanted to stay up all night. They'd spend entire nights round the fire doing sing-songs. It was getting even more like a Boy Scout camp every day.

One day Des and I were sitting in the van, looking out of the window.

'What do you make of that?' I asked, nodding back to Susanna's strange construction tied between her tent and my van.

'I dunno, mate,' he said. 'But I'd watch out if I were you.'

I was beginning to feel trapped. What if I wanted to leave? I had all these obligations to people. And then I had Des's musical equipment in the front, and Susanna's weird ceremonial knots tying me down at the back. I had visions of screeching off insanely, kicking Des's equipment out of the door, while dragging Susanna's tent behind me. I was having those feelings again, like I did at Pilton: *I hate festivals. I fucking hate them.* Everything was such a hassle. Here we were, sat on top of a windswept hill overlooking Warminster, and all anybody seemed to want to do was squabble. The whole exercise seemed pointless somehow. Pointless and irritating. I got Des to move his musical equipment into one of the yurts, while I made Susanna untie her contraption from the back of my van. Even so, she still left one tiny piece of string, as a kind of symbol.

One night I went to bed early. I was tired of it all. I was fast asleep, when there was a loud metallic rap on the back door. I jumped up, wondering what was going on – where's the fire? – and caught my finger in the catch as I slammed opened the door. There was no one there. It happened again, later, just as I was drifting back to sleep again. Only this time there was a drunken Tim booming, 'Come on, C. J., we know you're in there. Open up, open up. I want a fucking drink. Let's have a drink, you bastard. We're thirsty out here.'

'Fuck off!' I said. I was being diplomatic.

The trouble with hippies is that often they haven't taken the necessary step out of own glorious (or self-glorified) past to make their peace with reality. It's like they're stuck in a time warp, somewhere back in the late sixties or early seventies, still dreaming of the New Age that is to come, still waiting for the dawning of the Age of Aquarius, still plying the same old rhetoric, doggedly rewriting the script of a soap opera that no longer makes any sense.

That's what my stay at the Big Green Gathering began to feel like: like some crazy soap opera whose plot had gone horribly wrong.

First of all it was the High Priest. He was ranting at everyone. He'd been up for about four nights by now, with hardly any sleep. I wanted to tell him off. 'Just go to bed and get some sleep.'

Another day he 'showed' an axe to someone. It was a young man dressed (pretentiously) as a Mayan priest, and called (pretentiously) Sky. He was sitting by the fire, and said (pretentiously): 'Are you afraid to go into the void?'

The High Priest leapt to his feet. 'Get out of here, demon,' he said, taking a patrician stance and pointing theatrically to the exit.

And when Sky refused to go he picked up an axe and 'showed' it to him. 'Go! Go! I banish you from this fire.'

Someone else protested.

'This is not your fire,' the High Priest roared. 'You're not Merlin. This is my fire.'

'Put that axe away and stop your theatrics,' said Rob. But the High Priest had a mischievous twinkle in his eye.

He also 'showed' an axe at some people who had inadvertently parked their tent beneath a couple of tied-up twigs. I mean thin, twig-like branches, pressed into the ground about a yard apart, and tied up at the top to make an arched doorway at the edge of the Druid circle, opposite the entrance. The people who'd set up their tent there hadn't realized that the tied-up twigs were meant to represent a portal marking the symbolic and ceremonial exit from the Druid circle. They thought they were a couple of tied-up twigs. Some people just don't know anything do they?

And by now everyone else was ranting too. It wasn't always angry or autocratic. Often it was meant to be humorous. It's just that someone had turned up the volume. It was like they were all at a party somewhere, and shouting to be heard above the roar of the sound system. Except there wasn't any sound system. And none of the jokes was funny.

It was like that over the whole site. I went for a walk one night. I couldn't get to sleep. So I wandered over to where a couple of friends were running their mobile solar-powered cinema. This was Nancy and Moffs of the Groovy Movies Picture House. They were situated across the site, opposite the Permaculture tent. As I approached I could hear all this screaming.

'Fuck off!'

'No, you fuck off!'

'No, you fuck off. There's people trying to sleep here.'

'Well, there's people trying to watch a film over here.'

'You don't know what this all about, do you? What do you think this festival is all about?'

'I'll tell you what it's all about, mate. It's about us offering these facilities to the Permaculture exhibition this afternoon.'

'No it's not. It's about people trying to get some sleep.'

'Well fuck off and get some sleep, then.'

'No, you turn the volume down first.'

'No. Fuck off.'

'No, you fuck off.'

And on and on and on. Two hippies screaming abuse at each other across a windswept field in the middle of nowhere in the dead of night.

'What was that all about, Moffs?' I asked when I got there.

'He says we're keeping him awake. It was even worse at the Buddha Field festival last week. They were always telling us to turn the volume down. Trouble is, our system's so good, we can't make it any quieter. Green fascists,' he added.

And he told me this story.

It was while they were at the Buddha Field festival the week before. In the afternoons they showed films for the kids. One day they were advertising *Bugsy Malone* for that afternoon's showing. A woman came over as the delegate for the Mothers' Union.

'We are very concerned about your choice of film,' she said. '*Bugsy Malone*. It glorifies violence, doesn't it?'

'Which part of it, exactly, are you concerned about?' Moffs asked.

'Oh, you know: all of it.'

'No, but which part of it do you think glorifies violence?'

'The, er . . . you know. Everything.'

'You haven't seen it have you?' Moffs asked.

'Er . . . Well, no actually. But we've heard that it glorifies violence.'

'And how do you know whether it glorifies violence or not if you haven't seen it?'

188

'Well it does, and the Mothers are concerned,' she said.

And it was in the Buddha Field Café the following day that I had my own little revelation. The Buddha Field Café is what the Buddha Field festival organizers do when they're not running their own festival. Des was playing there, with Rob and Andy. They were trying to run their AC amps off DC batteries by using an inverter. The trouble was, the technology just wasn't up to it. There was a constant buzz from the amps. Des was barking orders at everyone as usual, people were tuning up, the amps were buzzing and humming and, occasionally, cutting out. Nothing was working. The café started off busy. By the time they'd got round to playing a number, an hour or so later, the audience had cleared off.

So I was standing there, waiting, in the dim spluttering light of the Tilley lamps, listening to the hiss of the Calor Gas stoves. They had wood-burners too and there were candles on the tables. I thought: *So what's so alternative about Calor Gas and candles? Or burning wood for heat and paraffin for light?* The only alternative aspect to it seemed to me to be the fact that none of it worked all that well. But I was reminded of something, something from my own past. It was strangely familiar. The smell of wood smoke. The hiss and splutter of the Tilley lamps as they flickered and cast dim shadows around the walls. Where had I experienced this before?

Then I knew. It was in those cafés in Nepal. Even the decor was the same: native art and dangling drapes. It was like being in the Third World.

So the festival had nothing to do with alternative energy sources, then, I decided. It was just a way of saving the flight to Nepal.

The trouble with hippies is their arrogance. They're the representatives of a new kind of consciousness, remember. They are the product of an evolutionary shift, the vanguard of the New Age, an entirely different species of human being altogether. That's one hell of a burden to carry. Hubris. The burden of an overbearing vanity.

It was Monday morning when things finally came to a head for me. It was just complete madness.

189

I got up and everyone was still round the fire from the night before. There was a bloke called Mushroom Tom, standing on one leg on a box, declaiming loudly. He was Doing His Own Thing, telling the same three jokes over and over again.

First of all he would take a small wooden sign attached to a stick.

'How does a fly commit suicide?' he'd say. And then he'd hit himself with the sign and fall on the floor.

Then he'd hold a glass of water behind his back.

'How does a fly eat its food?' he'd ask.

And he'd take a mouthful of water and spit it at whoever he was talking to.

'How does a fly sleep?' he'd ask.

And then he'd lie on his back with his arms and legs in the air.

He must have repeated those jokes about twenty times in the five minutes or so I spent listening to him. I went back to the van.

Meanwhile the High Priest was standing in the kitchen area. I'd been observing him for a while. You'd see his face go blank for a second, as if he was thinking what to say next. And then he'd step forward and start ranting at the crowd. When he saw me his face would change, and he'd suddenly become normal for a moment. 'Ah yes, you old reprobate. Lovely morning,' he'd say, straight-faced, in a normal voice, before reverting to type again. No one was listening.

But, in fairness to the High Priest, I have to say that he suffers from a certain blood disorder which is exacerbated by the excess of sunlight in the summer months. So I could forgive him for his rages, and the way he 'showed' his axe to people, and his huffing, autocratic manner. What I can't forgive him for is the way he played the bongos – no, sorry, the drums. I think he's quite possibly the worst drummer in the world.

How can I describe his technique to you? Try this.

Imagine a pneumatic drill. That has a certain rhythm. Now imagine the thrub of a diesel engine. That has a certain rhythm. Now imagine the rustle of the wind through a grove of trees. That has a certain rhythm. Imagine the ticking of a clock, and the sound of someone chopping wood. Imagine the pounding feet of an early-morning jogger, and the click of the freewheel of a downhill bike. Imagine an audience enthusiastically clapping their favourite cabaret act, and the sound of water dripping into a sink. All of these sounds have a certain rhythm. Now imagine all of these sounds piled together, shifting around intermittently, totally at cross-purposes, crunching chaotically from one to another. That would have no rhythm at all. And that's how the High Priest played the drums, Doing His Own Thing with no sense of rhythm whatsoever.

At one point he was standing in the kitchen, when a stranger asked him for a cup of tea. 'Festival's over, mate,' he huffed. 'No punters. Staff only. Go home now. Festival's over.'

That's when I lost my temper. I went to the entrance to the circle, where there was a sign saying TEAS, COFFEES, with an arrow pointing the direction, and brought it back to show him.

'What's this?' I asked. 'What does this sign say? Look. It's inviting people in for teas and coffees. See? And what does that sign down there, say? TEA, 50P. COFFEE, 70P. That's what it says. You invite them in and then you have the nerve to tell them to go away again.'

'Festival's over,' said the High Priest. 'They can get their teas and coffees somewhere else.'

'Well put the fucking sign away, then,' I said.

'The sign's just a lure,' said Denny, intervening. 'It's so we can bring the punters in and then play with them.'

'Oh, is it?' I tutted.

Later she apologized to me. 'I just didn't want you to upset the High Priest,' she said. 'You know what he's like. You realize that everyone is scared of you?' she added.

'That's because I don't have to shout to get my voice heard,' I said.

She was wearing a sort of Chinese dressing gown. She opened it up to show me what she was wearing underneath. Not a lot. She has a very brown body.

Breaking point came when I was listening to someone's performance round the fire. Everyone was performing round the fire. No one was having any conversations, they were just declaiming, roaring, raging, talking nonsense. And if anyone spoke, no one else listened. This particular guy was playing the guitar. He was singing a song, a parody of one of the songs from *The Jungle Book*.

'Oo oo oo, don't wanna be like you-oo-oo,
'(with your nine-to-five)
'Don't wanna walk like you, talk like you, oo be do', etc., etc.

So who was he talking about. Who is this 'you' that he was referring to, this person he doesn't want to be like?

Well: YOU, of course. You, dear reader, if you happen to be straight. You, if you happen to get up in the mornings to go to work. You, if you happen to have a mortgage, if you happen to be married, if you happen to send your kids to an ordinary school, if you drive a car, if you like books about war or romance, or if you like Blur or the Spice Girls (or Abba or Elvis) or anyone else, in fact, who's not got some sort of cult superiority status. You, if you happen to fancy Pamela Anderson or Mel Gibson or that woman from the Peugeot advert. You. Me. Anyone. Everyone. Everyone, in fact, who is not a hippie. The whole of the rest of the human race.

The trouble with hippies is that they have defined themselves, not in opposition to other cult groups – like the Mods and the Rockers or the skins and the punks – or to the followers of rival football teams, like everyone else: but in opposition to the whole of the rest of society. They are the hippies. We are the straights. They are the Alternative Society, the Counterculture, the harbingers of the New Age. They represent what the New Age will look like and think like and feel like.

It is a thought of the most monumental vanity, vainglorious in the extreme. Vainglorious, note. It's the only word to describe it.

And if this is what the New Age feels like, I thought, *I want the old one back.*

Later I met Emma on another part of the site, pushing her pushchair with the two kids in tow. She was glowering. 'What's wrong, Emma?' I asked.

'I'm fed up with all the ranting,' she said. 'On and on and on. I want to go home.'

It was just the excuse I was looking for.

'I'll take you,' I said, Doing My Own Thing.

And we left that afternoon.

14 Des

*'We are not now an anarchic community. We're a survival unit
... emotional, financial, physical and psychic survival. Perhaps
the basis of the Dead's popularity is that their struggle is the
struggle of ordinary people to find pleasure in their everyday
life on this planet.'*

Bob Weir, The Grateful Dead

I got to know Des quite well over those weeks at Pilton and the
Big Green Gathering. Or I thought I did. It was only later that I
found out the real story.

But I always knew that there was some fragility there, some
deep ache behind the bluff and bluster of his masculine persona.

Well, he says he's a hippie. I was never so sure myself.

One day I suggested we could get all his hippie friends
together, so that they could remember the old times. I was going
to record the conversation for the book. I mentioned one person's
name.

'He's not a hippie,' said Des.

'What do you mean, he's not a hippie?' I said, startled. 'He
smokes dope, goes to festivals and he lives in a bender. You can't
get more hippie than that.'

'No. He's the enemy,' said Des, darkly. 'He has no love in him.'

This kept on happening. Every time I mentioned someone's name, it was the same thing.

'Denny?'

'She's not a hippie.'

'The High Priest?'

'He's not a hippie.'

Which means that, according to Des's analysis, he's the only hippie left. And he wasn't the only old hippie to do this. Other people I spoke to denied that Des was ever a hippie either. They all did the same thing. None of them could recognize each other as having any relevance whatsoever. They were all, according to their own analysis, the last of the hippies. 'Last of the true spirit,' as Swami Barmy put it.

A bunch of old men squabbling amongst themselves, is how it seemed to me.

I interviewed Des on three separate occasions, always in his council-owned bungalow on the Windmill Hill estate, always occupied by a beer or two, or a bottle of good whisky. Des has a taste for good whisky, like he has a taste for venison and fine wines.

He's from an Irish working-class background, he told me. Came to England when he was ten. Father was a postman. So nothing out of the ordinary there. But he was clearly aware that there was something happening in the world from an early age. He picked it up from the airwaves.

'You mean, like, telepathy?' I asked.

'No. I mean like the radio.'

It was Dylan and the Beatles. There was a quality in John Lennon's voice that made you trust him like an older brother. Later it was other things. Hendrix. The Grateful Dead. Des is a Dead Head. A Dead Head is a Grateful Dead fan, in the same way that other people might be fans of Elvis, say, or Abba. Except that Elvis and Abba don't come with a philosophy attached. The Grateful Dead do. The Grateful Dead philosophy is the pure philosophy of psychedelic hippiedom.

He worked on the main stage at Pilton for many years. It wasn't the money. He was always hoping that the Grateful Dead would appear. As he said, 'Where better to watch the Dead than from the sidelines on the main stage at Pilton?'

He first took LSD when he was fifteen or sixteen. There was a series of trips. And it wasn't just any old acid. This was '67 or '68. It was Californian acid. Owsley acid. The purest and strongest black-market acid ever made. Or, as Des puts it, 'it was . . . .
. . . . . . absolutely . . . . er . . . .
. . . . fucking . . . .
. . . .
. . . .
. . . . transformative stuff, man.'

The dots there represent Des's phrasing. It's how he talks. Long pauses while he searches for the appropriate word. Sometimes the pauses take over and you look up to see a man deep in thought. All you can do then is wait.

I was trying to pin him down to the exact moment when he became a hippie. But he was having none of it.

'I've been at it all my life. It's like, trying to find a moment that you can say, "well that's the moment that . . ." you know . . .'

'Well maybe there wasn't such a moment, then,' I said, giving up. 'Maybe it was just an assumption that that's the way it's going to be.'

'Yeah. That was very much what it was like.'

So there were a series of incidents and encounters that backed up his already burgeoning philosophy, throughout the late sixties and into the seventies. Hendrix at a concert in '66. A free festival on Hampstead Heath. The Paris revolt in '68. Dylan at the Isle of Wight in '69.

'I remember crossing the water and . . . got off the ferry and somebody gave me a ticket. That was what it was like. The movement was inventing itself on the ground. There's a sense in which the whole thing was being created before our eyes. I mean, regardless of what the organizers thought they were getting out of it, the crowds just weren't interested in being contained and controlled.'

He went to France in 1971. Got back to London, and the squatting scene had started. People were finding empty properties that could be renovated, and moving in. 'Borrowed from oblivion', to use Des's phrase. Various communities were being formed. 'Some with clear principles. Some eccentrically drug-based. Some visionary. They were pioneering sustainable lifestyles. It was the beginning of the eco-war, attempts to recycle properties to break the stranglehold of the developers. Also an attempt to create a sustainable resource system, like wholefood co-ops, housing co-ops, workers' co-ops, musicians' co-ops. It was the beginnings of the tribal approach. Not tribal through blood, but through a shared vision. They were prototype eco-villages. Psychedelic colonies. You could actually follow your heart without money.'

And then, after the break-up of his first relationship, he went into a café in the basement of some squat somewhere. This was in Maida Vale. There were squats all over London, but particularly around Ladbrook Grove and Portobello Road in Notting Hill, which was the hippie heart of London at the time. Maida Vale was running a close second. Elgin Avenue. Bristol Gardens. And he walked through the door of that café and it was like entering another world. Spray-paint psychedelia, like the Magic Theatre in Herman Hesse's *Steppenwolf*: 'For Madmen Only'. He stayed.

He says they were often targeted by the police.

'If you were a freak you had thereby torn up your ticket of acceptability and were available for whatever crap anyone wanted to dish out. It was the test of the mutation. If they couldn't distract you through argument, if they couldn't distract you through threats and intimidation, if they couldn't distract you through starving you out, then basically you knew the next stepping stone was creating itself,' he said.

'The truth is, you didn't know what you were doing really, Des,' I said.

'Still don't,' he said, and laughed.

In 1973 he went on a summer hitchhiking trip. It was a spur-of-the-moment thing. He just upped and went and hitchhiked into the sunset. He had his guitar with him, and some provisions. Just after his first lift, the heavens opened. Torrential rain. The driver dropped him on a slip road when the rain stopped. Someone picked him up and – the same thing – as soon as he got in the car the heavens opened. So the journey was conditioned by the rain. By the end of the night he found he was in Dorset. He pitched camp somewhere, but was moved on. He pitched camp again, in a grove of trees on top of a cliff, but was moved on again. In the end a couple of climbers told him of a cave where some Buddhists had been staying, down at the bottom of the cliffs. So he climbed down to find what turned out to be a Buddhist hermitage. There was an *Om* sign carved into the rock, cooking pots, a tea chest and a wok: everything he needed. He ended up spending the summer solstice there.

So he was hanging round in this cave, meditating in the darkness, playing guitar on the rocks outside, living on brown rice, completely drug free, in touch with the elements, buffeted by the wind, swimming in the sea. He says it taught him something about the primal pulse of life. He could have drowned in that cave. And he also became aware of how important the solstice was. 'I felt that there was this point of stillness in the centre of the universe, and that the solstice was the still point of the year,' he said.

The following year he went to Stonehenge for the first time. And the year after that, and the year after that. He had recognized the solstice as an important time, and decided that the thing to do was to hook up with the English network at this time of year. Stonehenge was the place. So he was at the festival all the years down the line till it was smashed into oblivion by the hyped-up goon squad in 1985.

Nineteen seventy-six was the best year for Des. There he was, on the main stage, in the same field as the stones, aligned to the sunrise on midsummer's morning, just as the sun lifted above the horizon, sharing the stage with a middle-aged American in a cowboy hat playing rhythm guitar, a pirouetting ballerina, the twelve-year-old son of the American, playing synthesizer, a large body-painted man with a grass skirt and wellies, and a one-eyed black drummer. The audience was tripping, and the band was playing this wired-up, wild, psychedelic, spontaneous music, warping their minds. The whole thing, in Des's words 'had manifested itself for that occasion, on that occasion'.

And there you have it, in a nutshell, the essence of the hippie philosophy. 'For that occasion, on that occasion.'

Do Your Own Thing. Go with the flow. Where the spirit moves you.

It could only happen at Stonehenge.

Des's first daughter was conceived in Tally Valley in West Wales in 1979. Tally Valley – also called Tepee Valley – is one of those hippie colonies that has survived the decades. It's still going. It's a village in a Welsh valley made up entirely of tepees. Like everything else in Des's life, ending up there was an accident. Or rather, to use the hippie jargon, it was 'synchronicity'. He followed his nose and ended up there. The woman was called Jean, a profoundly spiritual woman by all accounts. There was an immediate spark between them. They got together on the full moon. They stayed together for a while and Jean got pregnant. Then Des got ill. He kept getting cuts that would not heal, which were then turning into festering sores. There was something in the soil, some kind of animal disease. He was a city boy, stranded there in the country, suffering from chronic blood poisoning. He decided he had to go back to London, while Jean decided to press ahead with being a single parent. They parted. Later a child was born of the union. The child's name was Kiera.

Back in London Des sorted himself out and got on with his life. He was clean in those days, into yoga and brown rice and playing the guitar. There were still colonies of what Des refers to as 'evolutionary hippies', taking acid and dope (good acid, good dope): 'as tools of the trade, to re-write the script', as he puts it. But a change had come over the scene in the intervening years. Various other drugs had turned up: prescription drugs, downers and heroin. There was suddenly a lot of heroin about. Des puts this down to the fall of the Shah of Iran. He says all these wealthy Iranians were fleeing the revolution. And that they brought their wealth over in the form of brown powder. That was what was on offer in Maida Vale: Persian Brown.

A lot of the squats had become official by now, leased from the GLC as a housing co-op. Des had his own place. There was a couple living next door. The guy was selling off his musical equipment, which, of course, Des was happy to buy. After a while he realized that they were strung out: selling off the equipment to buy heroin. The woman was heavily pregnant. Des was worried about them. He said, 'It's about time you sorted out your lives. You've got the baby to think about now.'

So she disappeared off to mid-Wales. When she got back she'd kicked the heroin. Somehow or another she ended up staying in Des's flat. And then Des became aware that she was making a nest for herself and her baby. Well, he was supposed to be going to California. He'd got a place in a music college there, in San

Rafael. It later turned out that, had he gone, he would have met members of the Grateful Dead there, who were attending the college at that time. But here was this pregnant woman in his house, kind of settling herself down, making herself comfortable, ready to give birth. Something of the protector came out in him. The child's father was a heroin addict and didn't want to know.

So he hung on, waiting for the baby to arrive. It was already a month overdue by this time. Des was sitting round burning logs on the fire and singing 'Dear Prudence', while Nanette, the mother, was going into and out of labour. Obviously the heroin in the early months of the pregnancy had affected her. Things were starting to get desperate, and they called up a friend of theirs, a practising homeopath, who recommended a startling treatment. He said that someone should have sex with her. Nanette had this large grin on her face while this was being said, and was staring straight at Des. 'Well someone had to do it,' says Des now.

'All in the interests of medical science, Des, is that right?' I said.

'You've got it.'

The treatment worked. Des delivered the baby himself, catching her as she shot from Nanette's loins like a bowled cricket ball. And that was his second child, Tui, born at around the same time as Kiera.

Well he wasn't the genetic father, of course. But he brought her up as if she was his own daughter.

Des had three children with Nanette after Tui was born. Heather, born in 1981, Jonjo, born in the winter of 1984, and Angelina, of course, whom you've met.

I'm not going to go into the complications of Des's personal life with Nanette. It wouldn't be fair to tell that story. And anyway, it's the story of our time, as I said to Des. 'People get together. They separate. That's how it is these days.'

So there were times in his life when they were all a family together. Lots of times. And a few years when he was bringing up the kids by himself. And about two years when he saw nothing of any of them except Angelina. That's been the case for these last two years, in fact – an awful silence.

It was after Heather was born that he started getting into coke.

Before that he'd had nothing to do with it. It was like this. Des had done someone a favour. He'd rushed around London in a frantic attempt to collect money people owed, for a friend who was in serious trouble with a South American drugs gang. The friend was in fear of his life. It was a substantial amount of money: £23,000. Somehow he managed to get it together and then took it to the appointed place, where he was met by the South Americans. They were every bit the cliché: a bunch of swarthy men with moustaches, and bulges under their jackets. Des handed them the money.

'It's all right,' they said. 'We don't know you. You can keep the money.'

But Des insisted they take it, and that they should let his friend off the hook. At which point the South Americans laughed. 'Mucho cojones,' they said. And Des found himself suddenly within easy reach of a perpetual supply of high-grade Colombian cocaine. Well he could have made himself very rich, and with no more risk. But he didn't. He started snorting it. He started supplying it to his friends, at cost price. They became a wholesale drugs co-operative. It was party time. It was party time all over the country for that select few who had access to the drug.

A few things had happened which had got him down over the years. He'd lost the housing co-op due to the back-room machinations of the GLC and a few sell-out hippies. Then he'd been ripped off in Norfolk over a festival he'd organized. He began to feel that the movement was being taken over by people on the make: 'middle-class infiltrators', as he refers to them. Meanwhile he was living in this grim South London squat, while outside, in the Big World, Thatcher and the Special Patrol Group were strutting about like storm troopers, putting the boot into anything that stood in their way. And then this magic supply of coke turned up. 'No one had planned it,' he says. 'The whole community were suddenly in this complete, fucking . . . . hedonistic haze, you know.'

It was the perfect antidote to Thatcher.

This went on for about three years. Or as Des puts it: 'I was three years before the mirror.' It was three years of not just good coke: good acid, good hash, good brandy. Good everything.

Cocaine is the hedonist's drug, a rich person's drug, pure indulgent fantasy. Everyone was taking it. Everyone who could pay for it, that is. Rock stars. City whiz-kids. The aristocracy. The captains of industry. Newspaper editors. TV producers. People on the boards of directors of prominent companies. The high-grade whores that served them all. And a bunch of wired-up hippies in a nest of run-down squats in South London. 'It was a Furry Freak Brothers fantasy,' he told me; 'the dispossessed inadvertently democratizing the good life.'

The South Americans were fascinated. One day one of them came round with a bag.

'Where are the guns?' he asked, looking round.

'No guns man. Good karma.'

'The South Americans didn't know what to make of it,' says Des now, laughing.

'The Lost Three Years,' as he calls that period. 'We were allowed to indulge our fantasies to the hilt. We wanted to snort our way to the other side to see through the illusion. It's just that we never realized that the other side was so far away. We were not criminals. We were a bunch of lunatic party-heads just . . . .
. . . . . partying.'

But then it started to turn bad. There were bad people associated with that scene, people who would hurt you and yours for very little. Des was putting himself on the line. And it was always a question of coming up with the money. Sometimes people would run off with some of it, and they'd have to find ways of replacing it. It was getting very dangerous. The worst point was Stonehenge in 1983. Des had given it up by now, beginning to realize the danger. But some friends cajoled him into supplying them with a bag. He was doing people a favour. He got the bag, which then disappeared off to Stonehenge. Now there's a problem with cocaine. It's a desperately moreish drug. It's not addictive in the way that heroin and nicotine are. It doesn't cause a cellular dependency. Once you've used up the supply, you can get on with things. It's just that when it's there, if you like it – if you've got the nose for it that is – you'll just have to keep on taking it. It's psychologically addictive.

And there's a problem with hippies too, that once they've got hold of any drug they'll take it and forget the consequences.

Which is what happened to that bag of cocaine at that festival. They lunched it out.

So now Des had to go to Stonehenge to try and recover the money. There was no money. He was wandering about for days, but people were avoiding him. Nanette was pregnant again. He saw her. And then she told him that 'she wanted to go walk-about', as he puts it. Also he was under the impression that he was under police surveillance. And then he got the feeling that the South Americans were chasing round London looking for him. What if they had realized that their product had gone missing?

Cocaine tends to create paranoia. Des had every reason to be paranoid. Paranoia feeds paranoia. And paranoid fantasies were turning into reality.

The hazy hedonistic dream had turned into a nightmare.

He went back to London to face the consequences. He went to see the South Americans, and told them what had happened. 'The hippies have spaced the coke out. Stonehenge has been turned into a . . . . communal ceremonial experience. Whatever you want to do, it's up to you,' he shrugged.

He was dumb, but honest – these are his words – the South Americans could see that. They gave him some mad and danger-ous task to perform – he wouldn't tell me what it was – and after that they were evens. But it was also the end of the cocaine binge. Or nearly the end.

It was a year or so later. Des was back with Nanette again, but, once again, things were going wrong. It's probably easy to try to blame one of them or the other. That's what couples tend to do when things go wrong. She was an ex-junkie, and he'd been a rabid coke fiend for years. I'm sure they got on each others' nerves. And I'm sure it was 50 per cent of one and half-a-dozen of the other. But there was a gulf between them. Des's solution, as usual, while everything else was going wrong around him, was to go on a massive coke binge.

He was actually building bunk beds for the kids. But he was also snorting lines of coke. He had packets and packets of it. When one wrap was finished he'd stuff it in his pocket, kind of to keep track. This went on and on. And then, in the midst of all this – in the midst of the quarrels, and the bunk-bed building, and the lines of coke – two bags of grass turned up. Someone wanted him to look after them. 'Yeah, yeah, sure. Stick 'em over there.' And then he forgot about them.

'That's when the doors were booted in, and the guys with the blazers and the police-issue revolvers were suddenly pinning me to the wall and terrorizing my kids and giving us the whole treatment, you know.'

Busted.

That led to four and a half months on remand. And then the trial.

The police had offered him a way out. 'Tell us who the bad guys are,' they'd said, 'and we'll be easy on you.'

'I honestly don't know any bad people,' he told them.

Come the trial they were trying to make out that he was some kind of big-time dealer. They knew perfectly well that he wasn't. The police had concocted his statement. And he'd been without proper legal representation while on remand. The barrister was a last-minute replacement, whom he'd never seen before that morning. So he was trying to explain. He was trying to be honest. He was trying to point out that in his culture marijuana and cocaine were just recreational drugs. He told them that he had a particular penchant for cocaine, and could get through heaps of it. He probably said it with the same kind of chuckle in his voice he had when he was recounting the story for me. 'You are the gin-and-tonic culture, and we are the cannabis and cocaine culture,' he said. So the basis of his defence was the absurdity of the law. 'Although I was breaking the law, it's not a very important law. It's just a matter of cultural difference. I don't think that the two bags of marijuana I'm being prosecuted for, or a few wraps of cocaine, is actually any more of a problem than the three or four gin and tonics you've had at lunchtime.'

This was his first time in the dock. He was having to learn about the process on his feet, as it were, while going through it. He thought that it had something to do with finding out the truth. Well he was telling the truth. He'd been building bunk beds for his kids while snorting lines of cocaine, and one of his mates had left a couple of bags of grass for him to take care of. So what? He wasn't going to be apologetic because, actually, he wasn't doing anything wrong.

Every time he looked over at the judge he could see a kind of taxi meter in her eyes, running up the fare.

In her summing up she said: 'Mr Moore is a hard-working family man with a highly developed social conscience and a history of good works for charities, who has openly stated that he has no respect for the law. As such, people like him are the greatest threat to society as it stands.'

He got three years.

'I genuinely thought it was possible to have a dialogue with the authorities,' he says now. 'And while they were mugging me in broad daylight, with such finesse, they were also being congratulated for it. Crucial thing: I didn't say sorry. I didn't know what I was supposed to be apologizing for. I felt that it was important to give them an insight. "This is actually what it's like. This is where our heads are coming from." In reality I was taking a hammering for a whole colony of people.'

In the debriefing afterwards his barrister said, 'I forgot to tell you, Des, these are not courts of truth, they're courts of lies. It's down to who tells the best lies, not who tells the truth. You were the only person in there telling the truth, and you've suffered the consequences.'

It was 3 May 1986. He was down in the courtroom cells, talking to Nanette and his mum. Outside he could see an avenue of trees heavy with blossom. He thought, *This is karmic overhaul. Prison is the only place I have left to get in touch with my own inner life.* He had a certain pride that he'd been honest and courageous and told the truth, but a certain trepidation that he was now about to enter the belly of the beast. (These are his words.) He hadn't grovelled or sold out or buckled. But he was anxious about the well-being of his family.

And that was it. He was stepping through the portal into an unknown world.

An old lag he'd shared a cell with while he was on remand had said to him: 'Let me give you a bit of advice. You'll meet some of the best men you'll ever meet in your life in there. And you'll meet some of the worst men. All you have to do is be able to tell the difference.'

And that turned out to be sound advice. It was difficult to tell the difference between them. The Worst and the Best seemed like one and the same thing.

Des did OK in prison. Some of those old hippie pastimes stood him in good stead. He took it as a period of enforced meditation. In the end, in the last months of imprisonment, he'd even been allowed a Buddhist meditation teacher who had come to see him every fortnight. He was reading books of philosophy, thinking, dreaming, writing poetry. And he'd got a guitar with him. The prison officers all said the same thing: 'People like you should not be in gaol.'

It was only hard when he thought about the kids. One day – it was during Pilton – he was looking up at the sky and thinking about them all. That's all he could see: a patch of sky through his cell window. He was in Wandsworth Prison by now. And he wrote this song. It was kind of wrung out of him, from the depths.

'I asked the Moon to ask the Sun to shine a light on everyone.
Asked the trees, asked the breeze,
To sing a song for you and me.
I asked the sky to shine a star
For each of you
Because you are
So dear to me.
I'll see you soon.
Just ask the Sun to ask the Moon.'

He sent them a letter, with the words of the song. He sent it to the following address:

Toby Truck,
    Rainbow Village,
        Green Fields,
            Pilton Festival,
                Worthy Farm,
                    Pilton,
                        Somerset.

And it got to there.

He was in prison for nineteen months before being let out on parole.

Toby Truck. He'd bought it a couple of years before, at an auction. It was a Leyland F9, 'a gorgeous green thing'. He'd rebuilt the engine and fitted it out with mahogany panelling and a lovely little pot-bellied stove. It was like a log cabin inside.

One time he was on holiday with the kids. They were in the West of Ireland, on a cliff overlooking the Atlantic. It was late in the year. There was a storm brewing, churning dark clouds and lashings of rain. And there he was, in the driver's seat, dressed only in a pair of shorts, with a glass of Irish whiskey in his hand, feet up on the dashboard, kids playing happily out the back, the pot-bellied stove gurgling and spluttering playfully like a jolly fat little gnome. *This is the life*, he thought.

He went all over the country in that truck.

Another time he was in Glastonbury, parked up beneath the Tor, when Kiera turned up. She was having a wander. She was about twelve years old by now, dressed in a top hat and a frock coat, with Doctor Marten boots with rainbow laces. Like the Artful Dodger, he thought. She'd actually arrived on a horse. And she spent a day or two with Des and the rest of the family. It was a good moment for him, having the whole family together. But that was spoiled when they were attacked by vigilantes with axes and rocks in one of the small villages outside Glastonbury. It was a regular feature in the area at the time.

Actually he'd not seen much of Kiera over the years. The mother kept him at arm's length. He had no real idea what was going on in her life.

I said, in an earlier chapter, that Des isn't like a hippie in one respect. He's always been very strict with his children. 'I saw my job as protecting them from harm. Providing security. And if that involves reining them in every so often . . . Well they can spit on my grave when I'm dead. But I'll go knowing that I did my job.' I had the feeling this was his Irish background talking. What he didn't know about Kiera is how wild she was. She'd been brought up with absolute freedom. She wasn't just wild: she'd gone feral. Everyone in Glastonbury can tell stories of her, how loose and uncontrollable she was. But Des didn't know this.

So – and now the story moves up a gear – he'd finally split up with Nanette. He was seeing a woman in Ireland. Another one of his disastrous affairs. While he was there he had this feeling of impending doom welling up inside him. It was like something dark and terrible rising above the horizon. He drove back from

Ireland in turmoil. Toby Truck was playing up. He had to keep stopping to fix it, dragging himself under the body every few miles. It was like Toby Truck was dying. He had Angelina with him, but the rest of the kids were with Nanette. And two weeks after he got back he heard that his sister had died, in a medical accident. And then, on the day of his sister's funeral, there was a phone call. He didn't say who the phone call was from. But it had a stark message. Kiera was dead. She was fourteen years old.

It was a bizarre and tragic accident. She was driving a car and there were other people in the car, including a baby. It was at a crossroads. She put her foot on the accelerator instead of the brake. There were two other cars involved. A complete mash-up. Several people died. He didn't know the details.

You may ask, how come the adults were allowing a fourteen-year-old girl to drive a car on the public highway like that?

That's easy. They were letting her Do Her Own Thing.

Sometimes I'd felt that Des was too hard on Angelina. Now I knew why.

So we're sitting in his pleasant little council bungalow as he's telling me the story. There's a Grateful Dead poster on the wall. It shows two skeletons on a hill looking over San Francisco bay. I'm looking at it while I'm waiting for Des to finish. The pauses are becoming longer and longer, and he's starting to take deep breaths. The lines on his face are becoming more marked, as he looks down into some middle distance, playing with a pair of curtain rings.

And then it was the funeral, he tells me. Over two thousand people turned up. The entire festival community was there, all the people he'd known down the years. But when it came to shovelling soil on Kiera's grave, he was alone.

'It was like . . . . every moment of crisis or distress . . . . had prepared me for this moment . . . . . . filling in my daughter's grave . . . . and emerging with the possibility of . . . . of sanity. I wasn't interested in people's tears or platitudes. They were like a Band-Aid on a leaking dam. No relevance . . .'

Des is slowing down more and more as he's talking. The pauses stretching out, longer and longer. Still looking down at those curtain rings. Still taking deep breaths between words.

I asked him if he'd known how wild Kiera had been and how he felt about that.

'It . . .'

Breath.

'was . . .'

Breath.

'my understanding that . . .'

Breath.

And then he stops, and I look up to see him deep in thought. I'm waiting for him to complete the sentence. Des is just sitting there, quietly engrossed, staring at the curtain rings in his hands, perfectly still. In the end I realize that he's not going to finish the sentence. I think, well, maybe the silence is far more eloquent than words.

There's a tape playing in the background. It's Des's version of the Grateful Dead's version of 'Not Fade Away'. 'Love is love and not fade away.' Des is drifting off, just listening to himself on the tape player. The chorus finishes and Des is launching into one of his solos. A flurry of notes over the relentless surging power of the bass and drums, like shimmering ripples across a booming ocean. More like Jerry Garcia than Jerry Garcia himself, I think. This goes on for some time, perhaps five minutes or more, and I'm loath to interrupt his reverie. Just looking down into some dark middle distance, not focusing on anything.

Suddenly he brightens up. 'I haven't heard this for a while. I forget. I'm a fucking good guitarist.'

'Yes Des. You are.'

We're nearing the end.

For the past two years Des has been in recovery. He was like a coiled spring for a while. People didn't dare come near him. If anyone had touched him or said the wrong thing, he would have killed them.

And it was in this state that he approached the Council. He said, 'I need a safe place where I can look after Angelina and get on with my grieving.' They were in a hostel for a while, and after that they moved to their present home. It's been from this place, on the mystical council estate of Avalon, that he's made a safe place for Angelina. And for himself, of course, to put his life back together.

But in all this time he still hadn't heard anything from the rest of his family. He'd sent cards at Christmas, and birthday cards and letters. But no reply. He was anxious about them, worried. Then one day – this was recently – the phone rang. It was Heather and Tui. They'd taken the initiative themselves. 'Hi Dad!' they chirruped. He spent a delightful half an hour on the phone with them. But afterwards he was circumspect, worried about the effect it might have on Angelina. After all, she'd grown up with them. He thought, *What if this is just a blip? What if she has to lose them all over again?*

Then he got the letter from Nanette. It was an apology, asking him if he wanted to see the kids. She said it was important that they showed they were capable of healing and progression. 'We are their role models,' she said.

So they came down for a few days, for his birthday. Nanette, Heather and Jonjo (Tui was in Spain with her boyfriend). And there they were, all grown up: his kids. Heather, a very striking young woman, and Jonjo, a sensitive, intelligent, amusing young man. He was proud of them.

They went for a walk one day, and Jonjo and he climbed a tree together. Then Des said, 'Come here,' and he embraced his son. 'See, that's what you get for having a hippie Dad. Bonding in an oak tree under Glastonbury Tor,' he said, laughing.

And they spent one afternoon playing songs together. Heather had the most gorgeous voice, and she was playing stuff that she and Nanette had written together. She sang one of her own songs, in a voice like sparkling crystal:

'I am restless like the river as it washes pain away.
I am breathless like the wind as it cries from day to day.
If only life could be something that we share.
Dissolve the separation, celebrate the differences that are there.'

He was delighted that they turned out to have the same tastes in music as him. He played them 'I asked the Moon':

> *'I asked the sky to shine a star*
> *For each of you*
> *Because you are*
> *So dear to me.'*

Finally it was time for them to leave. It was a Sunday afternoon, bright but chill. Des was playing a gig in a pub that afternoon, so he was loading a friend's car with all his gear. The family were going to wait at the house till after he'd gone. Jonjo came out and watched him for a while. Then Heather came out. He'd packed the car and it was nearly time for him to go. Then Jonjo leapt forward. He grabbed Des in an awkward embrace. 'We're really glad you're our Dad, Des,' he said, before dashing back inside.

And Heather hugged him too. 'I love you,' she said. 'We all love you.'

And that was it. The moment of peace. The moment of redemption. The moment when he knew that he hadn't, after all, wasted his life; that it all really did mean something. That the last seventeen years really did mean something. That it had all been worth while. And the pain, and the confusion, and the sense of loss, and the anguish, and all that buried anger burning away inside of him, it just seemed to drift away, like a fog lifted in the morning breeze.

The boat hasn't capsized, he thought. *We've made it through.*

15 Glastonbury

I'm sitting on top of Glastonbury Tor as I'm writing this. It's Imbolc – early in February – a surprisingly warm afternoon. I'm leaning against the tower of St Michael's chapel, on the lee side, so there's no wind. The sun is hot against my face.

There's a dowser wandering round with his dowsing rods and a man in the tower playing his didgeridoo. The sounds are reverberating up the tower like some kind of electronic signal. And – who knows? – he might actually be trying to contact something out there. Perhaps he's another one of Steve's alien tribe, still waiting for the Mothership to arrive. There's also an ordinary-looking French family sitting on the grass, looking chic but baffled, and one or two other tourists wandering about. There's always tourists on Glastonbury Tor. Mystical tourists, mainly, all milling about, trying to find a space to do their spiritual practice.

People dowsing. People praying. People meditating. People playing the drums or the didgeridoo. It's always busy, Glastonbury Tor. It's the spaghetti junction of the spiritual journey.

I was up here first thing this morning too. It was frosty then, with a heavy mist across the levels. I was halfway up before I noticed the mist. I stopped to get my breath back, turned around, and there it was, like a huge, rolling, white ocean. The hills were like islands. Only the occasional tree rose above it, drifting in and out of view like dark ghosts. And a single chimney, letting off a plume of smoke, like a medieval pennant fluttering in the breeze. I was so startled by the sight I let out an involuntary exclamation. 'That's it!' I said. What I meant was, that's how it used to look, in the days of my map, before the levels were drained, when Glastonbury had really been an island.

It was like looking back through the centuries, into another time. Except for the sound of traffic, that is. You had to ignore the traffic in order to imagine it was another time.

This is where I've been living these last three months, in Glastonbury. Parked up in a witch's back garden in the shadow of the Tor. It was Jude who found the spot for me. She said, 'I don't know what it is about you. I always seem to be able to find things for you. Normally I wouldn't bother asking.'

The reason I moved here is that I wanted to be nearer the source of things. By that I don't mean that Glastonbury Tor is actually the source of all things – though it may be, who knows? No. I mean that Glastonbury town is the hippie capital of the world.

It's dominated by hippies. There's hippies everywhere. Half the shops are hippie shops. Half the cafés are hippie cafés. Half the pubs are hippie pubs. Needless to say, I avoid them all.

There's even a hippie bed-and-breakfast or two. 'Bed and breakfast with a sacred space.' Muesli for breakfast. Massage for tea.

It's a peculiar little town. For several hundred years, from the dissolution of the monastery in 1539 – when the last Abbot was hung, drawn and quartered on top of the Tor at the orders of Henry VIII – to the arrival of our own particular brand of mystical bohemians in the late 1960s, it was just a sleepy little market town in the West Country. There was a cattle market and a sheepskin factory. The people were farmers or tradesmen or labourers. Nothing much happened. The hill was there, of course (that's what 'Tor' means: hill), and – this being the West Country – populated as much by ghosts as by people. There were superstitions attached. It was hollow, they said. And somewhere there was a concealed entrance, a portal to the underworld, a passageway to the otherside.

Then, in the late sixties, everything began to change. First of all it was Sir Mark Palmer, former page of honour to the Queen, with his buckskins, flowers in his hair, living in a horse-drawn cart and accompanied by a ragged band of followers out of Chelsea and Notting Hill. Glastonbury's first hippies. They were all aristocrats of course, and a peculiarly naïve bunch. Brought up with servants. One of them was asked who would look after the hospitals if everyone dropped out.

'In the coming future,' he said, 'no one will be ill.'

More hippies arrived with Andrew Kerr and Arabella Churchill after the 1971 free festival at Pilton. This was the upper-middle-class variety. Nearly, but not quite, aristocracy. And they were still coming throughout the seventies. The first hippie/mystical bookshop/head shop, Gothic Image, was opened in 1975. Which signalled the arrival of the merchants.

Then Glastonbury festival at Pilton became a regular event. This was after 1979. And so more hippies were encouraged to come. These were the first 'punters'. That means working people, who can only get out at weekends or when they're on holiday. And then someone invited the convoy down in 1985. These were the intellectuals: poor, but idealistic and proud. And more and more and more hippies were arriving. Some of them were mad types, like the Brew Crew, the Underclass. These are the burdens that everyone in society has to share. It's an influx of aliens that looks as if it will never stop. The town is getting heavy with hippies.

It's left everyone baffled. The locals simply didn't know what to make of it all. They still don't. And neither do the hippies, for that matter.

Glastonbury is possibly the only small town in the world where builders are also astrologers, where accountants sing in Bulgarian choirs, where shop assistants are witches, and librarians do the tarot. Where carpenters listen to ambient New Age electronic music while they work, and go home afterwards to meditate. Where people 'attune' before meetings, and 'de-attune' at the end. Where vegan restaurants are the norm and where you can find two hundred different types of crystal in a twenty-yard radius. Where a newsagent's shop window offers several varieties of healing. Where you can attend dance workshops and drum workshops and Bridie-doll-making workshops almost any night of the week. Where the bookshops are full of books about witchcraft and healing and tantric massage. Where you can buy hemp seed from a high-street shop. Where one man (a Brummie, bless his soul) takes his pet owl into a pub and says things like, 'I was a warrior of the sword, but now I am a warrior of the heart.' Where one shop advertises its wares saying, 'Kindness is more important than Wisdom, and the knowing of that is the beginning of Wisdom.' Where bumper stickers say things like 'Back Off I'm A Goddess' or 'Peace Through Love'; and where one high-street shop – called Archangel Michael's Soul Therapy Centre: Providing Tools For Personal And Planetary Ascension – sells geometric constructions made out of copper piping, and nothing else. Soul plumbing. Plumbing for the soul. Even the shop assistants don't know what to make of that.

Everyone in Glastonbury has something to sell you. Not just artefacts: a line. The common question here is, 'What are you into?'

I never know what to say when people ask me that.

I was sitting in a café one day when a young German tourist started talking to me. She said, 'Do you believe in the darkness?'

'Pardon?'

'The darkness,' she said. 'When I first came to Glastonbury all I could see was the light. Then, when I had been here for a while I began to notice the darkness too. It is inside you. It is all around you. I can feel the two forces struggling inside me now. Sometimes the darkness is winning, sometimes it is the light . . .'

She was going on like this. I had no idea what she was talking about. Then Sky came in, the pretentious young Mayan priest-type, whom the High Priest had banished from the fire at the Big Green Gathering. He overheard what the German tourist was saying. 'You are becoming a multidimensional being,' he said.

'Pardon?' said the German tourist.

'A multidimensional being,' Sky repeated.

'What is that? What is a multidimensional being?' asked the German tourist, reasonably.

'It's, er, you know . . .' he stumbled, 'like, a multidimensional being.'

'He doesn't know either,' I said. 'He just read it in a book.'

'Pardon?' he said.

You only have conversations like that in Glastonbury.

A number of people have read the book so far. Jude has read it, and so has Des. Chris the carpenter (Jude's partner) has read it. Graham, my friend from Birmingham, and Rose, my first ever girlfriend, they've both read parts of it. Beverley has read parts of it too, and Lois, my ex-wife. And Dave the communist, of course. You've already heard his comments. I sent Tim the Archdruid a copy of Chapter 13, The Trouble With Hippies, and he passed it on to the High Priest, so they've both read that much. Steve has read it. He thinks the bits with him in it are among the funniest things he has ever read. But, then again, he thinks everything with him in it must be funny, by definition. He's right. Steve is funny, by definition.

A few other people have read the book too, most of whom don't even get a mention. It's a widely read book, and I haven't even finished it yet.

Des was very disappointed. I think he thought we were engaged in some sort of propaganda exercise for the hippie movement, even though I was warning him all along.

'I don't like the hippie philosophy,' I'd told him, several times. 'I think it threw the baby out with the bath water.'

He said, 'But that's what you're doing now. You're throwing the baby out with the bath water. Sure, a lot of it was wrong. But a lot of it was right too,' he said. 'You've used the word "hippie" like a dustbin, to chuck everything in you don't like.'

'That's true,' I said. 'That's what it means to me. But that doesn't mean I want to undermine anyone's ideals. I just want people to be aware of what was wrong, that's all. I want people to learn from our mistakes.'

He said, 'You're taking the piss.'

'That's true,' I said. 'I felt I had to represent my generation, the ones who came after you. I'm a Brummie. We always take the piss.

Anyway,' I added, 'a philosophy that can't laugh at itself can't be taken seriously, isn't that true? That applies to people too.'

He said, 'You've used the authority of the authorial voice to undermine the things we were saying.'

'That's right,' I said. 'But I've also used the authority of the authorial voice to undermine the authority of the authorial voice. No one comes in for more criticism than me in this book.'

I hope you noticed this too.

Des particularly objected to the 'Trouble With Hippies' chapter. He said, 'You've misrepresented what we were saying.'

'No,' I said. 'That's precisely what all the hippie leaders were saying.'

'But that's a contradiction in terms,' said Des. '"Hippie Leaders". The hippies had no leaders. Anyone calling himself a leader could not be a hippie, and vice versa.'

Tim the Archdruid didn't like the 'Trouble With Hippies' chapter either. He said it didn't have enough jokes in it, and he was offended I called him 'the most completely useless person I've met'.

The High Priest sent a letter threatening to sue. He objected to several of the statements I'd made about him. On my account of the axe-wielding incident, he wrote:

> The pretend Mayan priest was not fucked off because he said pretentiously 'Are you afraid to go into the void', but because the night before he had tried to interfere with three women, two of whom were married, all against their will. Even then, 'took an axe to him' suggests an attack, which did not take place, whereas in fact he was shown an axe, in order for him to know and understand quite clearly that the men of the camp would defend their women were he to be so stupid as to try again.

On my account of his drumming he wrote:

> For a start, I don't, and never have, played the bongos. I do play an African concert drum, and whether you like it or not, I have played with the Van Morrison band, Hawkwind and many other world famous artistes. I can't be bothered to argue with you about this, but if you want to print I'm sure

that the legal department of the Performing Rights Association who ensure my royalties will get round to dealing with you in the usual way.

And then, at the end of the letter, he put in what amounted to a thinly veiled threat. 'And don't try and cross any more so-called hippies,' he wrote, 'most of them are not as feeble as they look, and their bite is far worse than their bark.'

I must admit to being worried about this. What did he mean? In my confused state I imagined him taking part in various magical rites, with me as the focal point. I imagined him putting a hex on me. I was nervous and jittery for a few days. Eventually I wrote a series of letters to friends in the magical and mystical professions, asking them to do spells, or to say prayers, or to chant for me. That cheered me up straight away. The mere act of writing them was enough to make me laugh. Not because any of my friends would be doing spells or saying prayers or chanting for me, but because I'd asked them to. I don't believe in such things. But you never know, do you?

Chris the carpenter was disappointed, he told me. He said that he'd been reassessing his life recently. He said that he had been worrying whether what he had spent his life doing had been worthwhile. I know what he means. It worries me too, about my own life.

He said, 'A lot of my friends went to the Big Green Gathering and had a really nice time.'

'Well I didn't,' I said.

Jude said, 'Well if you will go in the Druid circle with the High Priest, what do you expect?'

Jude liked the book but was profoundly embarrassed whenever she saw her own name mentioned. So this is one more embarrassment for her. But, as I pointed out, most people reading the book won't even know her. And those who do know it's all a cock-and-bull story anyway. It's my fiction, disguised as fact.

Chris the carpenter said, 'You obviously don't know Willow if you think she was only crabby after her parents died. She's always been crabby.'

Jude said, 'You'll lose all of your friends if you carry on writing about them like this.'

'I already have lost all of my friends,' I said. 'Anyway, I told you I'd change your name, and miss anything out you didn't like. I'd have taken anything out. It's only words on paper, after all.'

'Yes, but I didn't want to appear too precious,' she said.

Rose read bits of it and was very upset. I'd said some unfair things about her. Then I realized that I was simply retelling the story as I'd told it to myself at the time. I realized it was the same story I'd been carrying around in my own head all these years: my fiction, not hers, and I changed it.

Graham was really angry. He accused me of wanting to write like Julie Burchill. He said, 'Why do you think that writers don't use people's real names? Don't you know how much it can hurt people? It's fiction you're writing, not fact. You're turning your life into a fiction. It's crap, Chris. It's really crap.'

I said, 'But there's as much truth in fiction as there is in fact.'

Graham was right about using people's real names, though. So I changed many of them. I would have changed Graham's too, only he didn't ask me to. He was more concerned about Rose than he was about himself.

On the subject of fiction, I lied to you at the end of Chapter 11, when I said that I wasn't a hippie any more. I still am a hippie, albeit a critical one.

My disillusionment with a number of the dumber aspects of the hippie philosophy happened over a number of years. It didn't all happen all in one night, the way I've put it in the book. That was one night, but there were many more after it. I've cut off my hair and then grown it again. I've changed my opinions on this and that. I've rejected the hippie philosophy, and then reconsidered it again. In the end my philosophy has been just like my hair. No matter how often I've cut it, it's never stopped growing back.

I still hold to some of the ideals of my youth. I think it would be a crazy person indeed who didn't hope that, by his actions and his beliefs, he couldn't at least make some difference to the world.

Being a hippie was never only about taking drugs and having sex. It was also about believing that the world could be a better place, and that we have a duty to try to change it.

Most people I know wish that the world was a better place.

Most people are hippies in some form or another, without even knowing it.

That's why the hippies set up the free festivals. The free festival movement was the hippie way to try to change the world.

Tell me: what do Canterbury Cathedral, the Poll Tax marches, your local music venue, a fruit and veg market and Christmas have in common?

Absolutely nothing.

And yet this was what the Stonehenge Free Festival managed to combine. A sacred site, a political protest, a social occasion, an alternative economy, and a time for spiritual worship.

It was an act of the most audacious intelligence on the part of a movement that largely decried conventional intelligence.

It was the fulfilment of Simon's story in Chapter 2, 'The Time, The Place and The People'. The time was the summer solstice. The place was Stonehenge. And the people were all the disaffected youth of Britain and the world, come together to laugh and have fun under the stars, to listen to music and feel the deep-earth stirrings in their bones again.

It might have worked. It did work for a number of years. But then something happened to change it. More and more people were turning up. It stopped being an experiment in alternative living, and it became more like a drugs supermarket.

There was a stall called Coco Loco, which sold lines of coke. It was a pound a line. At the beginning of the night the lines would all be of a reasonable length. But by the end there would be maybe half a gram in each line. The stall holders had stopped caring. People would take their line, then go to the back of the queue and start again. Over and over again.

Tim the Archdruid told me this. He also told me a story about when the Chief Constable of Wiltshire had invited some of the organizers to go and meet him.

'What's it all about?' he asked. He genuinely wanted to know. He was particularly puzzled by the sight of all these Anarchy flags flying. People had flags with Big A's with rings around them, and words like, 'Southend Anarchists' and 'Aberdeen Anarchists' in scrawled white letters on the black and red of the material. There were hundreds of these flags. It had the air of some vast, threatening conspiracy. Tim had to explain. 'It's just so people can find each other,' he said. 'People know where they are by the flags, that's all.'

People would steal cars from whatever town they were coming from and drive them down to Stonehenge. And then, when the festival was over, they'd torch them. There were always piles of torched cars left on the site, burnt-out wrecks, like the wrecks of what had once been people's minds.

Des said, 'In the end Stonehenge was like a sick dog. It needed to be put down.'

So maybe the thinking was just too grand, too big. Maybe we should all be setting about trying to make the world a better place by being better people ourselves.

It's one of the things I noticed about a lot of the hippies I met: that they were all very big on grandiose forms of rhetoric. They liked to emphasize their place in history and in the great scheme of things. But not very many of them were kind.

Kindness never earned you a place in the history books.

Incidentally, Des and Jude both singled out one particular passage in the book which they disagreed with. It was the bit in Chapter 2 where I suggest that it is a form of vanity to say that LSD changed the world. LSD did change the world, they say. It made Jude think about God, she told me. 'That's all I saw: God, God, God,' she says. And she told me the story of when she first saw God, emerging out of Roath Park lake in Cardiff.

She said she felt this terrible thing emerging, rising up and up out of the waters of the lake, like a many-tentacled octopus, writhing in its loathsomeness, so that she had to rest her back against a tree for fear of falling over. And then, when it did emerge, it was not a loathsome thing at all. It was many-armed Vishnu, shining like a sun, radiating pure bliss, pure love, pure beauty, orgasm incarnate, the most lovely creature in the Universe.

Des, on the other hand, found himself empathizing with the struggle of the Vietcong in South-East Asia. A whole generation in the West took to the streets, he says, because for the first time they knew empathy: they knew what it felt like to be in a guerrilla army in the jungles of Vietnam.

'And it was more than just a few thousand of us,' said Des. 'Many, many more. What was it that Abbie Hoffman said? "We are all Vietcong."'

And they both agreed that the passage from Chapter 2 was wrong.

What is most interesting about this is not so much what Jude and Des had to say about their own experiences. It's the fact that they agreed at all. Jude and Des are as different as chalk and cheese. They're as different as an elephant and an opera house. Neither of them would ever dream of being friends with the other. And, despite the fact that I am friends with both, I think that's just as well. Some things, by their nature, just do not mix. You can't write on a blackboard with a piece of cheese, and chalk doesn't go too well with a tossed salad. Elephants should never go to opera houses. Opera houses are not safe with elephants inside them.

So it kind of proves my point, in a way. If both Jude and Des are agreed on this, on the philosophy of LSD, then the philosophy must be so vague, so diffuse, as effectively to have no meaning.

Either that, or it is a philosophy that can encompass the whole damned Universe.

It was while I was living in Glastonbury that I got to know John Pendragon, to whom this book is dedicated. I'd met him before, of course. It's a small world. It's especially a small world amongst the hippies. There's not many of them left.

The first time I'd met him was at an anti-Criminal Justice Bill lobby of parliament in 1994. He spoke in a whisper, and had long grey-blond dreadlocks snaking down his back. He seemed like a total anachronism even then, with his baggy colourful clothing, and his passive manner; with his whispering voice and his cosmic imagery. He made a short speech, and the chairman just looked at him with a kind of soft indulgence, before getting on with the rest of the meeting. No one paid any attention to what he'd said. He was like a piece of flotsam washed up on the beach from some past time, some crazy old man without relevance or purpose any more. Or that's how I viewed him at the time. Later I came to respect the man.

In fact the description of the archetypal hippie on the cover of this book – fluffy and idealistic, with a cosmic turn of phrase, a middle-aged pot fiend sporting dreadlocks and baggy trousers – is actually a description of John Pendragon. He was the archetypal hippie.

He was known as 'Y-fronts John' by his peers. This was because he would always do his t'ai chi exercises at Stonehenge wearing only a pair of Y-fronts. He never took his Y-fronts off, even in the sweat-lodge. Whereas all the other hippies would strip completely and dangle their body-parts about, John would always keep his Y-fronts on.

And later travellers didn't have a lot of time for him. His fluffy cosmic waffle got on their nerves. He was seen as an anachronism even in the seventies.

I'd meet him occasionally, here and there. I'd always talk to him, but he'd never remember who I was.

'I met you at an anti-Criminal Justice Bill lobby of parliament in 1994,' I'd remind him.

'Oh yes,' he'd say, and shake my hand.

When you shook hands with him he would do an odd thing. He would take your hand and, inclining slightly at the neck and shoulders, raise it to his forehead. Always. It was like a blessing. He had a thin, bony hand.

And then, while I was in Glastonbury, I heard that he was ill. He was living on someone's floor, too tired to get out most of the time. No one had any idea what was wrong with him. I'd meet him on the street occasionally, and would always promise to come round and see him. But somehow I never managed to do it.

Meanwhile I was going through a hard time myself. I'd spent all the advance on this book, and had no more money coming in. I was broke, and fairly desperate. I started eating at the soup kitchen put on by the Christians. Beans and baked potatoes, every night. And John would always be there too.

One night he said, 'I was talking to someone at the soup kitchen the other night. He'd been an oil-rig worker in the past. He said, "Who'd've thought it twenty-five years ago you'd've ended up in a place like this?" I said, "Or even five years ago."'

'Or even five weeks ago,' I added.

John hadn't signed on for many years. He'd made his money through the free-festival network, year by year, selling incense and candles and all the rest, or by doing casual work. But this year he'd been too ill to work. He was nearly destitute.

I bumped into him one day. He was with Percy – short for Percival – who I knew as Mick. There was a police car parked by the side of the road. The policemen were out, talking to a shop keeper. Suddenly John laughed. He grabbed my back, and made a play of running to steal the police car. He had a mischievous twinkle in his eye.

It was after that I heard he had lung cancer. By the time they found that out he only had about a fifth of his lung left.

He was dying.

He moved in with Charley Barley and Kate. Charley Barley is another archetypal hippie. That description on the cover fits him too. Except for the 'fluffy and idealistic' bit. Charley isn't in the slightest bit fluffy or idealistic.

I'd see him on the street, and ask about John's health.

'He's dying,' Charley told me, with a strange chuckle. And he told me that the house was full of presences, like shining balls draped in black cloth. He used some Egyptian word to describe them. 'They always come when someone is dying,' he said. And he laughed coldly.

Once more I promised to visit. I even rang up one day, to ask if I could come round. But John was too ill to see me then. And in the end I couldn't face seeing him.

It wasn't only the fact that he was dying, and that that scared me – though it did – it was also because I knew I would feel like a vulture sitting in his presence, pumping him for stories for this book, while he lay dying in front of me. After all, he was never a friend of mine.

My relationship with him was purely literary. He would have made an interesting addition to this book.

So I never did go round to visit him.

He died on 13 April 1998, just after the manuscript of the first draft of this book was delivered to the publishers.

RIP.

There's one last story I have to tell you, before I finish.

I hadn't wanted to include it, but Des urged me to.

I said, 'But it will only make what I'm saying worse, Des. I was even more pissed off after Hallowe'en than I was after the Big Green Gathering.'

'But it was a good night,' said Des. 'I think you should write about it.'

So this is what this last story is about. It's about Hallowe'en in Glastonbury, and then at Stonehenge, in the Year of Our Lord 1997.

Des had hired the Glastonbury Town Hall for the night. Several bands were playing, including his own. I was late, having been to another do at the Assembly Rooms with Chris and Jude. Which is an extraordinary thing in itself. Jude never goes out.

By the time I got to the Town Hall Des's band had just started playing. It was actually the live tape from that night that Des was listening to when he was telling me about Kiera, the daughter who had died in a car accident.

The band is called the Ripple Effect, which is a good name, I think. I believe it describes Des's philosophy. It refers to the psychedelic experience as like a stone thrown into the waters of Time. The ripples go on for ever.

There were two drummers. A vast, cavernous, relentless rhythm, like the boom of the ocean heard from a cathedral. A girl singer. Bass and rhythm. And Des's psychedelic guitar on top, playful, erotic, soothing, yearning, faltering, lonely by turns. Psychedelic dance music, he calls it.

What I liked about this gig, as opposed to the alternative one at the Assembly Rooms, was that all the Glastonbury locals were there too, the lads and lasses from the council estates. It wasn't an exclusively hippie affair.

Well I got drunk as usual. Denny was there, and she made me a proposition. She and the High Priest were off to Stonehenge that night to meet up with King Arthur. And she said I could share her bed at the High Priest's house until it was time to leave.

It was too good a proposition to turn down.

At the end of the gig I went up to Des on stage. He was wearing some kind of a dress, with a feather in his hair. There was one young female admirer still on the dance floor, looking up at him admiringly.

'You're not a hippie at all, are you, Des? You're a punk,' I said. It seemed like punk music to me, raw and energetic.

'That's right,' said Des, rumbling with laughter. 'I'm a hippie-punk.'

So after that we went back to the High Priest's house, where a bottle of brandy appeared. At least I think it was brandy. It could have been cold tea for all I knew.

I was raving by now, talking gibberish. And at some point I found myself in bed with Denny, but I fell asleep halfway through our lovemaking. In the morning she said, 'I don't like booze. It sends you to sleep before you're finished.'

I said, 'Will you stay with me for ever?'

'I don't "do" for ever,' she said. She has a particular way of saying 'do' which makes it doubly emphatic. She also doesn't 'do' (in no particular order): going to the park with her kids, going to pubs, 'wanky-bollocks' (which is anything vaguely New Age), and anything, in fact, which she doesn't want to 'do'. Which includes me, as it happens.

We were driving to Stonehenge and I was still raving. I had my head in Denny's lap, and I was raving at the High Priest's choice of music. He had on 'When the Music's Over' by the Doors.

'Why are we still listening to this after all these years?' I asked. 'Jim Morrison was in his early twenties when he wrote this, and here we are, all in our forties, still listening to it.'

It got to the bit where Jim Morrison is intoning 'I want to hear, I want to hear,' in his theatrical way.

'Listen to him,' I said. 'What does he want to hear?'

'I want to hear, I want to hear,' crooned Jim Morrison, 'I want to hear, the scream of the butterfly . . .'

And I laughed derisively. 'It's complete crap,' I said. 'What the hell is the scream of the butterfly? I guess he thought it was poetry when he wrote it. He must have thought "the scream of the butterfly" sounded like poetry or something. It sounds like crap to me. It doesn't mean anything. It's nonsense. Stupid little man. And here we are still listening to him after all these years.'

The High Priest said, 'What about the "What have they done to the earth?" lines? It was the first eco-song, surely?'

But I was too caught up in my own rhetoric, too drunk to listen to him. 'It's all nonsense,' I said. 'That's all it is.'

When we arrived at Stonehenge the High Priest said, 'How can you be an atheist in this day and age? You must be the last atheist on the planet.'

'Well that's what I am, an atheist. What does it mean, A-theist? It means you have to do without belief. It means no god. And that's what I believe in. No god. And no bloody goddess either.'

Actually I was lying to him, again. I often do that. I take a position actually opposite to what I believe in order to watch people's reactions. I'm an agnostic really. Meaning I have no idea what's going on.

King Arthur was there. King Arthur is one of my favourite people, and I'd like to write a book about him one day.

He's an ex-squaddie and ex-biker who has taken on the mantle of the historical King Arthur, in order to bring 'Truth, Honour and Justice' back into the world. That's his slogan: 'Truth, Honour and Justice'.

And you can't argue with that.

At one time he was claiming to be the reincarnation of the historical Arthur. He's not so literal any more. He says, 'There have been many Arthurs throughout history. There was a pre-Roman Arthur, and a post-Roman Arthur. And now there's a post-Thatcher Arthur too, and that's me.'

He's a compact, muscular man with long, grey hair, and a grey beard. He wears the Druid's white robe, with a green cloak, and carries a shield and a sword. It's a real sword, the actual sword – according to him – made for the actual film *Excalibur*. So it's the real Excalibur in that sense. The modern Excalibur.

He certainly looks how you would imagine the real King Arthur to look. As to how he acts: well he acts like an ex-squaddie and an ex-biker. Roaringly, when he's drunk. Which may not be how the literary King Arthur would act. But it could easily be how a Celtic Chieftain (i.e., the historical Arthur) would have acted.

He's always bumming cigarettes off you. Actually he doesn't bum them. He doesn't ask for them. He takes your tobacco, rolls himself a cigarette, and then says, 'tax'. He does the same thing with your drink. In the end you give up. You buy him a drink of his own.

On this particular occasion he was planning to march on London, where his sword was being held by the Metropolitan police. They were threatening to melt it down.

Susanna and Denny were sitting together by the wood-burner in the cold dawn light, giggling.

'Look at that, look at that,' they said excitedly, indicating Arthur, who was bent over with one foot raised across his knee, with a look of profound concentration on his face, and a tube of glue in his hand. 'King Arthur gluing his shoes together before marching to London. That's one for your book.'

Tim the Archdruid was there. He was fast asleep in the back of a van. I thought, *Right, I owe him one.*

So I leapt over the front seat of the van right on top of him. It was his rude awakening as revenge for my rude awakening at the Big Green Gathering.

'Hello Tim,' I said brightly.

'Fuck off,' he said. He was being diplomatic.

After that we went over to the Heel Stone to have our Hallowe'en ceremony.

It was all the usual stuff. I-A-O this and I-A-O that, and the lovely open legs of the goddess, with the local press attending. I refused to join the circle, being shy, as I said before. Instead of which I stood behind the TV cameraman and made faces at whoever he was pointing the camera to at the time. It seemed to me, once more, that this was the only real reason for all this ritual. It was a way of getting your face on TV.

Druid rituals make as much sense to me as Christian rituals. Namely: none whatsoever. Druidism is not a pagan religion. The words 'pagan' and 'religion' are contradictions in terms. Religion is a tool of the State, paganism is the practices of the people. They have nothing in common. Religion is about ritual. Paganism is about celebration. Which is why I hate people who call themselves the High Priest of this, or the High Priestess of that, so much. They are doing a disservice to the people, and to the art of celebration.

Finally, the I-A-O-ing done with, and Arthur having stomped off determinedly towards London, surrounded by his entourage, and swishing his cloak dramatically behind him, it was time for me to go home to Glastonbury. Unfortunately there was no way I could get home. I had to beg a lift from the High Priest.

He played his Doors tape over and over again. The final part of the journey was through the winding, narrow, back roads of Somerset. He did it all at about eighty miles an hour, screaming round narrow corners, overtaking on blind bends, changing down, slamming his foot on the accelerator, changing up again, his knuckles white with rage clutching the wheel. I had to pretend I didn't care. He was obviously trying the freak me out. I think he thought he was being Neal Cassady.

He was Doing His Own Thing, but with me in the back.

So, having screeched to a halt on Glastonbury High Street, I went off to get myself some breakfast. I was shaking with fright, but doing my best not to show it.

There are a lot of cafés in Glastonbury. Unfortunately most of them are full of hippies. I'd had enough of hippies by now. But there's one – called the Monarch Tea Rooms, down one of the alleys – to which the hippies never go, on account of the fact that it serves bacon sandwiches rather than vegan mud-pie sandwiches. And I had a bacon sandwich with mustard, followed by a cup of coffee and a cigarette. After that I went back to my van.

I'd parked it in the twenty-four-hour car park. I'd tucked it away in a corner by a wall, out of the way, as I thought. What I hadn't noticed in the dark of the previous evening was that there was a gate in the wall which my oversized van was now blocking. The gate was open as I approached and there was another van trying to get out. It was a blue Transit like my own, but in the modern, aerodynamic style.

The man in the other vehicle was a Glastonbury local. The car park backed onto a council estate.

'Look, I'm sorry,' I said. 'I didn't notice the gate when I parked last night. It was dark.'

'What are you, fucking blind or something?'

'I'm sorry,' I repeated. 'I'll move it now.'

But it wouldn't start.

'It won't start,' I told the man in the other vehicle. 'Give us a hand and we'll try to push it out of the way.'

'Push it yourself,' he said.

So I tried pushing it. I don't know how heavy it is. It's a lot heavier than a car. More like half a lorry. I couldn't move it at all.

Meanwhile the man in the other vehicle was revving his engine, and inching forward. He had bull-bars on the front. He was threatening to push my van out of the way.

'Fuck off, you wanker!' I said.

'No, you fuck off!'

Things were getting out of hand.

'I'll call the police,' he said.

'Call the fucking police,' I said.

'You're a wanker,' he said.

'No, you're a wanker,' I said, as he edged his van ever closer to mine. I stood in the way. He got out of the van. I moved towards him, and he cowered. It's not often I make people cower.

Every so often I would go back and try to start the van. Eventually – miraculously – it started. I backed off, allowing the other Transit room to exit. Then I stopped to roll myself a cigarette, with the engine still running. I was shaking with rage.

I looked up, and the other van hadn't moved at all, despite the man's urgency. He was now standing glaring at me, with his wife and kids beside him. He had his arms outstretched around them, as if to gain comfort from his family. I glared back. I couldn't understand what he was waiting for.

And then it clicked. He would have had to pull out in front of my van. The man thought I was going to ram him.

That cheered me up. I laughed at the absurdity of the situation, lit my cigarette, and then drove away.

I went round to see Jude, who made me a cup of coffee, while I told her what had happened: about my argument with the High Priest, about going to Stonehenge, about the insane drive home, about the man with the blue Transit, the screaming abuse, and the way the man had cowered when I approached him.

Jude laughed. 'Well,' she said. 'If you will go to Stonehenge with the High Priest . . . And on Hallowe'en too. Ha!'

She seemed to think that going to Stonehenge with the High Priest on Hallowe'en inevitably brought on all the rest.

Then she pointed something else out to me.

'He thought you were a hippie,' she said. I was quite grubby by now, having lived in the van for several months. I'd also stopped shaving. It was too much trouble. I was beginning to look like a hippie. 'The locals round here hate hippies,' she added. 'Now you know what it feels like to be a hippie.'

'But I'm not a hippie,' I protested feebly. 'Honest.'

So that's it. My story over. A few years being a hippie, nearly a quarter of a century ago, and a year pretending to be a hippie, only last year. I hope it all makes sense.

At this point I'd like to reintroduce you to Piss-Off Pete, the man who started the book. I'd like to, but I can't.

It's where I wanted the book to end. I wanted to find Piss-Off Pete for you, to have a conversation with him – maybe in a pub somewhere, or some little smoky café, somewhere down-to-earth and ordinary – and finish the book on a happy note.

Unfortunately I couldn't find him.

Someone had said they'd seen him in Cardiff a few years back, and that he was healthy and normal-looking, dressed in a suit. I wanted to find him to see if it was true. It would have made the perfect end.

Steve even managed to get a phone number for me, of someone who claimed to have an address. But every time I rang the number the guy was out. I left several messages on his answer machine.

Finally I left a message with his landlady.

'Tell him I'll ring him again on Sunday morning. Tell him it's very important. If he's got Piss-Off Pete's address it would make the perfect ending for my book.'

So I rang him on Sunday morning.

'He's gone out,' his landlady said. 'He's gone to the pub.'

'But didn't you pass on my message? I told you it was important.'

'Of course I passed on your message. He says he's told you everything he knows.'

Which was precisely nothing.

The only thing I knew was that Pete came from Nottingham originally, and that that's where he probably moved back to after he left Cardiff.

So I tried ringing every entry in the Nottingham phone directory under Pearce (and Pearse, and Pierce, and Pierse too, for that matter). I got nowhere.

There I was in the Faber offices in London, listening to all these Nottinghamshire accents.

'Excuse me,' I'd say, 'I'm sorry to trouble you. You don't happen to know someone called Peter Alexander Pearce, do you?'

'Where does he live?' they might ask.

'I have no idea.'

One man laughed and said, 'Not with a name like that, I don't.'

He seemed to think that Peter Alexander Pearce was a poncey name.

Then I got a lead. An old woman answered. I said, wearily, once more, 'Excuse me. I'm sorry to trouble you. You don't happen to know someone called Peter Alexander Pearce do you?' I'd probably been on the phone for over an hour by now.

'Peter Alexander?' she said. 'Didn't he used to live in Woodside Road?'

'I don't know. He might have.'

'I think he moved to Matlock,' she said.

'Where's Matlock?' I asked.

'It's near Derby.'

'Are you his mother?'

'No.'

'Are you related to him?'

'No.'

'Matlock, you say?'

'Yes.'

I couldn't think of anything else to say after that.

So I rang all the Pearce (and Pearse, and Pierce, and Pierse) listings in the Matlock directory.

Same story.

No one had ever heard of him.

I was ringing number after number with one elbow on the table, and the handset pressed to my ear. My ear became numb and I got a scab on my left elbow. It hurt for days.

And I still couldn't find him.

It was only later that I realized that I should have taken note of that old woman's number so I could speak to her again. I was so excited by the lead (and exhausted by all the other phone calls) I forgot. I tried ringing through all the numbers all over again, working backwards this time, but I couldn't find her. It was like looking for a needle in a haystack. Or a needle in a needle-stack, rather. One Pearce (or Pearse, or Pierce, or Pierse) in a stack of Pearces.

I'd say, 'Excuse me, I'm sorry to trouble you. I don't know if I've spoken to you before, but you don't happen to know someone called Peter Alexander Pearce do you?'

'Yes you have rung me before, and no I don't know anyone by that name,' they'd say, curtly. It was embarrassing. I gave up in the end.

Finally I sent letters to the *Nottingham Evening Post* and the *Matlock Mercury*. This is what the letters said:

Dear Sir,

I wonder if any of your readers may be able to help me. I am trying to locate a man I believe to live in the Nottingham area. His name is Peter Alexander Pearce – or Pearse, perhaps? – and he lived in Cardiff between about 1973 and 1979.

The reason I'm trying to find him is that I have recently completed a book in which I tell the story of those years, and in which Pete plays a prominent part. I'd like to contact him so that he can see what I have written. My name is CJ Stone, and the book (out next May, published by Faber & Faber) is called *The Last of the Hippies*. Pete would remember me as Chris Stone. He would also remember a mutual friend of ours, Steve Andrews, at the time known as Droid.

Yours sincerely,

CJ Stone

I never got a reply.

The reason I wanted to find Piss-Off Pete – and the reason I started the book with him – is that he seemed symbolic somehow. He was a victim of LSD, as we all were.

We were the first LSD generation. It was this that marked us out from the generations which came before us. We were the first LSD refugees.

It's hard to describe the experience to someone who has never tried it. How can you explain something which lies beyond the compass of mere words?

Try this.

Imagine stepping into a World – a parallel World something like, but not like, our World – in which every moment, every ripple in time, every shiver of every leaf, the very air, is vibrant with colour, is alive, is resonant with a kind of Presence, something like, but not like, human; and then, in the presence of the Presence, to realize that this Other is Yourself, something like, but not like, You. You and yet not You: your Beloved Other. And then to know that this Presence, this Beloved Other You, was present when the Universe began, was somehow responsible for it, that He/She made it, and was part of It when It began.

As I said: it lies beyond the compass of words.

But then, imagine, on returning from this Other World, that all you were left with was the clear impression that You were there when It began.

Hubris. The hippie disease. The human disease.

It was this that destroyed Piss-Off Pete. This was the reason he assumed the grandiose title of Creation Number One.

And it was hubris, too, that was the downfall of the hippie movement. A whole generation feeling that they were somehow special, somehow different, somehow more important than all the generations that had gone before; a whole generation with the weight of history on their shoulders; a whole generation with the ultimate responsibility for the fate of the world. All blessed, all blissed, all burdened with the embrace of the Stranger/Beloved. All bombed out.

It was too much for some of us to bear. It was too much for Piss-Off Pete. His mind became buckled like the substance of Space–Time in the presence of a black hole.

Jude said, 'There should be a warning when you take LSD. "Leave your ego at the door."'

'Otherwise what?' I asked.

'Otherwise you end up like Piss-Off Pete.'

Jude's Dad asked her one time why she took LSD.

'Dad,' she said, 'you had the War. We have LSD.'

So that's why I wanted to find Piss-Off Pete. I wanted to find out if he'd survived the War or not. Because that's what this book is all about, really: war and survival. The people in this book are survivors of the Great Psychological Wars of the seventies.

Piss-Off Pete might not have survived. But then again, he might have.

And if he has, and if he reads this book, and if he contacts me through the publishers because of it, then I'll have to rewrite this section, and you'll have to wait till the reprint to find out how he is.

And I will get double the royalties.

Ha!

So in lieu of a meeting with Piss-Off Pete, I went back to Stonehenge instead, one year after the meeting with Des and Denny and the ceremony on the traffic island at Amesbury. The Druids had been let back in to the monument itself this year, for the first time in over ten years.

I drove over with my old friends Polly Pot and Simon, having sold the van by now. Neither of them is a hippie.

234

It was about midnight when we started off. Simon and Polly were squabbling all the way. Who says only hippies squabble? Simon is very methodical and slow. Polly is quick, sharp and impatient.

We stopped off at a service station so we could get some petrol and Simon could find out the time. He wanted to pace himself. He always drives at exactly sixty miles an hour, which is infuriating if you're in a hurry. Fortunately we weren't in a hurry.

He was fiddling about in the back of the car.

'What are you doing now?' asked Polly, impatiently.

'I wish you'd stop asking me what I'm doing all the time.'

'Well, fuck off then,' said Polly, and stormed off into the night.

Simon got back into the car. He'd been fixing himself a sandwich. He chomped on the sandwich nonchalantly, with his feet up on the dashboard, drank a cup of tea, and then started up the engine. He was ready to drive away.

'Where's Polly?' I asked.

'Don't know,' he said. 'She's fucked off. Probably trying to hitch home.'

'Well we can't leave her here,' I said. 'We can't leave her to hitch home by herself in the middle of the night.'

So we went over to pick Polly up again.

'Take me to the nearest railway station,' she said.

'There's no trains,' I told her. 'Not at this time of night.'

So she agreed to continue the journey with us.

We were coming from Kent, which is where I'd moved to by this time. We drove the back way, over the downs, to avoid the M3, and got lost once or twice. Simon said, 'You should see the view.' Unfortunately we couldn't see the view, as it was dark.

Later Simon was playing Clash tapes very loud to keep himself awake. Polly likes seventies disco.

'Switch that fucking noise off, will you? It's driving me mad,' she said.

So, with a surgeon's precision, and without taking his hands off the steering wheel, or swerving one degree to left or right, Simon kicked the cassette player off the dashboard. Just like that. Kick, kick, kick. Crunch.

Silence.

We got to Stonehenge as dawn light was beginning to play across the horizon, like the faded backdrop of some long-passed psychedelic band. It was pink and grey with a splattering of orange. Later it was just grey. The sun stayed determinedly behind the clouds.

The police were there, though not nearly in as much evidence as they had been the previous year. There was a road block on the Stonehenge turn-off of the A303, and that was it. We drove passed, and then took a right, hoping to approach Stonehenge from the rear, but there was a road block there too. Simon parked the car, and I went to talk to a policeman.

I was trying to pretend I was there to write an article for the *Big Issue*. I showed him my out-of-date NUJ card.

'I'll see if you are on the list, sir,' he said.

'What list?' I asked.

'It's ticket-holders only, and designated press. I'll see if you're on the press list.'

Well I wasn't. I'd never heard about any designated press list.

'I'm sorry, sir, I can't let you through,' the policeman said. 'It's not people like you we're trying to stop.' He was being very polite. I no longer looked like a hippie.

Meanwhile some German tourists had arrived. He was polite to them too. When asked why no one was allowed entry, he told them about the festival. 'It was all down to a few trouble-makers damaging the stones,' he said. Which, I have to say, is a lie. The festival had not been stopped because anyone was damaging the stones. The reason English Heritage and the National Trust had given for stopping the festival was that someone had dug an earth oven into a burial mound one year. Which is a small irony, to say the least, since much of the area is owned by the MOD, who regularly allow tanks to do wheelies over the burial mounds. But – no matter – at least the policeman was civil to us.

And then an old hippie turned up. He tried walking through the police cordon. We watched them beat him up. As we left he was on the floor. Several policemen had surrounded him and were giving him a good kicking before dragging him into a van.

After that we drove into Amesbury and then out the other side. We parked up on a side road, just off the A303, not a half a mile from Stonehenge, by a police encampment. There were no bollards. Simon and I went into the compound to ask if it was all right to park there. The police were just standing about, drinking tea and joking amongst themselves.

'As long as you are not creating an obstruction,' we were told. And then we were given leaflets explaining about the four-mile exclusion zone. 'We wouldn't want to see you get into any trouble,' one policeman said.

This is what the leaflet said:

WILTSHIRE CONSTABULARY
Notice regarding Stonehenge

1 With the consent of the Secretary of State, the Salisbury District Council has made an order under Section 14A(2) of the Public Order Act, 1986, full details of which are contained herein. This order is effective for the period – 2359 hours, Thursday, 18th June 1998 until 2359 hours, Monday 22nd June 1998 – covering an area up to a radius of four miles from the junction of the A303 and A344 roads adjoining Stonehenge. The area concerned, termed the 'prohibited area', is shown on the map contained in this leaflet and lies within the boundary marked upon the map in black (but referred to in the Order as 'edged in red').
2 The effect of a Section 14A(2) Order is to prohibit all trespassory assemblies within a radius of four miles from Stonehenge. 'Assembly' is defined as an assembly of twenty or more persons.
3 Any person knowingly organising, taking part or inciting others to take part in such an assembly, commits an offence and may be arrested by a Constable in uniform.
4 The Stonehenge Monument will remain closed to the public outside normal opening times throughout the period of the Order, notwithstanding that the English Heritage Commission retain the right to close said monument at any time.
5 In the County of Wiltshire, the provisions of the Public Order Act, 1986 and the Criminal Justice and Public Order Act, 1994 will be vigorously enforced, particularly where there is criminal trespass on land.

Signed Elizabeth NEVILLE
Chief Constable. 9th June 1998

Barring the particulars (such as the date, and the name of the Chief Constable) this is the same leaflet which has been given out for several years now. I only quote from it so extensively so that members of the public less interested in the goings-on around

237

Stonehenge might wonder where such powers came from? And you thought it was a free country.

So, having read our leaflets, and proceeding in an orderly fashion, as a group of no more than three, Polly, Simon and I set off for Stonehenge. There were several other groups also making their way towards the monument, but there were no trespassory assemblies, since none of us were assembled in any way. I hadn't even managed to assemble my thoughts as yet.

I saw Tim the Archdruid and ran ahead to meet him.

'C. J.!' he boomed, and put his arm round me. 'Greetings from the most useless Druid in the world.'

He'd read Chapter 13 by now.

He was wearing his Druid's cloak and carrying a staff. It's the same staff he always carries, with a brass crescent on the top, and broken about two-thirds of the way down, bandaged with pink ribbons to keep it from falling apart. I'd seen him break it two or three years before. It was over an argument about tobacco.

So not all the Druids were being allowed into the monument. At least, not useless Druids with broken staffs.

We came to the police lines at the junction of the A303 and the A344 and were told that we could proceed no further.

I asked if King Arthur had turned up yet. All the policemen knew him. He's famous for constantly being arrested. 'He's been arrested,' one policeman told me. Which was odd, as King Arthur actually had a ticket to get in. But that's Arthur for you.

Tim was also determined to be arrested. He was booming at the policeman, telling them that he intended to proceed to his 'temple', as he called it, and that legal proceedings would follow if he were arrested. He was drunk.

Proceedings following proceedings; and this was not a procession, but the due process of law. It was all very confusing.

Meanwhile Simon and Polly had arrived. Simon was getting agitated (he's been here before) and was whispering that we should keep moving. I was too intent upon watching Tim's heroic stance, as they bundled him into a meat-wagon. Heroic but useless as usual.

Then the police began to amass. We had accidentally, without knowing it, become an assembly. There were twenty people there by now. The police asked us to walk back up the road towards Amesbury.

So that's what we did. We trudged back towards Amesbury, to the top of a rise, with the police marching in a line behind us, where we were left alone to watch from a distance the goings-on inside the monument.

As we were walking I overheard two kids talking. They were about ten or twelve, and were here with their parents.

'This is dumb,' one of them said. 'It's as dumb as . . . as dumb as . . .' searching for the right image . . . 'it's as dumb as sliced ham.'

'No it's not,' the other one said. 'It's as dumb as high-heeled shoes.' And they both giggled.

Polly was admiring one policeman's belt. It was like Batman's utility belt, strapped around the waist of the fluorescent yellow coat he had on. He had all sorts of things: a truncheon, handcuffs, radio, bits of this and that, and several leather pouches which might have concealed all kinds of high-tech gizmos. Maybe he had a Batarang or two.

Polly is a bit of a fetishist. 'I like your belt,' she said, laughing huskily. 'I like a man in uniform.'

The policeman coughed, embarrassed.

As for the proceedings inside Stonehenge, all you could make out were these little white flecks flitting about. But across the road from the monument, in a field, there were these other, patchy flecks, which looked like a herd of cows. And then a line of fluorescent yellow flecks began bearing down towards them. It was a line of policemen.

'Look at that,' someone said, 'they're going to arrest the cows.'

After a while, and as our eyesight began to grow accustomed to scanning the distance, the patchy flecks resolved themselves into two separate camps. There were, indeed, cows among them. But there were people too. The line of police had soon dispersed them.

And that was that. One hundred people were allowed into Stonehenge to prance about mystically, while the rest of the world was kept outside.

John Pendragon's ashes were spread, to join those of Wally Hope, and countless other hippies.

239

The sky remained resolutely grey. The sun refused to shine. The rest of us grew bored and set out for home. I have to say, however, in deference to the High Priest, that it was principally his efforts that got the Druids back into Stonehenge this year; and that, although only a hundred people of mystical persuasion were allowed in this time, that the High Priest is in favour of open access for all.

On the way back I apologized to Simon and Polly for bringing them all this way on a completely useless exercise. Simon is an ex-traveller, so he already knew what Stonehenge was all about. Polly Pot, on the other hand, had no idea. She'd thought that we were going to a party. She'd thought she might be able to score some Ecstasy there.

'No, Polly: you've got it wrong. There used to be parties at Stonehenge, before 1985. A quarter of a million people would turn up, and it lasted for a month. It was the biggest free party in the world. Not any more though. There hasn't been a party at Stonehenge since 1984.'

Also there'd been a solstice party in Kent the night before which we all might have gone to. The usual thing: drink and drugs and the boom of the bass. And, as we were driving to Stonehenge, we'd heard all these parties going on throughout the night. And one time we stopped and we heard the steady thud of the bass in the distance, beating out the solstice rhythm, and saw the lights like an alien landing beacon flitting playfully about in the night sky. It was alluring. It was captivating. It drew you across the indistinct landscape like some mesmeric rite of darkness. I wanted to go, but I knew we couldn't.

'Forget Stonehenge,' Polly said, already starting to writhe and jolt to the rhythm, winding her hands in the air, 'let's find the party.'

'No, no, no, I can't. I musn't go to any parties,' I said. 'I've got to get to Stonehenge, Polly. I'm under orders from the publishers.'

You see: the party doesn't happen at Stonehenge any more. It happens everywhere else instead.